Contents

CANCELLED

I dedicate this book
to my two grandchildren
Jacleen Sarah Passman
and Adam Maurice Passman,
with love from their Oma.

Acknowledgements

I wish to gratefully acknowledge a number of individuals and organisations.

My thanks to my lawyer and friend, Mr James Macdonald, for his encouragement to write this book; my friend, Joan McCreed, for her help and assistance with getting the book published; my publisher, Ray Coffey, for his help and guidance.

My sincere thanks also to all my friends who have, over many years, given me help and encouragement when, at times, the pain of recalling the past became too much.

My gratitude is also due to the BBC for kindly allowing me to use the transcripts of my April 1945 interviews with Patrick Gordon Walker, and to the Imperial War Museum, Documentation and Archives Section, for the use of the photographs in its collection.

Glossary

Appel – Roll-Call

Appelplatz – Roll-call Area

Arbeitsführer – Task Master

Häftlinge – German Slave Labourers

Hauptaufseherin – Technical Sergeant (Female SS Guard)

Hauptsturmführer – Captain

Kapo – a prisoner chosen by the SS to head a work gang made up of other prisoners. Often chosen for the criminal element, the Kapos were treated better and, more often than not, brutalised other prisoners

Ober Scharfürher – Staff Sergeant

Prominent – prisoner granted special privileges by SS, and one who keeps other prisoners under control

Scharfuhrer – Sergeant

Prologue

A translation of the BBC interviews recorded in German between Patrick Gordon Walker and Hetty Werkendam after liberation. Recorded at Bergen-Belsen 18 April 1945.

What is your name?
Hetty Werkendam.

And how old are you?
Fifteen years.

How long have you been in this camp at Belsen?
Fourteen months.

Did your parents come with you?
Yes.

And are they still with you?
No.

Your mother, for instance, what happened to her?
My mother drove away from here.

Drove away or taken away?
Taken away.

By the Germans?
Yes, the Germans took my mother away. They made her drive away.

And your father?
My father drove away a day earlier than my mother.

Now tell me, what is the worst thing you have seen in the camp?
The time my father wore two scarves around his neck, and then the Germans came and they said, 'Ha! Ha! scarves around your neck. we cannot tolerate this, come here.' Then they took each end of the scarves and they lifted him off the floor with the intention to hang him by his own scarves.

* * *

Recorded 21 April 1945.

Now tell me what is your name?
Hetty Werkendam.

And how old are you?
Fifteen years.

How long have you been in this camp?
Fourteen months.

Are you with your parents here?
I was ten months with my parents here.

What work did your parents have to do?
My father worked in the shoe factory and my mother in the peel kitchen.

And at what time did your mother have to wake up?
At three o'clock in the night.

Why so early?

So early because my father at noon … (corrects herself). So that my mother could give her food at midday to my father. My father was so very hungry that my mother gets up early so that she in the kitchen can get some extra food. That is why my mother got up at 3am and came home at 8pm when it was dark already.

Did you not get enough to eat?

No, we had terrible hunger and we scraped with twenty-five men the remains of the food from the empty food kettles.

Can you remember any of the names of the Nazis and the SS here in the camp?

Yes.

Which one for instance?

Herr Müller. Er . . . (hesitates).

And what did Herr Mueller do?

He has beaten people and when he came into the barracks he did cupboard control and when the people had saved a bit of soup to eat at night, he would take the dish and throw it through the barracks, he would take their clothes and throw them in their faces.

And other SS men?

Lubbe. That was the one who took Appel and left us standing once for nine hours in the snow.

He left you standing in the snow?

Yes, and there were children there from three years old.

One

'What now? What now?'

My family – mother, father, myself and younger brothers Max and Jacky – lived in Amsterdam, in the Jewish quarter. It never used to be a Jewish quarter, as the Dutch people did not know the word 'segregation', and everybody could live wherever they wanted. Religion and belief were not considered an issue. Then, in 1941, during the German occupation of Holland, the Germans decided to concentrate the Jewish population in Amsterdam East. I was eleven years old.

There were many raids in the Jewish quarter during the summer of 1942. We saw families dragged from their homes, never to be heard of again. Some of these people were crying when they were taken away, others were relieved that the suspense of waiting was over. We watched through the curtains as the Germans marched long columns of people down the street to the station, where the trains would take them far away from the things they loved and lived for. My family used to feel very sad after each of these raids, as our friends and relatives disappeared, and God only knew what was happening to them.

For a while we were lucky. My father was a well-to-do textile merchant. When the raids started, someone told my father that we could buy our freedom from the German SS Commander, Auster Funken, in the form of a work deportation exemption. We could then be exchanged for prisoners of war via Portugal.

My father did not hesitate. He sold most of his valuables and my mother's jewels and managed to get about 500,000 guilders together. He did not know whether this was enough money, but after talking it over with Mum, he decided to give it a try. The question was, who was going to approach Auster Funken? The person would have to go to SS headquarters. This was dangerous – many people had gone there and not returned. After a long discussion, Mum persuaded Dad to let her go. She reasoned that a woman might have a better chance of being admitted to see Funken.

On the sunny morning of 22 September 1942, my mother set out to walk the eight miles to try to save her family, as Jews were not permitted to travel on buses or trams. All day we lived a nightmare, trying not to think of all the things that might happen to our mother. The day dragged on, until at five o'clock the telephone rang. After some hesitation my father picked up the receiver, afraid of what he might hear, but then his face transformed into a smile. Mum was all right and on her way back home. Imagine our happiness when Mum arrived, tired but safe, a few hours later. Dad said that he would never permit her to do a thing like that again, as he had died a thousand times during the day. Mum smiled happily, her mission completed. She had spoken to Auster Funken, and was told to come back with the money and our passports the next week. She was also instructed to have suitcases prepared with clothes for all of us so that we could be ready at a moment's notice for our trip to freedom. How wonderful! Our spirits lifted. Soon we might live in freedom again, as human beings, without being shunned or hunted.

The next day we all had our pictures taken and our fingerprints were put on our passports. The week passed and Mum set out once more for the SS headquarters. Another unbearable day loomed ahead of us, but this time Mum came home earlier, with photocopies of our precious passports, stamped by order of Auster Funken: 'The holder of this passport is exempt from work deportation.' The work deportation exemption protected us from being taken away during the raids which went on night after night. We desperately wanted to believe Auster Funken's verbal promises that we would be exchanged for prisoners of war.

* * *

My grandfather was already in a camp in Groningen, put to work there by the Germans. He had been a merchant in the meat industry when, early in 1941, the Germans forbade the Jews to enter abattoirs. My grandfather had to make a living somehow and, with the help of his non-Jewish colleagues, he was able to slaughter some cattle and sheep on a farm near Amsterdam. I was living with my grandparents at the time and had to vacate my bedroom for the work. My room was transformed into a sausage-making factory at night, while during the day it looked like my bedroom again. At times the dining room table was used to bone the meat. A gate in the fence gave the men who helped my grandfather a chance to get away if there was a raid.

Woken by the activities during the night, I volunteered to help. My grandfather showed me how to cut the last remaining meat from the bones with a razor-sharp knife, and he was proud when I proved to be an apt student. But one night the loudly ringing doorbell sounded disaster. I could hear my grandfather helping his two friends escape through the fence before my grandmother opened the door to two Dutch detectives, who entered without permission. There had been no time to disguise the equipment and the sausage meat, so my grandfather was caught red-handed. While one detective questioned my grandfather, the second one leaned against the doorframe, his eyes wandering over the room before coming to rest on a quantity of first-class fat my grandfather had laid out to dry on top of my wardrobe. Everything was covered hygienically in white fat-free tissue paper. When the detective brought the attention of his partner to his find, my grandfather was so disappointed. The detectives made up a report and confiscated all the meat, sausages, salamis, fat and the sausage-making equipment. About an hour later, a truck arrived to take it away. However, the Dutch detectives did leave my grandparents six salamis and a large piece of fat for their own consumption.

In May 1942 my grandfather was summoned to the Court in Amsterdam and given a choice of the four-month gaol sentence or going to a work camp. One Saturday afternoon my grandfather told me he was going on a vacation for four months. My grandmother's sadness gave away what was really happening and I told my grandfather I knew he had to go to gaol. I will never forget the look of shame on his face. The thought of going to gaol as a God-fearing man who had never done a criminal thing was nearly unbearable. He then told us of his decision to go to the work camp. Now, all these years later, I know that if he had chosen to go to gaol, he probably would have survived the war.

After my grandfather had gone to the work camp, my grandmother always came to our house, as she lived just down the street from us. She was my mother's mother, and the most wonderful person. She would not hurt a fly, and was loved by the entire neighbourhood. Everyone called her Oma (Grandma) Judy. My wonderful grandmother, she looked after us like no one else. When we finished our delicious dinner each night, she would ask, 'What would you like to eat tomorrow?' With full tummies, we did not have much of an appetite to think about tomorrow's dinner.

On Friday 2 October 1942, my Oma cooked a sweet pear cake for us, a dish which took hours of patient preparation. When she served it at dinner, we told her how tasty it was.

'Eat well, my children, and may God bless you all. I am sure it is the last time Oma will cook it for you,' Oma said.

'But Oma,' I said, 'this is nonsense. What are you talking about? You will be with us for a long time yet.'

'No, my darling,' was Oma's reply, 'I know. I can feel it, tonight they will come to get me.'

'Please Oma, don't talk like that.' I was in tears. 'If you do feel like this, stay with us tonight. Don't go home – and if you do go, I am coming with you.'

'No.' Oma was firm. 'Tonight you sleep in your parents' home.'

Sometimes I slept at Oma's place so she would not be so lonely at night, although it was forbidden by the Germans to stay the night in someone else's home. (The Germans had declared a curfew from eight o'clock at night until six o'clock in the morning for the entire Dutch population.)

Before eight o'clock, Oma prepared to go home. She kissed us all with tears in her eyes and said, 'Be good, my children. I love you all very much.' With those words she left.

From that moment Mum stationed herself in front of the bedroom window where she could see Oma's street. The Germans started to arrive at about a quarter past eight. The raid was on. Through the curtains we could see them going from door to door to bring the people out of their homes. This time they took the people to the station in trucks because it was quicker. My brothers and I were in the lounge when my father called out, 'Quick children, run to the bedroom, they have got Oma. Be quick and you can say goodbye to her!'

From the bedroom window we could see Oma with her bags, waving and calling to us. Mum opened a window, despite strict orders from the Germans not to do this. 'Mother! Mother!' she screamed, 'God, don't let them take my mother.'

She was waving frantically, and the next minute she was halfway out the first-floor window. My father grabbed her and pulled her inside. In the meantime, the Germans motioned Oma to move on.

'Goodbye my children!' she called while she walked on. 'Goodbye, goodbye.'

They were the last words we heard from Oma. My lovely sweet grandmother! We had heard people calling goodbye many times before, but this time the Germans had hit hard at our home and family. That terrible Friday night I will never forget as long as I live.

* * *

Months passed but the Germans did not let up on the raids. Our neighbourhood became very quiet. The houses were empty because the Germans picked up people and, a few days later, Puls, a carrier contracted by the Germans, would come and take all their furniture and belongings. All the goods from Jewish homes were sent to Germany. Since then, the Dutch language has derived the word *gepulst* – 'taken away'.

Our school in the President Brandstraat also emptied. Most of the students had been deported to Germany and Jewish teachers replaced all the gentile teachers. It was a sad day when our head-master, Mr Douwes, and our favourite teacher, Mr Tettelaar, were replaced. Both were loved and respected by all the students. After Mr Tettelaar had to leave, about twenty of us, including my girl-friends Sonia and Blondy, had a photograph taken by the photog-rapher on the President Steynplantsoen. When it was finished we took it to Mr Tettelaar's home. Although it was forbidden to have Jews to visit, Mr Tettelaar invited all of us in and we spent a lovely afternoon with him and his wife. Our photograph was given a place of honour on the living-room wall.

* * *

Many older Jewish people had been hiding in hospitals with pretended illnesses to avoid being sent away to a camp in Germany or Poland. By the end of February 1943 we had some inkling that the Germans did not have much good in mind for us, as we never heard a word from those who had gone away after they had received an order to go to work in Germany. The families or loved ones of those people who had been removed from their homes during the raids of the past terrible month had not received any news either.

My father's father was in hospital as he had been very ill with a life-threatening infection for some weeks. Now he was on the way to recovery, but every day huge bandages were required to clean out the painful wound on his bottom. My other grandmother, Oma Hetty, was also in the hospital, not because she was sick, but because it was too dangerous for her to stay at home.

Rumours had circulated for days that the Germans were going to evacuate the hospitals. My parents were so concerned that they decided to bring my grandparents home. They managed to hire a pushcart from some good Dutchmen in the market, who also offered to bring my grandparents back safely. My parents accompanied the men to the Jewish hospital and they managed to put my still very sick grandfather on his mattress and onto the pushcart, with Oma Hetty sitting beside him. After a walk of about two hours, my grandfather was put to bed in our home where he could rest. The hospital had supplied my mother with lots of bandages and medicines, and the nurses had explained to her how to keep the wound clean. After some embarrassing moments when my mother had to touch my grandfather's bottom for the first time, she turned out to be such a good nurse that my grandfather was fully recovered before two weeks had passed. My grandmother could not thank my mother enough, as she had been unable to do this unpleasant task herself.

All Jewish hospitals were raided on 1 March 1943. The Germans had no mercy and filled the trucks with the very sick.

* * *

Our gymnastics club, Bato, organised a competition with the other clubs still operating to take place on Sunday 20 June 1943. I had trained for weeks on the rings and parallel bars at the playgrounds close to our school, determined to have a good chance of winning. The night before the competition, I laid out my training suit and all the things I needed.

I was awake early on Sunday morning, a brilliant summer's day. All of a sudden I heard announcements from cars with loudspeakers being driven through the streets ordering Jews to get ready for immediate transportation. I ran to the window and could see lots of German police, assisted (as we later found out) by security police of the transition camp, Westerbork, and many Dutch Nazis, who were being paid five guilders per head. The whole neighbourhood was surrounded and sealed by the SS so no one could escape. The rest of the residents were told to stay indoors. Heavily armed police went from door to door checking passports and other documents. They drove the people out of their homes to an area right across from our street. The people were forced into an enormous queue on the corner of Hofmyerstraat and President Steynstraat and guarded by German soldiers with drawn bayonets. Through the curtains we could see the people in deep shock and trauma trying to keep their dignity. A man approached a German soldier. In his hand he held a document, which I supposed was a deportation exemption. Gesticulating with his hands, he tried to persuade the soldier to let him and his family go. But the soldier took one look at the precious document and tore it into small pieces. Defeated, the man returned to his family in the queue, realising that no one could help him.

For five hours the people, young and old, stood huddled together without food or water, until they were ordered to start walking to Amstel Station, where they would board a train for Westerbork.

The whole city of Amsterdam was raided that day and only a few families were allowed to stay. Our family was one of them.

*   *   *

During 1943 my father's parents went into hiding, and a man from the Dutch Resistance came occasionally to tell us how they were making out. He would bring us letters and news about the war, about the movements of the Allies, about how they had defeated General Rommel in Africa. It would cheer us up, and hope would flare that we would soon see the end of the war.

Through a strange quirk of fate, my father was still allowed to trade during all this upheaval. Shortly after the German occupation, every Jew who was in business was ordered to register the business and apply for a licence to operate. By that time my father was a well-established textile wholesaler, and his large stalls with magnificent fabrics were well known in the markets of Amsterdam. He had applied for two different licences, one for the markets and the other for the wholesale business. Both licences were granted after an accountant and the Germans had checked the books for days on end. The Germans were very meticulous in these matters and every detail was recorded. For a while everything seemed all right; it was business as usual. But then came the order that everyone with two licences had to return one. Mum and Dad argued for days over which one of the licences they should return. Dad wanted to keep the wholesale licence and Mum wanted to keep the one for the markets. In the end Mum won: Dad surrendered the wholesale licence and sent in the market licence for renewal. About a month later the market licence was renewed, and my father continued to trade.

The people who had kept their wholesale licence were not so lucky. Their businesses were confiscated by the Germans, whose agents, Lipman and Rosenthal, took over the businesses and capital, giving the luckless owners thirty minutes' notice to leave the premises. Those people were left with nothing. They had no money to buy food for their families as they had no income. Many of those once very wealthy people suddenly had a lot of time on their hands. They came to visit our home in the afternoons and soon devised a plan: my father would buy more goods than he needed for his own business and allow those poor people to sell the surplus to their own contacts, so they could make some money in order to eat. Of course, we had to do this very carefully as traitors were watching and would report to the SS. The other problem was that textile stamps were needed so my father could buy the extra fabrics from the distributors. That is where the man from the Resistance came in. During the past months, members of the Resistance had raided the Office of Births, Deaths and Marriages in Amsterdam and acquired a lot of textile stamps. My father bought the stamps from the Resistance, which desperately needed the funds. For many months my father bought extra goods with his own money.

Our attic soon became a warehouse where many rolls of fabric were neatly stacked on shelves. It was there that I escaped to do my homework very early in the mornings, as I was sitting for my final exam to enter secondary school. One of these mornings at about five o'clock, as I was climbing the stairs to the attic, I met a man carrying down rolls of material. I asked him what he was doing. He said he had to make an early delivery. I did not like something in his manner and I asked him for his name. 'Jan,' he told me as he raced down the

11

stairs. Suspicious, I ran up the stairs to the attic. The locks on the door were broken and only a few rolls of material were lying on the floor. The room that had been chock-a-block full was empty. I ran downstairs and into my parents' bedroom to wake my father. When I blurted out that we had been robbed, my father ran down to the street in his pyjamas in an effort to catch the thief, but to no avail. My father and I went up to the attic to view the damaged locks and the now-empty room. He was furious, as most of the goods had arrived only two days before. After a while he calmed down and we both went downstairs where my mother was waiting, wanting to know what had happened. Without giving an explanation, my father went to the telephone and rang the police. My mother became very worried and said, 'Don't do this, Maurice. It can be very dangerous to bring attention to us as Jews. Better forget about it.'

But my father was so furious that he did not want to think about the consequences. He told my mother to be quiet while he reported the theft to the police.

Two Dutch policemen arrived about half an hour later at our home. One was an elderly man and the other was a very tall young man with blond hair and sparkling blue eyes called Henny. Henny asked me questions about what the man looked like, what he had said to me, how tall I thought he was and other details about what had happened. He was such a nice policeman that, by the time he finished questioning me, I adored him as only a young girl can. Mum reminded me that it was time for school. After a quick breakfast in the kitchen, I said goodbye to Henny and the other policeman and went to school. When I came home again at about 4.30 that afternoon, my father told me that they had caught the thief in the morning, with the help of my description and his knowledge of the market helpers. Most of the goods had been recovered and returned already. Now my father could keep on helping those poor Jewish people without an income.

* * *

Henny became a good friend of our family's and he would often drop in after his afternoon shifts. If I happened to be home, he would give me one of his beautiful smiles and look down at me from his six-foot height and say, 'How is little Hetty today? Did you do your best at school?'

He was such a wonderful person – his smile, the open look of his eyes. Everybody loved him. One day I came home from school and found my father and Henny in serious conversation. I heard him say: 'No, Maurice, not this time. First we will see if they arrive safely. I tell you what we will do. Tear a 100-guilder banknote in two and I'll give one half to the doctor who is going with his family and ask him to post it back to Amsterdam when they arrive in Switzerland. When the half of the banknote arrives, we'll join it with your half and if it fits then we'll know they have arrived safely and you and your family can go on the next trip.'

Reluctantly my father agreed. He took out his wallet, pulled out a 100-guilder note and tore it into two, creating a zigzag pattern. He handed one half to Henny and carefully put the remaining half back in his wallet. Henny got up to leave when he noticed me for the first time. He did not smile at me. He looked strained and tense. I remained silent.

'Good luck, Henny. Be careful,' my father said, and extended his hand.

When Henny had gone, my father confided in me what it was all about. The Resistance, of which Henny was a member, believed they had found an escape route. A Rhine barge would take thirty people up the river to Switzerland. The people would be hidden below the deck. The barge would leave from the Zuider Zee and travel through Germany to Switzerland.

'I wanted us to be on the barge,' Dad said, 'but Henny wants us to wait for the next trip.'

I was glad Henny did not want us to go, and I told my father so.

'It's much too dangerous. The idea of going through Germany scares me. I think the other way to England is a much better idea.'

'Yes,' Dad said. 'I understand that, but a Rhine barge is not built to go on the sea.' He let out a deep sigh. 'We now have to wait to see if that doctor sends the banknote from Switzerland. I do hope so, for the doctor's sake.'

'When is the boat going?' I asked.

'In two days,' Dad said.

We both were silent, each busy with our own thoughts. Four days went by. We had expected Henny to come but he did not. Dad was nervous and we were worried as well. On the fifth day, Dirk, the elderly policeman who had accompanied Henny when our attic was robbed, came to see us. He told us that he had heard at the police station that Henny had been arrested by the SS two days previously and taken to the Euterpastraat SS headquarters. We were appalled; we knew about the atrocities committed by the SS there. Dirk told us that as far as he had been able to find out, thirty people (about five families) had boarded the barge. They had paid large amounts of money to the crew, and the barge had left safely early in the night. When the barge was in the middle of the Zuider Zee, at about midnight, the crew started to throw the families overboard. Their screams of terror were so loud that a German patrol boat came to investigate and, of course, everyone was rounded up, with disastrous results for our Henny. Dirk told us that Henny was now in a very bad state in the Wilhelmina Hospital and under SS guard.

'My God!' Mum wailed. 'How they must have tortured him.'

I was still sitting frozen in my chair. My mind would not accept the truth. Our beautiful, wonderful friend. Twenty-one years old, he had risked his life to help desperate people.

'My family owes their lives to Henny. He advised me not to go on this trip but to wait,' my father said, his face ashen. 'How can I thank him enough for stopping me from doing something foolish. Oh God! Let him get better!' He banged his fist on the table. 'Yes, please,' he repeated, 'let him get better.'

At that moment my father's niece Sonja walked in with her friend Johnny. We were a bit scared of Johnny as we did not know if he was 'safe'. He claimed he was a detective from the Dutch police, but Dirk had investigated this and could not find his name on the register. Johnny was madly in love with Sonja, and when he was around we were very careful about what we said. Therefore, all that we told Sonja and Johnny was that Henny was in the Wilhelmina Hospital after a serious accident and that a police guard was sitting at his door.

'I'll go and have a look at him tomorrow,' Johnny said.

Dirk got up and said goodbye. 'Let me know if you have some news from Johnny tomorrow,' he said to Mum as she escorted him to the door.

Later in the kitchen Mum related the horrible story to Sonja, after which Sonja told Johnny that they were leaving. We were glad that they had gone. In our depressed condition we did not feel right about entertaining anybody.

The next night Dad told me that Johnny had gone to see Henny in hospital. Henny was in a very bad condition. The SS had beaten his head into a bloodied mess and whipped him until his kidneys had ruptured. Mercifully, our courageous Henny passed away the next day.

* * *

The Germans had checked our passports a few times, but left after seeing the exemption stamps on them. Until now we had not heard anything about our trip to Portugal, but our suitcases remained packed under our beds in case the summons came. On 29 September 1943, at four o'clock in the morning, the doorbell began ringing urgently, accompanied by loud banging on the front door. The banging woke everyone in the house. I heard my parents moving about in their bedroom, my mother saying, 'They are here, we had better open the door.' From my bedroom I could see into the hall. I saw my mother open the door and there stood an SS officer and a German soldier with a drawn bayonet.

'Jews?' the officer asked.

My mother nodded.

'Passport,' he snapped, 'quick.'

By that time my father had already come with the passports, sure that the stamp would work its magic again. He confidently handed over the passports to the SS officer, who examined them carefully and ordered all five of us to line up in the hall. There we stood in our pyjamas, my mother holding her pink dressing gown tightly around her to stop herself from shaking. The SS officer told the soldier to keep watch over us while he had a look around to see if there was anyone else in the house. 'Oh dear God,' we silently prayed. In the confusion we had forgotten that Sonja and my mother's cousin Morris were in the house. To top it off, Morris had been hiding for a year and had come for a short visit only the day before. He had no passport or papers. Sonja had been born from a Jewish mother and a gentile father, and had papers to prove it. While the SS officer searched the house, we held our breath. We could hear him opening doors and banging them closed again. All this time, the soldier stood in front of us with his drawn bayonet. The officer returned with Sonja. He had found her in the lounge. We were all wondering what had happened to Morris. Where was he? Why hadn't the SS officer found him? Our family tried to talk to each other with our eyes, wanting to know the answer to this unbelievable thing, but we weren't left with much time to ponder over it.

'Your papers?' the SS officer asked Sonja.

She handed them to the officer.

'So you are half-Jew. And may I ask what you are doing in this house? I suppose you know it is forbidden to stay overnight in someone else's quarters?' By this time, he had worked himself into a temper. 'Answer me!' he shouted.

We all froze, looking at Sonja and the officer. Sonja was very pale, but proudly held her head up high and looked the officer straight in the face. Softly she said that during the day she had paid us a visit, and by the time the curfew came around she had a migraine headache, and it had been impossible for her to get home safely.

'You're lying!' the officer screamed. 'I'll keep your passport and you will come with the rest of them to the station. There someone else higher than me will deal with you.'

The officer turned to us and said, 'Jews, I'll give you one hour to get ready.' He ordered the German soldier to watch us carefully until he returned to take us to the station.

My mother told us all to get dressed. 'We don't know where we are going, so to keep warm is a good idea. Come on, boys, I'll help you get dressed.' She pushed Max and Jacky in front of her towards their room.

Of course, I thought, she's going to find out what happened to Morris, and I motioned Sonja and my father not to follow them. My father looked dejected.

'Dad, you had better get dressed or you'll catch cold, and we have to go soon,' I said.

'Yes,' Dad said, 'I had better go and get dressed. I hope they have made a mistake. Maybe we will be home again tomorrow morning. I can't understand it, they promised me we would be going to Portugal.'

Sonja and I said nothing. Mum came back down the hall, and in her eyes we could see that Morris was okay. She drew us all into the main bedroom. Whispering, she told us that when the Germans banged on the door, Morris had hidden himself under the bed among the suitcases. He had a bad moment when the officer searched the room – but he did not look under the bed.

'Good,' Dad said. 'For a minute I thought he had jumped out of the window again like he did the last time they came to pick him up.'

'What's he going to do now?' Max asked Mum.

'I told him to stay where he is until after we are gone, and to give our neighbours any valuables that are left. It's better that they have it than Puls,' Mum said.

'I suppose we'd better get ready. Hetty, after you get dressed, I would like to talk to you and the boys before we go,' Dad said.

After I got dressed I went to find Max and Jacky, and the three of us went to my parents' room. In the hall, we had to pass the German soldier, who by that time was tired of holding his bayonet. He had placed it against the wall, and was leaning beside it. Dad was sitting on the side of the bed. He looked very upset.

'Children, I'm very sorry this has happened,' he said. 'I've done everything I could so we didn't have to go to Germany. I have worked very hard for all of you, to give you a lot of things I didn't have when I was a boy. I gave nearly all of my money to the SS to save you. I'm very, very sorry.'

By now Dad was crying and we all tried to tell him it was not his fault.

He hushed us and said, 'We don't know what is going to happen, but you must promise me faithfully that if you are alive when this terrible war is over, no matter where you are, you must try your utmost to come back to Amsterdam, to the Pomstra family, who live around the corner. They have some shares and some jewels that I gave them to keep until after the war. Even if your mother or I do not return, they promised that they will look after you, because the money, the shares and the jewels will be enough to pay for your upbringing and education. Now children, did you all understand that?'

The three of us nodded our heads.

'Come here,' Dad said. He held us close as if he wanted to protect us from the things to come. 'I'm sorry, I'm sorry,' he kept on repeating.

Mum walked into the room with Sonja. They had been looking after the luggage. Mum put her hand on Dad's shoulder, trying to reassure him. 'Come on,' she said. 'The SS officer will be back any minute now. Come on.' Sonja had just made some coffee. Reluctantly, Dad let us go, and we all followed Mum into the kitchen.

It was 6.30 when the SS officer returned. The hour had become two and a half.

'Are you ready?' he shouted.

'Yes,' my father said.

'You lead the way, the rest of us will follow!' the SS officer barked at the German soldier.

My mother was the last one to leave our apartment, with the SS officer. She locked the front door firmly. Nobody spoke as we descended the stairs to the street. When we were all down, the SS officer told us to wait in the porch. He said that he had to collect some more people from around the corner. Again he left the soldier to guard us. It was a beautiful morning, the sun was shining and the square was deserted – except for the trucks waiting to take us to the station.

'Psst!'

My mother and I heard the soft sound, and we turned to see where it was coming from. The door next to our apartment was opened to a slit and our neighbour was peering through it. Mum and I moved closer to the door.

'What's going on?' the neighbour asked. 'Did the bastards come to take you away?'

Mum nodded and rummaged in her handbag. She took out the keys to our house and handed them to the neighbour.

'Here,' she said. 'After we've gone, go inside and help Morris who is hiding upstairs. Also take whatever you want.'

'Of course,' our neighbour said. 'Leave it to me. In the meantime, look after yourselves, and all the best to you all. Let's hope that this lousy war will soon be over. Good luck.' Silently, he closed the door.

The SS officer returned with another family.

'Start walking!' he ordered, and we all set out towards the trucks.

How strange the square looks, I thought, as we were crossing the road. This could not be the same square I had crossed a thousand times on my way to school. But then, would anything be the same again? We arrived at the parked trucks and were ordered to get in quickly. All of us scrambled on board. We were standing up in the back with the guard where we could hear the SS officer laughing and joking in the front cabin with the driver. Yes, they could laugh! The two small children from the other family were crying. The mother was trying to hush them. Apologetically, she told us they had been awakened from their sleep.

The truck arrived at the station and we were told to alight. One by one we filed into the station. The SS officer marched Sonja away from us towards a counter where high-ranking SS officers were standing together. Our family was ordered to stand with a group of people. Although there were about a thousand people altogether, an unnatural hush lay over the hall. We made conversation only in whispers. It looked like all the remaining Jews in Amsterdam had been picked up in the raid. We soon found out that even the Jewish Council President, Abraham Ascher, and Councillor Abraham Soep and their families had also been picked up. Soon we saw some of our friends in other groups. More and more people were being brought to the station. By eight o'clock the hall looked like an anthill. People, young and old, babies and children were all huddled together. Some had walked over to family standing with another group. Rumours started to circulate. Some said we were going to Portugal, others that Hitler had sent orders that all the Jews left in Amsterdam were to be liquidated. We did not know what to believe, so we were torn between hope and despair.

The time moved on. By nine o'clock we were still in the station hall, but no one was standing with their appointed groups. The only SS guards were standing outside the station. Near the counter, we could see Sonja standing with her hands behind her back and her face to the wall. We did not go near her because we were afraid that it might make it worse for her, so we waved from a distance. The same thought was in everyone's mind: when would the train come?

'Hetty,' I heard a voice calling. I turned around to see my very special boyfriend.

'Herman, what are you doing here? Did they get you too?' I had gone to school with Herman for years. He used to carry my school case, and at the local gym we were always teamed up together as we were the youngest.

'Yes,' Herman said. 'They came at two o'clock last night and we have been here since three o'clock.'

'How's your mother? Is she all right?' I asked.

'Mum's all right,' Herman said, 'but Dad is taking it pretty rough. I'll tell you something funny. There's a man down there who's telling everybody that the train is not coming because it's got a flat tyre.'

We laughed. It was good to laugh in the midst of all this misery.

'Do you know where we're going, Herman?' I asked.

'Your guess is as good as mine, but I think we're going to Westerbork. Listen, Hetty, if you have a chance in the train, ask your mother to cut your hair short, because when we arrive in Westerbork you have to pass a health test by a German doctor. If he thinks that your hair is not clean enough, they shave it all off.'

'Oh no, Herman, that's not true.'

'Yes, my dear,' he said. 'It's a pity to cut it, but you'd better not take any chances.'

I was heartbroken. My hair! My shoulder-length hair had to be cut off! Before I could reply a whistle started blowing and a voice came over the address system asking for silence. The hall became very quiet, and no one moved. This was the moment. You could feel the tension rising. Then the voice said, 'Jews, we want you to pick up your luggage and proceed to platform 3, where the train will take you to Westerbork. Group A will come forward first. Group B will follow.'

It was chaos in the big hall. People were running everywhere to return to their groups. Mothers were looking for their children who had wandered off, fathers struggled with the luggage from whole families. Already groups A and B had passed through the turnstiles, and C and D were following. We were with group W, so we were not so pressed for time. When group S went by, Herman called out, 'Hetty, see you in Westerbork. Remember what I told you.'

Then Mum asked for my attention. 'When we go, Hetty, you hold Jacky by the hand so that we don't lose him in the crush. We must try and keep close together and not lose one another.'

'Sure,' I said, taking Jacky by the hand.

'That's it,' Dad said, 'they've just called out our letter. Let's go, and God be with us.'

There was a tremendous crush at the turnstiles, but we managed to reach the platform together. It was the longest train I had ever seen. The locomotive was already a long way out of the station. As each carriage filled up, it moved further out of the station. We were lucky: it was a passenger train, not the cattle wagons used to transport most of the people. (Westerbork was what the Germans called Vorsuchslager, which means a repatriation camp. From there, you were sent to different camps in Germany – Sachsenhausen, Buchenwald, Ravensbrück, Dachau, Neuengamme, Mauthausen, Oranienburg and Auschwitz. In Poland it was Birkenau, Sobibor, Blechhammer, Gleiwitz and Monowitz.) The Germans had told the Jewish population in Holland that we would be put to work there with plenty of food and family accommodation.

So now we were on our way. Slowly, the train left the Amstel Station. In our compartment there were only about thirty people. We were lucky. They must have put a lot more people in the first carriages, as some of them had to stand. At least we all had a seat. Silently we watched the passing scenery, the fields with the cows and the orchards. 'What now, what now?' sang the wheels of the train.

Two

'Oh dear God, help us!'

Suddenly the train came to a halt. Our first glimpse of Westerbork was a long platform with barracks next to it. Everybody alighted from the train and we were met by a group of nurses. They guided us to a barracks where a team of doctors, Dutch and German, was going to give us a medical check-up. First of all we had to be registered, and we also had to declare if we had any precious jewels, gold or money with us. This was our first encounter with the efficient registration system the Germans maintained. Hours and hours passed. Some 1,600 people had to be checked in, and we were among the last. It was eleven o'clock at night and we were very tired as it was long past our bedtime and we had not had much sleep the night before.

At last it was all over and we were taken to barracks 70. Our luggage was already in the entrance hall. The left side of the barracks housed the women and children, and the right side was the men's dormitory. The beds were very close together and the bunks were three beds high. My mother and I each occupied a third bunk, Jacky had the bed under mine, and Max was with Dad on the other side of the barracks. We were given coffee and sandwiches, as we had missed the six o'clock meal. We ate quickly so we could get some sleep. There were no sheets on the beds, but we had a grey blanket and a straw mattress. Exhausted, we slept.

We were woken up at 7 a.m. by our barracks elder, whose name was Walter. Every muscle in my body was complaining, but we had to make a move as coffee and bread would be served in fifteen minutes. We got into our clothes. There was no water in the barracks to wash ourselves. We had to walk to the washhouse, and the toilets were even further down the road. Inside the brick toilet block there were toilets without seats, and they were not very clean. There was no running water and no electricity. (Later, Max and Jacky would go there at night with a home-made lantern made of a small food tin with holes in it with a candle inside.) After we had washed ourselves, we went back to the barracks, where we found Max and Dad with our breakfast. We were all very happy that we could see one another again, and we had a reasonable breakfast around the table by Dad's bunk.

That day we decided to explore Westerbork. We found a small hospital, workshops and a factory. What they produced, nobody knew. In a separate part of the camp was a penalty barracks. This barracks was for people who had gone into hiding or underground and had been captured. There had been German–Jewish refugees in Westerbork for many years already, and they were put in charge of us. In turn they were responsible to the SS commandant, who lived in a nice home just outside the gate. We soon found out that life in Westerbork was not too bad, but we had to do without conveniences like showers and privacy, and although the food was not very appetising, you could receive parcels from friends to supplement your rations.

Sonja, who had been released by the SS, began sending us parcels of food, so we had enough to eat. She also sent a warm coat for me and a pair of warm slacks for each of us.

The days passed. I had met Herman a few days after arriving in Westerbork: he and his parents were in barracks 68. We spent as much time together as we could, and even went to gymnastics lessons given by Uncle Max to keep us fit and to stave off the boredom. (My father's younger brother Uncle Max and his wife Clara were picked up on the same night as we had been taken.)

About six weeks after our arrival in Westerbork, we heard that a transport of people was going to be sent away to Germany. Who would go and who would stay behind? Tempers flared. Early one morning a list of names was hung in the entrance hall of the barracks. Whoever had their name on the list had to be ready with their luggage by seven o'clock that night. From six o'clock, everybody would be confined to barracks. That whole day was bedlam in the camp. Families who were being separated were crying. A notice in the hall advised that Rabbi Bluhm would bless anyone if they were in need of it. Young and old were queuing up to be blessed by this wonderful man. I went as well, and as long as I live I will never forget the kind eyes that looked into mine before I bowed my head to receive my blessing. It was seven o'clock, and two guards came for the people who had to go on the train. It was a cattle train and on the roof of the cars were machine guns to prevent anyone from escaping during the journey. How can one express the misery of having to bid farewell those who were leaving? At about eight o'clock a parcel arrived for me – a watch with a photograph of Herman on it and a Swann fountain pen, a valued possession of Herman's. I knew that Herman wished to convey to me his sorrow and love with this farewell present. I cried. My heart was breaking to have us parted in such a cruel manner, and my mother closed her arms around me to soften the pain. At one o'clock in the morning the train left for a destination unknown. Herman and his parents and Rabbi Bluhm were on the train.

* * *

A few weeks after that horrible night, a transport of about one hundred people arrived for the penalty barracks. Soon we found out that my father's parents were with them. My father obtained a pass to visit them, and there he heard a pitiful story. My grandparents had been paying the people who were hiding them, and when the money ran out, the mercenary bastards delivered them to the Germans. For six weeks, my poor grandparents had been in gaol in Scheveningen, one of the worst gaols to go to during the German occupation of Holland. My grandmother was a diabetic and had been deprived of insulin for a long time. She told my father, 'I'm glad it is all over. I give in. I am half dead already.'

The following Sunday we were permitted to see our grandparents. Oma Hetty's hair had turned white and she was a ghost of her former self, she had become so thin. I had been named after her and was always her favourite grandchild.

'My darling,' she said, 'how much you have grown.' She held me tightly in her arms, tears streaming down her face.

'Please Oma, don't cry,' I begged.

'Here, young lady, don't I get a kiss?' This was Opa trying to break the tension.

Oma let me go. I ran over to my Opa and embraced him. He

was skinny as well, but he still had a twinkle in his eyes. My grandfather was always a cheerful, happy-go-lucky person. We stayed all Sunday afternoon together. We had brought food and clothing for them because they had nothing. During the next few weeks my grandparents stayed in Westerbork, and we visited them as many times as we were allowed, until on 25 January 1944 another train came and took them away to Auschwitz.

* * *

The fifth of December is St Nicholas' Day in Holland. This is the day that young children receive presents if they have been good all year round. Three weeks before I had taken charge of the children in the barracks and had put them to work making streamers from coloured paper and glue which Walter had organised for me. We were making trains and cars out of matchboxes. The youngsters had a wonderful time playing with them. The children's mothers were glad to have them off their hands for a few hours every day, and they promised to contribute flour and sugar for St Nicholas' Day, so we could make cookies. A spirit of goodwill pervaded the barracks. People would stop by the table where the little ones worked to give advice and help out when we got stuck. The pile of small presents grew until every child had a gift. Never mind that they had made their own presents, they had an interest.

A few days before St Nicholas, I went to Walter and asked if it was possible for him to arrange for a piano. No party is good without music. He promised to see what he could do, and the day before the party I was picked up by one of the camp elders to go to the German commandant to ask permission to use the only piano in the camp. I was very frightened but the elder held my hand while he spoke in German to the commandant, explaining to him that I had organised the party without help from grown-ups. We apparently struck the commandant in a good mood because when he talked to me, he smiled. I did not understand a word of German so I looked up at the elder questioningly. He did not bother to explain to me what was said, but he whispered, 'Say, "Yes, sir, thank you very much".' I tried as hard as possible to repeat the German words, and then we were out of the place with the promise that the piano could be collected the next afternoon. Walter was very happy when we told him of our success, and then surprised with more good news. The women of the barracks had put themselves to work and fashioned a bishop's robe and mitre. One of the fathers would act as St Nicholas. Every child went to bed that night at seven o'clock, and I am sure that nowhere in Holland were sweeter children. They knew that St Nicholas did not like naughty children who went to bed late.

There was great activity on the morning of 5 December 1943. Some women were making cookies and others were making sweets. The men also got in on the act, shifting bunks to make room for chairs. A special chair was decorated for St Nicholas. The colourful streamers the children had made were hung from the ceiling. Everybody was excited. At two o'clock the piano arrived. Six sturdy men had carried it across the camp. By now the news had spread that barracks 70 was having a party. We had many visitors that day from the other barracks. At six o'clock that night, the children were sitting in their best clothes, waiting for the big moment when St Nicholas would arrive.

A loud knocking on the door heralded his arrival. 'It's St Nicholas,' everyone whispered. The children began to sing, 'Welcome St

Nicholas,' and the adults chimed in with the youngsters. In the doorway stood St Nicholas, and he had brought Black Peter with him. He was carrying the large sack containing all the presents. Just seeing the children's faces, their eyes sparkling, was enough reward for the weeks of work I had put into it. At eight o'clock the children went to bed. They had all had a wonderful time, but the party was not yet over. The adults gathered around the piano and everyone began singing. Everyone looked happy for the first time in a long time. At 9.45, Walter climbed on a chair and asked for silence.

'Ladies and gentlemen,' he said, 'I would like to pay a tribute to a young girl within our midst, who has, by her own initiative and determination, given us much happiness today. Let it be known what co-operation means, because without the help of our wonderful mothers, this party would not have been a success, and I'm glad I could have been of some assistance. Hetty,' – he motioned me to come near him – 'I'm proud to know you, and I'm sure that I express the wish of everyone here that you and your family may come through these trying times safe and healthy, and that you may grow up into a beautiful young lady. As a memento of this occasion, I would like you to accept this beautiful mirror in gratitude from us all, and may you see yourself grow more pretty as time goes by.' Walter kissed me on both cheeks and handed me a beautiful hand mirror with a pink bow. Loud applause filled the room and everyone began singing 'For She's a Jolly Good Fellow'. I had never been praised in public before, and I did not know where to look or what to say. By now it was ten o'clock, the lights went out and the party was over.

* * *

31

Christmas came and went: 1944 had arrived. What would it bring us? The hope that this year would end our misery was in everyone's hearts. No transport had gone during the festive season, but we knew it would not be long now.

On 10 January 1944, a transport of eight hundred people with dual nationality went to Bergen-Belsen. On 1 February 1944, our names were on the list. That night, with about 1,100 people, we boarded the train. Surprisingly, it was a passenger train – but of course it was no Pullman.

At about ten o'clock, we left Westerbork and travelled all through the night. The whole of Germany was in darkness so we saw nothing. We stopped for one and a half hours at a very large station later on in the night. Then we were off again. When daybreak came we could see a bit of the country. We had tried to get some sleep during the journey but it was impossible as the uncertainty of our fate kept us awake.

The train slowly drew to a halt. 'CELLE' was the name written on the signpost. Curious, we looked out of the window and I heard Dad's shocked exclamation, 'Oh dear God, help us!'

On the platform, there were about thirty SS men with blood-hounds straining on their leashes.

'Get out!' someone screamed.

Bewildered, we left the train.

'Leave your luggage except hand luggage, and line up!' an SS officer shouted.

A long queue formed. Mothers held on to their children. Some of the men were told to come forward – Dad was one of them. They were told to pack the luggage onto trucks. The long columns of people started to move. I could see a small bridge over the railway line, and although it was early in the morning a few locals, mostly men, were watching us as we started to walk. We walked and walked and walked. When we left our luggage, we did not know if we would ever see it again, so we had all taken some small bags with us. Those bags became as heavy as lead during the long walk. Jacky, who had never been strong, was carrying a small rucksack. Now he looked green around the nose from weariness. When I saw his plight, I walked over to a man who wasn't carrying anything and appeared to be enjoying the walk.

'Please sir, could you be so kind as to carry my little brother's rucksack for a little while? He's only nine years old,' I asked.

'Look, you are not in Holland now, you are in my country,' the man answered, looking down at me from his six-foot height. 'Here you have nothing to say. Carry your own bag.'

Apparently, he was one of the German refugees who had been welcomed in Holland in 1937. (Poor man, his own countrymen later killed him – he was one of the first to die in Belsen of starvation.) I told Jacky to give me his bag and Mum and I carried it between us. Our feet were dragging, and the speed of the columns had slowed down. Behind us we heard the SS shouting, 'Hurry up, hurry up!' I glanced over my shoulder, and at the end of the column I could see two elderly people supporting each other and struggling along with their luggage. The woman was crying and the husband was asking the SS officer something. This resulted in the guard cocking his rifle at the couple and yelling, 'Forward, forward!' A young man came up to the nearly exhausted couple and took all their bags so they could walk more easily.

Where were we going? Would we ever get there? How long would it take? Dear God, help us! At least the road was made of bitumen, which was a blessing. We did not meet a soul – no cars, no people – only the guards and their dogs. If the circumstances had not been so miserable, we might have enjoyed the beauty of the surrounding forest of stately pines. The hours passed and we were still walking. Then at last we could see a high fence of barbed wire and a gate. On the other side was an office where SS guards were sitting. About five hundred yards further to the left, we passed another gate. We had arrived in Belsen concentration camp.

Three

'Why is it taking so long?'

Our first impression of Bergen-Belsen was of a big, open place. About thirty barracks were built in orderly rows of three or four, with about twenty-foot wide streets in between. Everything looked neat and tidy. When we first arrived, Belsen was a camp for prisoners of war, not the horror camp it later became. In size I believe it was about one kilometre by one kilometre, and I found out later it was divided into smaller camps. Our section was about the size of a football field. We had entered the camp by the main street, which divided the camp in two. The right side of the camp (as we later found out) was for Russian POW officers. The left side was divided into five parts: the SS camp and food store, an area which later became a camp for Häftlinge (Geman slave labourers), the Hungarian camp and our camp, which later was called the Sternlager (star camp) or Albela camp. Surrounding the entire camp was a strip of land, about twenty yards wide, dotted with skull-and-crossbones warning signs. High wire fences with watch-towers marked the perimeter.

Every camp was divided into smaller parts. Ours had the Appelplatz (roll-call) and the men's section together, then a fence with the customary gate to the women's section. We were received by Herr Albela, our camp elder, a Greek who had arrived with forty others eight weeks before us. Those Greeks, the dual nationalities and our group were the only prisoners in Belsen at that time. Herr Albela spoke to us in German, which was translated by one of our men. He told us that the gate between the men's and women's section would close at eight o'clock at night. During the day, we could be together. It was the same as in Westerbork.

We were taken to our barracks, where we got a pleasant surprise. The barracks was spotlessly clean and all the furniture looked new. It was divided into three sections: the dining room with large tables and chairs around them, a dormitory and combined laundry and washrooms. The dormitory had double bunks and plenty of windows for air and light. The washhouse had a cement floor with about ten washbasins, a row of laundry troughs and ten toilets.

The first thing we did after entering the barracks was to sit down and kick off our shoes. Did our feet hurt! Especially mine. Two days before we left Westerbork, I had dropped a pan of boiling water over my foot, and now it was all red and swollen. After we had rested for a while, we went and had a look at our beds. Mum and I took a top bunk each, and Jacky a lower bunk. Mum had not said a word about Dad but I knew she was worried. We had not seen Dad or the other men since we had arrived, and now it was about four o'clock.

Two Greeks brought us a large container with food. It smelled good. We were each given a bowl of soup and a spoon, knife and fork, and an enamel beaker. The walk had made us hungry and we had not eaten since the day before, but after trying one spoonful I looked at Mum. I could see that she did not like it. It was hot water, with a thread of sauerkraut floating in it here and there. We could not eat it and we were not alone. One lady decided to wash her feet with the soup, an action which was soon followed by others in our barracks.

It was about half past four when the truck carrying our luggage arrived. The men who had been ordered to stay behind at the station had loaded the luggage of the 1,100 people who had arrived that morning at Celle. As news of the arrival swept through the camp, everybody hurried to what became known later as the Appelplatz. We were just in time to see my father and some other men enter the camp sitting on top of the luggage on the truck. We called out to him and he smiled broadly when he spotted us. When the truck stopped, he jumped clear and, with the help of the other men, unloaded our luggage. Everybody surged forward to collect their belongings. We mustered enough strength to carry our cases to barracks 27, where my mother, Jacky and I were to stay. The blankets that we had brought from Holland were needed to get ready for the night. We also had some sheets with us, and we put some jumpers in a pillowcase to make do for pillows. We put our suitcase with the rest of our clothing on top of Jacky's bed near the foot end. This way we could keep an eye on them, as there was no other place to keep them.

Earlier that day two men had entered our barracks and asked if there was someone present who could speak German. A skinny lady of about forty years, with a hard face, came forward. She was one of those refugees who had been given asylum in Holland in 1937. She could speak Dutch but with a heavy German accent. A conversation took place between herself and the two men. Although we could not understand much of what was being said, we understood that she had been appointed as our barracks elder from that time on. When the men left, she took control as if she had done it all her life. She was the one who gave us the right to use a certain cupboard along the wall of the dining room. This created resentment as we felt at a disadvantage that we Dutch people had to take orders from this German woman, whom we had welcomed into our country a few years before. When we unpacked our suitcases, Mum moved the food, some cooking utensils, an iron and some other things we had brought with us , such as soap and some washing powder, into our appointed cupboard. In exchange for a jumper, Mum had got a hold of a lock to prevent pilfering.

At about seven o'clock, Max and Dad took their blankets and some clean clothing for the next day to barracks 14. They did not return until the next morning. Our barracks was the last to be occupied and although it had sixty beds, only thirty people were there, so we had been able to choose our beds at random. The barracks were new and the bunks only two-high. The straw mattresses were also new. They were, I suppose, worthy of people who would be exchanged for German POWs. There was a single row of beds along the length of the wall and windows, and double rows of beds in the middle of the dormitory. No food was brought to us that first night, so Mum gave us some biscuits. We were so tired that by eight o'clock everybody was in bed.

At first light the next morning, we awoke and surveyed our new surroundings. Although it was winter the sun was shining, which gave our dormitory a friendly atmosphere. Some women who had woken earlier had already been to the washhouse. Mum, Jacky and I set out with towels and soap to refresh ourselves. The washhouse was empty except for one elderly lady who was standing as God had created her at a washbasin. I had never seen a stranger naked before and it shocked me deeply. The woman took no notice of us and continued to wash herself. My God, I thought to myself, do all women look like this when they grow old? The woman was tall and very skinny. Her skin was yellow and very dry. Her breasts, like empty paper bags, drooped right down to her waist. My mother, seeing the astonishment in my eyes, whispered, 'Do not look. Give the woman some privacy.'

Jacky was also visibly shocked, but Mum turned him away firmly and told him to start washing himself. Jacky and I could not help ourselves. Our eyes wandered over to the woman, who, after a while, started to dry herself firmly and then, with a quick movement, threw her breast over her shoulder to dry the front part of her body. This became too much even for my mother. With our faces and hands still wet, she practically pushed us out of the washhouse. Once outside, the three of us burst into laughter and Jacky immediately dubbed the woman 'Mrs Cow'. The woman had shown no shame or embarrassment when we saw her naked, and we had to accept that our own inhibitions would no longer be considered. Although we did not realise it at the time, this encounter was the start of the degeneration of our values which we were to experience more of over the coming years in Belsen.

When we got back to the barracks we were told that black coffee had arrived, but when we tasted it, it was awful. It was only brown-coloured water. There was nothing to eat and we had to use some food from our cupboard. Max and Dad arrived at about nine o'clock. Their barracks was crowded and they told us that the Chief Rabbi was also in barracks 14. In the morning, those who practised their religion had held a secret prayer service. They also had this black coffee given to them, and we all agreed it was revolting. From somewhere, Mum produced some hot water and made us a cup of tea. She gave Dad and Max a few biscuits. We had eaten ours earlier that morning. Mum and Dad arranged with our barracks elder to receive the daily rations for Dad and Max in our barracks. This way we could remain a family unit.

For a few days, the SS left us in peace. Everybody tried to settle in and mentally adjust to our daily routine in Belsen. After about three days, our barracks elder advised us that we all had to attend roll-call the next morning at seven o'clock sharp at the Appelplatz. Everyone had to be up by six the next morning. We had a quick wash and dressed as warmly as we could, then went to the dining room where we received a beaker of warm brown water that was supposed to be coffee or tea. (Our bread rations were given to us at lunchtime, together with a bowl of soup. The soup was a half litre of warm brownish water with some pieces of carrot or parsnip floating in it.) At half past six, the messengers started calling, 'Everyone to roll-call.' Everyone who could walk, even babies as young as three years of age, had to go to the Appelplatz to be counted. We had to stand in rows of five and when the Scharführer came to count us, we had to stand to attention, with our heads up and eyes straight ahead. No movement or sound was allowed. The chaos that morning, and for many days thereafter, cannot be described. We were not used to lining up like an army or being counted like criminals. We were lucky that first morning. Either the figures were correct or the SS had something better to do. They let us get away after one and a half hours. The next day we were not so lucky. This time they let us stand for two hours at roll-call. Soon we found out that if we did not come up 'to standard', the SS would let us stand at the Appelplatz for hours on end. The barracks elders desperately tried to train us to behave the way the SS wanted. The agonising hours at the Appelplatz went by very slowly, and many a prayer went up from elderly people near death on their feet and children shivering from cold and hunger, their little faces becoming smaller as the days went by. Sometimes it was way past our lunchtime before the SS let us go. Herr Albela would blow a whistle and the music of a philharmonic orchestra could not have sounded sweeter. After the whistle, we would run as quickly as our legs would carry us back to our respective barracks. Our beds had become our home and the only place where we felt a little safe.

We had been in Belsen for about a week when the SS ordered all the men as young as fifteen years of age to come to roll-call at six o'clock to form work units. One of the toughest jobs went to the unit that went outside the camp into the woods to dig out the roots of tree stumps. It was hard and merciless work. My father and the Chief Rabbi were picked for this unit. They would leave the camp at six o'clock and return late in the afternoon. On the first day when they returned, my father brought back some berries he had picked off the bushes. He had filled his pockets with them and he emptied them into one of our soup bowls. It was not much, but the sight of these red berries cheered us. I was the first to try one. It tasted sour and bitter.

'Maybe they're not ripe yet,' Mum said.

Max and Jacky had a try but they could not eat them either. What a shame, they looked so appetising. We put the bowl of berries under the bed. Perhaps if we left them for a few days they would taste better. A few days later, with hunger gnawing at my stomach, I retrieved the bowl. The berries still looked the same as a few days earlier but I tasted them anyway. Brrr, how sour they were. A middle-aged man walking by saw the grimace on my face and noticed the bowl of berries.

'What a shame we cannot eat them. Perhaps they're poisonous,' I said.

He stuck his hand out and I gave him a few berries. He agreed that they could not be eaten raw but suggested that we try to cook them.

'How in the world are we going to cook them?' I asked.

My newly made friend said he would arrange something and left. He returned about twenty minutes later with a small spirit cooker, but we had no spirits. We removed the part that was the burner and were left with the frame of the cooker. I sent Jacky away to find some twigs or wood from somewhere, which we splintered on his return. After a few tries, at last I had the little stove going. I put the pan with the berries on top, but with no success. The fire burned itself out very quickly. There was no way I could bring the berries to the boil. I halved the amount of berries in the pan in an effort to get some result but this did not work either. My new friend, Henry, left when I lit the fire in the cooker because we knew it was punishable to light fires in the barracks. He returned occasionally to enquire about how things were progressing. After about an hour I was about to give up when Henry returned with some fire beads. Now it was easy. The water boiled and so did the berries. I had visions of being a famous cook who could create the most wonderful jam that we could put on our dry, hard bread rations, but the beads burned out very quickly and it became apparent that another supply was needed to finish the job. With pleading eyes I looked at Henry, who said he would try to get some more. He returned again with four small beads and told me that these were definitely the last he could obtain. Resigned, I lit the last of the beads and every nerve in my body was directed at the flame, imploring it to give out enough heat to make the berries edible. Slowly the flame became smaller and smaller until there was no spark left. Gingerly I tasted the gooey mess that lay at the bottom of the pan but it was still not edible. I gave Henry the remaining berries and returned the cooker to him. I told him that it was no good but he gladly accepted. He left with many thanks and I never saw him again.

All the women were called to roll-call. From them, the SS selected groups who had to work in the kitchens to cook the food for the camp. Mum was picked to work in the peel kitchen. She had to get up at three o'clock to go to roll-call and started work at four o'clock. She returned at six o'clock in the evening, so I had the task of looking after my two brothers, washing their clothing, making their beds and collecting our daily food rations.

We had been in Belsen for about three weeks now. The burns on my foot would not heal and the wound looked inflamed. The camp doctor advised me to rest for a week and gave me a letter so I did not have to attend roll-call. Our barracks was shiny-clean and pleasant, and I was quite happy to stay in bed reading a book that someone had lent me. It was peaceful in the barracks as nearly everybody else had gone to roll-call.

At the end of the dormitory another woman was sick in bed. She was sleeping. After about two hours, the women and children returned from roll-call, and soon after that our lunch arrived. It was not busy in the peel kitchen, so my mother had worked only a few hours before returning to the barracks. I decided to get up and join my mother for a little while in the dining room. Mum was sitting with some other women around one of the tables having a chat. I pulled out a chair to join them; planes were heard approaching. We could hear machine guns from the watchtowers going into action. Everybody was screaming. I panicked and started to run back to my bed. Bullets were flashing in front of and around me.

'Hetty, stop! Stop! Get on the floor!' my mother screamed.

I heard my mother's cries above the din. I threw myself on the floor, but before I landed I saw the sick woman in the dormitory coming out of her bed and running towards us. A bullet hit her and, as if in a dream, I saw her crumpling onto the floor with blood streaming from her wounds.

'She got hit! She got hit!' I crawled towards my mother, sobbing.

For about five minutes, the planes strafed the camp. When the planes disappeared, someone went to see to the woman. A stretcher was brought in and she was rushed off to the sickbay. She died that night. She was only thirty-two years old and was the first death from our barracks. I stayed close to my mother for the rest of the day, and when we went to bed that evening I found two bullets in my bed. One of them had made a large hole in my book.

Small groups of people began to arrive in our camp: gypsies from Hungary and Jewish families from Italy. Barracks were needed to house these people. Trucks arrived with dismantled barracks from other camps in Germany. The men from our camp were ordered to erect the barracks, but most of the men did not have skills in manual labour, so they went up very slowly. The barracks were erected on parts of the Appelplatz and to speed matters up, the SS brought in prisoners from the camp annexed to ours. It was the first time that we had seen these poor creatures up close. They were dressed in the white and grey cotton cloth, the uniform of the concentration camp. They would march into our camp early in the morning, trained into perfect precision. The kapo (overseer) would scream when they passed through the gate, 'Hats off, face right' in a salute to the SS Scharführer, who counted them as they came through. When their hats came off they revealed their shorn heads. They looked skinny and drawn. Their kapo would scream his orders, and how quickly those men moved. They lifted and carried and hammered the barracks together. They knew how to evade the monstrous whip from the kapo, which they would suffer if they did not work hard enough. They were from Eastern Europe, and I thought they spoke Polish or Estonian. We could not understand them. I was standing among a group of young children, watching from a distance. After about an hour, I left for our barracks. I could not watch any more, and yet I remembered the smile one of the prisoners gave me when he spotted me just as he was about to lift a heavy wooden part of the barracks with another prisoner. His drawn face had come alive with this smile as if he wanted to tell me, 'I have not given up yet'.

Our barracks had become very crowded. Jacky's bed was claimed so I had to share my bed with him. Luckily, I was not a tall girl, so we slept head to tail, and we moved our cases to Mum's foot end. Mum went to work in the peel kitchen every morning at three o'clock. Dad left his barracks at six o'clock to join the work detail. We only saw him at lunchtime and after he was finished at night for about an hour. I used to wait near the gate for him and when he arrived deathly tired, often he would say to me, 'I can't go on any more. How long before we are free again? Why is it taking so long?'

I used to take my father's hand, my heart bleeding to see him so depressed.

'Come on, Dad, you can do it. Don't lose hope. I am sure it won't be long now,' I said.

'Do you think so?' he said.

'Yes, I'm sure of it,' I answered. 'Remember the saying, "The last boxes are the heaviest".'

We used to walk, without many words, to our barracks where Jacky and Max were usually waiting for him on top of our beds. At the end of the day Dad, along with the boys, would meet Mum near the gate. She went to work dressed in long leather boots she had brought from Holland. In these boots covered by trousers, she would hide small pieces of carrots and smuggle them through the gates back to our camp. She risked her life doing that, but she wanted to bring some food back for her very hungry husband and children. She risked her life twice: first, by putting food in her boots in the peel kitchen, and second, by marching through the gates with it under the watchful eyes of the SS.

The food given to us became worse and worse. At noon we would get four centimetres of dry, hard bread. The barracks elder would cut up the square loaves of bread with a ruler while a group of people watched her like hawks to make sure no one got a fraction more. Sometimes we would get a tiny square piece of butter or a spoonful of jam, but most of the time it was only bread. We also got soup, the coloured water with a piece of parsnip or carrot floating in it. We were all terribly hungry and we became masters at dividing our food rations so they would last for twenty-four hours.

The news got around that the Rabbi was going to hold a meeting to discuss different things behind barracks 17 at about four o'clock. I decided to go. When I arrived there at the appointed time, only eight men and no women were present. The men stood closely together and asked the Rabbi questions, gaining comfort from the quiet religious man.

'What are we to do? We are hungry and the food we get is not kosher,' one man asked the Rabbi.

'God has told us that we must only eat kosher food, but he has created life and I therefore say that this is a time of emergency when life must come first,' the Rabbi answered. 'As a servant of the Almighty, I do hereby decree that you can eat anything even if it is *treife* (not clean). Your first duty is to stay alive.'

I was deeply shocked when I heard these words, as was the man who asked the question. He confessed that hunger had already made him break the commands of God, but he was deeply troubled by it.

'In the eyes of God, you have not done anything wrong, so do not be troubled any more,' the Rabbi reassured him.

After the meeting I walked back to our barracks and although we never kept a kosher home, I could not shake the impact of the Rabbi's words. I somehow felt betrayed. The Rabbi, of all people, had told us to give up part of our deepest beliefs and rules that guide the life of a Jew – even for those who have strayed, somewhere, somehow, deep-seated there is a spark that will never die. A spark that tells us we belong.

The people in our barracks were angry. During the night someone had broken into the private cupboards in the dining room and stolen bread rations and other food. Lots of suggestions were made as to who could have done it. It was even alleged that Max and Jacky were the guilty ones. My father questioned Jacky and was satisfied that he did not commit the crime. Max could not be the guilty one either as he slept in the male section with Dad. Every night the stealing continued. An old lady was crying because the little food she had in her cupboard was taken.

Some of the men decided to hold a vigil during the night to try to catch the thief. The next day it went all around the camp that the men had been successful. The thief turned out to be Emile, a twelve-year-old boy. The elders of our camp had previously formed a sort of court, as they thought it was better to deal with offenders themselves rather than the SS. Whenever necessary, court was held near Albela's office. A trestle table was set up and five men, some with legal backgrounds, would try each case that came before them. The accused was allocated a 'lawyer' who would plead for him. The hearing never took long, so as not to attract too much attention from the SS. Joseph Weiss, a wise man respected by everybody in our camp, was present at the hearings. Emile was brought before the court and given cleaning in the barracks for one month as punishment.

'Hetty, if things don't get better soon, we will lose Dad,' Mum said.

I nodded agreement.

'Would it be possible, Hetty,' Mum continued, 'that you and I share one bowl of soup each day so Dad can have two bowls of soup?'

'But then you'll be very hungry, Mum. You need it.'

'Yes,' Mum said, 'but we women don't have to eat as much as men.'

For a moment I considered the proposal and then agreed. Mum hugged me and said she would bring me some carrots every day. She could eat raw carrots in the peel kitchen.

'Hetty, the barracks elder wants to see you.' An elderly man standing near my bed delivered the message.

'What for?' I asked.

'You'd better come quickly to the dining room,' the man said as he walked away.

I climbed down from my bed and went to the dining room. Frau Müller, the barracks elder whom I distinctly disliked, beckoned me to come near.

'I want you to clear out your cupboard straight away,' she said.

'What for? We need the cupboard,' I objected.

'Do as you are told. I have given the cupboard to Mrs X,' she insisted.

A wave of disgust swept through me. Mrs X was one of a group of slimy, slippery people who competed for favours from the barracks elder. This German bitch, I thought, she was a refugee in Holland. While here, because she could speak the language, she had powers to humiliate the Dutch people who had given her shelter. I went back to the bedroom for the key to the padlock. Max arrived just as I got the key.

'What's the matter?' he asked, when he noticed my upset face.

'That barracks bitch told me to clear our cupboard. You had better give me a hand to put everything on the bed.'

We returned to the dining room and cleared the cupboard of our meagre belongings: our rations for the day, a few containers of vitamin tablets, calcium tablets, some pans, our soup bowls, spoons and forks, a few tea towels and our toothbrushes. We dumped everything on top of the bed. I hid the bread rations in one of the suitcases, out of view of the people in the barracks. There were three other families whose cupboards were confiscated that day. I told Max and Jacky, who had just returned from a stroll in the camp, to keep watch over our goods on the bed, as I wanted to collect some of our underwear from the washing lines before it disappeared.

When I returned with the clean washing, our bed was deserted and Max and Jacky were nowhere in sight. A woman came over and told me what had happened. Apparently my father had come home early from work and the boys had told him about the confiscated cupboard. My father became furious and, being a very short-tempered man, had stormed into the dining room and taken the barracks elder to task, voicing his disapproval in no uncertain terms. The barracks elder complained about my father to Albela, who summoned my father to his office. Albela, surrounded by his 'lieutenants', told my father that he was no longer allowed to enter our barracks and that he would lose two days' rations. This was the last straw for my father. He grabbed Albela by his necktie, and just as he was about to punch him, Scharführer Lubbe entered the office.

'What's going on?' he shouted. 'Lock up the criminal!'

Four strong men took hold of my father and dragged him across the Appelplatz to the small bunker.

While this was happening in Albela's office, I was waiting in the barracks for my father and brothers to return. Suddenly there was a knock on the window next to our beds. It was the same old man who had told me to see the barracks elder. He seemed very agitated and short of breath, and motioned for me to open the window.

'Your father had a fight with Albela and now they've put him in the bunker,' he gasped.

I went limp with shock.

'Oh God, what will happen to him?' I started to cry. The man tried to comfort me.

'I'm sure Mr Weiss will help as much as he can,' he said.

'I'd better get to the gate and meet my mother,' I said. 'I don't want her to hear it from someone else.'

I met Mum at the gate. Max and Jacky were also there. After Mum kissed us, she looked around for Dad.

'Where is your father? Hasn't he come back from work yet?' she asked.

The boys put their heads down to avoid looking at Mum. It was left to me to inform her of the afternoon's happenings. It was not easy. How do you tell your mother that your father is in the bunker? I started to say something, but was lost for words. Mum became alarmed.

'What's the matter, Hetty? What's wrong?' she urged.

I blurted out the whole miserable story, as horror and shock registered on my mother's face.

'Let's go to the barracks, it is getting very cold,' she said, when she had recovered. 'Then I'll go to Mr Weiss to find out what happened and see if we can get some blankets and food to the bunker for Dad.'

Mum tidied herself up, and then left with Max to find Mr Weiss. They were gone for about an hour and it was about seven o'clock when they returned.

'Hetty! Quick! Give me two blankets and a pillow. I have to get this to Mr Weiss as soon as possible,' Mum said. 'The curfew starts at eight o'clock. I'll be back soon, and while I'm gone, make some room for Max. He'll sleep with us tonight.'

'Wait, Mum, take a bread ration for Dad,' I said. I quickly opened the suitcase containing our rations. I wrapped it in the first available clean garment – a pair of Mum's underpants – and

51

handed it to her. Then she was on her way with Max, and all I hoped for was that they would return before curfew.

It was only minutes to eight when Mum and Max returned, and although Mum was near exhaustion, I could see that she felt a little more at ease. The four of us sat on top of the bed as Mum related what had transpired. Mr Weiss had told her that the offence Dad had committed in attacking the camp elder had been taken very seriously by the SS and this was punishable by being sent away to a concentration camp. However, Albela and Mr Weiss had persuaded Scharführer Lubbe that our leader would put my father on trial the following day and that he would be suitably punished. Lubbe had agreed, but said he would also consider what additional punishment he would give.

That night Mum and I could not sleep, not only as a result of the cramped conditions caused by Max sleeping with us, but also because our thoughts were constantly with Dad. The wind was howling through the camp and it was very cold. I prayed that Dad would be okay and I was happy that he had some of our blankets. Mum and I talked softly so as not to wake the others in the dormitory.

'Tomorrow I'll go and see Lubbe,' Mum said.

'Why Mum? It's too dangerous – please don't!' I said. 'Think about it and wait and see what happens tomorrow. Try to get some sleep, you have to be up at three o'clock.'

Mum agreed and then tried to make herself a bit more comfortable. 'Try to get some sleep too, Hetty,' she said, as she closed her eyes.

I watched my mother's face: her eyelids were transparent blue-white, her face had become small and her skin showed a very white contrast to her jet-black hair. Despite all this, she was still my pretty mother. Her breathing became deeper, telling me that she was asleep. I carefully bent over and gently kissed her cheek, which felt hollow under my lips.

'Oh dear God,' I prayed, 'help us so all this will be over soon.' I turned on my side to get some sleep. Someone was snoring and sleep would not come. I stared at the outline of the sleepers in the dormitory as the hours went by slowly.

Herman's watch, which had never left my wrist since he had been sent to Treblinka, showed three o'clock. Gently, I woke Mum and told her that she had to go to work. She was so tired. She dressed herself on top of the blanket and then put on her boots after she climbed down from the bed.

'I'll see if I can get back at lunchtime,' she whispered, so as not to wake Max and Jacky. 'I'll pretend to be ill and I am sure that Koch (the SS officer in command of the peel kitchen) will let me go. He is the most reasonable SS man of the lot here. When I can fix it, then I will see Lubbe or Rau when the work details go back to work after the lunch break.'

There was nothing I could do. Mum had made up her mind. It has been said that a yiddisher mother will fight to the death for her family, and here I had the living proof. With no regard for her own safety, she would go and plead for her man.

'Look after the boys,' Mum said. She pulled my head down and kissed me. 'I had better go now, as I'm running late. Try to get some sleep.'

She left. My dapper little mother. Oh, how I loved her.

I must have fallen asleep as I woke up to the sound of roll-call. I quickly put on my clothes, and called Max and Jacky over. I told them to dress very warmly as it was sunny outside but still cold. I wound a scarf around Jacky's head and did the same for myself. Max was wearing a balaclava, the one Oma Hetty had knitted while she was in hiding. The man from the Resistance had delivered the parcel, which also had contained a pair of knitted knee-high socks for me. I had been wearing them since we had arrived in Belsen. Those wonderful socks kept my feet warm and dry during the long hours at the Appelplatz.

'Come on, let's get to the Appelplatz. Most people have left our barracks already,' I urged Max and Jacky.

When we arrived at the Appelplatz, the people from our barracks were lined up only five metres away from the bunker where Dad was. I had never given the bunker a second glance before, but it was different now Dad was inside. In the sunlight, it looked like a square building about two metres by four metres. It was built of brick, with a heavy padlocked door. There was a square opening in one of its walls, presumably a window, but this was nailed up with a thick piece of plywood. The SS had not arrived yet, so I had an opportunity to get close to the wall with the covered window without arousing suspicion.

'Dad,' I called softly, 'are you all right?'

I heard my father's voice. 'Is that you, Hetty?'

'Yes,' I said. 'Are you okay?'

'I'm okay,' Dad said, 'there's not much light. They blocked the window up.'

'I can see that,' I answered. 'Are you warm enough? It was so cold last night.'

'Yes, yes, don't worry. I'm warm enough.'

I could hear the barracks leaders calling the people to line up properly.

'I have to go now Dad, I'll come back later.'

The SS were at it again. They had counted us three times already and made out that two people were missing. They screamed that we were not standing in line correctly and, at times, indiscriminately hit out at the unfortunate person in front of them. How could people go missing? There was no way out. There were guards everywhere.

As we resigned ourselves to being at roll-call for a long time, a small party of men approached. Lubbe, the Scharführer in charge of roll-call, Albela and two of his lieutenants walked past us towards the bunker. My heart was pounding. What was in store for Dad? The bunker door was opened and my father ordered outside. I strained to see what was happening through the crowd of people, but could only hear the loud voice of Lubbe as he addressed my father. I felt helpless. What could I do? Then, it was over. We heard the door of the bunker being shut and the party went back in the direction of Albela's office.

It took more than three hours that morning before Albela blew the whistle marking the end of roll-call. Usually after roll-call I would return to the barracks immediately, but this time I was in no hurry. Max also stayed behind. Together we walked slowly towards the bunker. With about a metre to go, we stopped. Max turned towards me and making out that he was speaking to me, he called out to Dad in the bunker. Dad answered immediately. Max asked what had happened when Lubbe and Albela came to the bunker during roll-call.

'Lubbe told me to apologise to Albela, and after I did he gave me two hard whacks about the head,' Dad said.

'Are you all right now, Dad?' Max asked.

'Yes, I'm okay. Don't worry. Can you get me something to eat, Hetty? She is with you, isn't she, Max?' Dad asked.

I told Dad that I would see Mr Weiss and ask him to bring one of our food rations and something to drink.

'Okay,' Dad said. 'See what you can do.'

Max and I left for the barracks. I collected our daily ration from Frau Müller. She gave me four rations. For two days Dad would get nothing. No words were needed. One ration would go immediately to Dad, and the four of us would share the other three bread rations. One bowl of soup would go to Dad, and Mum and I would share a bowl of soup. At about one o'clock Mum came back as she had intended. We told her what had happened at the Appelplatz that morning and assured her that Dad was okay.

'I know,' she said. 'I went to speak to him before coming to the barracks. But now I must go to the camp doctor for a certificate that my stomach is upset, and after that I will see Lubbe.'

'I'll go with you, Mum,' I said.

At first Mum refused, but when she saw my determination, she agreed. She made Max and Jacky promise to stay clear of the Appelplatz, and we set off to obtain the doctor's certificate. After that Mum and I went to the Appelplatz. We arrived at the same moment as the last work detail was marching off. Lubbe was in conversation with Albela. He seemed to be in one of his good moods.

'Wish me good luck,' Mum said, and squeezed my hand.

She started to walk slowly towards Albela and Lubbe. At a respectful distance she stopped and waited. Albela spotted her first and spoke to her. Albela said something to Lubbe, who turned towards my mother and I could see them conversing. How courageous she looks, I thought. Her head was lifted, to look up to the towering SS man. After about two minutes the conversation was over and I saw Mum coming back towards me.

'Let's go to the boys,' she said, smiling.

On the way to the barracks, she told me what she had said to Lubbe. She had addressed him as 'Hauptsturmführer', knowing quite well that Lubbe was only a Scharführer. She had flattered his ego this way. She had apologised to him in broken German for what my father had done, and portrayed him as a worried parent. His children were without supervision every day of the week, as she, my mother, was working seven days a week, and therefore could not attend to them at all. It seemed that Lubbe could understand this, and he told her that children needed discipline. He said that the matter had already been reported to Berlin, but that he would give it some thought. Although we could not be sure that Dad would not be sent away, we had some hope that Mum's appeal would work. That afternoon, the court gave my father four days' bunker time, which meant that in two days Dad could come out again. We all went to bed early that night as the emotional pressure had worn us out completely.

I woke Mum at three o'clock for work. After she left I went back to sleep until morning call. Max and Jacky had gone to see Dad early in the morning and they had not returned by the time we had to go to the Appelplatz. So I went there on my own and was glad to see Max and Jacky already standing with our barracks group. The boys told me that they had spoken to Dad and he had told them that Mr Weiss had brought him some food last night. I had no time to go and speak to Dad as we were called to line up. The Scharführer had already started to count the first barracks groups. There were always two of them, with Albela a respectful step behind them. It was deadly silent. Slowly the counters came nearer. Suddenly there was a loud bang-crash-bang that seemed to shatter the silence of the Appelplatz. It came from the bunker and I turned to see what had happened. There was my father looking through the hole in the wall. With his bare fist he had knocked the wooden cover loose so he could look out. The Scharführer was approaching our barracks group and, from the corner of my eye, I saw my father pulling away from the opening so he would not be spotted. A sigh of relief escaped me when the Scharführer passed our group without noticing the hole in the wall of the bunker.

It was a bitterly cold morning towards the end of April 1944. Although we had all dressed ourselves warmly, the wind made us shiver. The Hungarians standing in the group next to us were moaning and crying, 'Oi, joi joi joi', and were stamping their feet to get the circulation going. Some of them were middle-aged and had blankets over their shoulders. We were cold too, but we did not cry. For four long hours we stood at the Appelplatz – four long hours designed to break our spirits. I went over to Athena, an Italian girl. She and her mother had arrived a few weeks ago. I had tried to befriend her as she was my age, but there was a language difficulty. Somehow, I had learned that she had been buried for three days under the rubble of her house in Milan, which had been bombed. Athena was very beautiful but I could not help noticing how frail she was. She had a face like a Madonna and her serene looks reminded me of a statue of Sachsen porcelain. I sensed that she was in a world of her own. Perhaps it was the terrible experience of the bombing that had broken her spirit. One thing I had found out was that she had a beautiful voice. I put my hand on her arm but she looked at me with vacant eyes.

'Athena!' I said, 'please sing for us?' There was no response. She stood there without moving a muscle, oblivious of everything around her. I shook her arm.

'Athena, please sing for us?' Still no reaction. I softly started to hum the tune of 'Santa Lucia'. As though a magic wand had been waved, Athena came to life; slowly at first, but then she put herself into the song with full force. The song went up like a prayer and was a diversion from our misery. It filled our hearts with hope and when I turned towards the group of Hungarians, I could see they were listening, and their moaning had stopped. At long last, after four and a half hours, Albela blew his whistle. The Appelplatz emptied, with everyone hurrying to get back to their barracks as quickly as they could. The Hungarian group brought up the rear and I could see some of the young children supporting the elderly, who could barely walk. I sent Max and Jacky back to the barracks to collect our rations, but I stayed behind because I wanted to talk to Dad. I walked towards the bunker where I could see Dad's face peering through the hole in the wall.

'Hello, Dad. How are you?' I asked.

'I'm fine,' he said.

'Aren't you cold in there, Dad?' I asked.

'No, I have the blankets and while roll-call was on, I had a sleep,' he said with a mischievous smile.

I did not believe a word of it. Dad would not sleep while we were freezing during roll-call. At that moment I heard movement near the fence. A small private gate had opened and there stood Lubbe. There was a Häftling with him, a prisoner from the camp next to us. But that man is a kapo, I thought with shock. Lubbe ordered the man to open the door of the bunker. My father was ordered to bring the bucket out, which had apparently been used as a lavatory. I saw my father bring the bucket out and then Lubbe ordered him to stand at attention with his back against the wall. I stood frozen to the ground. 'Oh God, what is he going to do?' Fear grasped my whole body.

'You criminal, why are you in the bunker?' Lubbe shouted at my father.

'I have been bad to Herr Albela and I apologise for that,' my father said.

'You deserve to be shot!' Lubbe said.

I must have made an involuntary movement, because Lubbe noticed me standing nearby.

'Lock up the criminal!' he told the kapo, who roughly shoved my father back into the bunker.

'Well,' Lubbe said, turning towards me, 'do you want to go into the bunker too?'

'No, Herr Scharführer,' I answered, after some hesitation, fearing what would follow next.

Lubbe smiled at me.

'I don't want to go in there either!' he said.

With those unexpected words, he turned and left through the private gate. Phew! I let my breath escape. My legs were still shaking from fright. I saw Mr Weiss coming towards me. He had witnessed the whole thing.

'You're a very lucky girl!' Mr Weiss said. 'You know you aren't allowed to go near the bunker. I'm telling you, Hetty, your father will be out in a few days and I don't want you to go near the bunker again. You don't only put your own safety at risk, but also your father's.'

I had not thought of that, but now the realisation hit me.

'I promise, Mr Weiss. I'll stay away,' I said.

'That's my girl,' Mr Weiss said. He put his arm around my shoulders and we crossed the deserted Appelplatz to the barracks.

The next day Mr Weiss told us that the SS had given my father another four days' time in the bunker by order of Berlin. We were relieved that he was not going to be sent away to Sachsenhausen.

More and more people started to arrive in Belsen. The Hungarian camp next to ours was now empty as it appeared the SS had transported the inhabitants away. We noticed that the Hungarian camp became joined with what we called the New Camp. Later it was called the Häftling camp. The men in this camp had their hair shorn and were dressed in grey and white pyjamas. Some of them had no shoes. The weather started to get cooler and it rained sometimes, which turned the Appelplatz and roads into quagmires. The SS let us stand for hours at roll-call, and from our position we could observe that the Häftlinge in the camp next to ours experienced a similar fate. Sometimes, long after we were allowed to go back to the barracks, those poor creatures were still standing at roll-call without food. Their faces were grey, their cheeks hollow, their eyes deep in their sockets, and some of them had the look of cornered animals.

For the thirteen long weeks since our arrival in Belsen, we had been given that inferior brown murky soup. It started taking its toll. Men were the first to die from hunger, especially the tall men. During a roll-call earlier in February, Scharführer Rau selected two young men for special work. As young as I was, I noticed that they were handsome young men: tall, blond and blue-eyed with a sporty, outdoor look about them. They had to leave our camp at a minute's notice without their belongings and were escorted by a guard. It was observed that they did not go towards the exit of the camp but the opposite way. We worried about what would happen to them and we thought the worst. About four days later we saw one of them walking along the main road to the kitchen to collect his daily rations. Some men near the fence called out to him, trying to find out why they had been isolated, but he did not answer and kept his eyes straight ahead. It was obvious that he was not allowed to make any contact with us. We could see them in the distance during the day at the far end of the camp. It appeared that they worked outside their small hut making brooms. Every day they deposited those small bundles of what appeared to be broom heads made from twigs near their gate for collection. After a week it became known that they were in charge of the small crematorium at the far end of the camp.

'How did they find out, Dad?' I asked when he told me the news. 'They are not allowed to talk to us.'

'Well,' Dad said, 'when one of them went to the kitchen, he told someone in sign language what they were doing. In the beginning there had not been much work for the crematorium, but now it must work day and night, as day by day more and more people die.'

Dysentery was rife in the camp and at night the people who had to get up to go to the toilets kept us awake. Sometimes a person did not make it in time, and the vile stench penetrated the nose even during sleep. Our family was lucky, none of us had dysentery. Could it have been something to do with our constitution or was it the food we had eaten before we were interned? I remember the beautiful juicy brisket my grandmother used to cook for us, which Opa brought home from the abattoirs. I could see it: Opa cutting the meat with a very sharp, long knife into even, thick slices. He would serve each one of us a generous portion before he served himself. He always started his meal with the meat, which he meticulously cut into small square pieces and then topped with a small square piece of juicy fat, relishing every bite. He taught me to eat the juicy fat as he said that it was good for my bones and brains. Never ever did Opa eat meat with other food or vegetables. When he finished with the meat, Oma handed him a fresh plate, fork and knife for his vegetables.

Opa had been a respected member of the meat industry in Holland. As a boy of ten he had attended the cattle markets in Holland with his father and learned the trade from the bottom up; wholesale in sheep, cattle, goats, and so on. He knew his trade from buying and selling, to slaughtering, manufacturing of fine foods and marketing. As I sat on my bed in Belsen I saw my grandparents' living room in front of me and recalled the happy faces around the table from a time that seemed so long ago. I saw the spread of food and my Oma's happy smile, and my heart was crying that this was gone for ever.

My tummy reminded me that I was very hungry. I laid my two hands on my stomach to stop the hunger pains. After a while the pains subsided. I decided to change my clothes, or at least my jumper. For some months now I had worn the same jumper and I felt uncomfortable. When I pulled the jumper over my head, it turned inside out. I was in the process of correcting this when my eyes fell on something crawling – lice. The area under my armpits was putrid with nits. I started to kill them between my thumbnails but it was useless. I looked in the suitcase to see if I could find another jumper. I found one that was not as warm, but I still changed. I put the offensive jumper in the suitcase hoping the lice would die. I did not tell a soul, I was so ashamed. Hygiene had deteriorated to a standard that cannot be comprehended: no soap, no water. I had been wearing the same clothes for months. My underwear was also not so clean. The only place on my body that I protected from dirt was the wound on my foot, the result of the boiling water accident in Westerbork. How many months was it? Five months, and there was still a deep open wound. I could see down to my bone. Every few days I would change the bandage, a paper bandage obtained from the camp doctor. I had no medicine or antiseptic, so I covered the wound with a clean square of paper bandage and re-used the winding bandage again and again. One day the wound stopped secreting fluid, and I watched my body start to rebuild, as very slowly, red flesh grew at the bottom of the hole.

At the end of May 1944, a transport of about eight hundred people had arrived from Westerbork. The group was made up of 'diamond people', that is, they were diamond merchants or tradesmen. Special barracks had been erected for them near the hospital barracks. The diamond people were given special privileges. They did not have to join work details and were given double food rations. The weather had improved again, and during the day you could see the diamond people sunning themselves near the clothes line or just strolling through the camp all nicely dressed. A few weeks after their arrival we observed that two special barracks were erected just outside the fence of our camp under the trees. The camp telegraph soon informed us that those barracks would be fitted out to house a diamond factory. Dad, who had come back from work with this information, told us that he was going to Albela's office to try to get his name on the list with the diamond group. Dad had been trained as a skilled diamond tradesman and his father and brother were excellent diamond polishers and cleavers. Before he went to Albela's office, he went over to Uncle Max to discuss the situation. They both agreed to give it a go, as the prospect of not going to work at six o'clock in the morning was worth a try. After a few days Dad told us that all our names had been registered with the diamond group. However, things did not turn out as we hoped. Dad and Uncle Max still had to go to work every morning and they did not receive double food rations.

The talk Mum had had with Lubbe when Dad was in the bunker had a pleasant result. From the end of May, the women who worked in the kitchen were allowed half a day a week off so they could look after their families. How happy we were to have Mum with us for a half a day. Mum and I attended to such tasks as washing our only sheets, and other laundry. During the months Mum had worked seven days a week, I had done the washing, but now Mum taught me how to wring the sheets so that most of the water was removed from them. We had long run out of the packets of soap we had brought from Holland, so we used to soak our washing in salt. When our laundry was on the line, I would sit near the clothes line to keep watch so it would not be stolen.

The area around the clothes line was deserted. I was the only one there. People are not looking after basics any more, I thought. I was sitting on the ground with my back against a pole about ten metres from the danger strip with the skull-and-crossbones signs warning everyone not to trespass. I could see the SS in the watchtowers who, after giving me a fleeting glance, totally ignored me. Now and then I could hear one of them call out to the other man in the next watchtower, but that was the only sound.

It was peaceful under the clothes lines. I looked at the blue sky and saw a small white cloud. I looked at the shimmering distance of the Lüneburg Heath, and as my gaze travelled through the wire fences, I saw a bird high in the sky and I felt a deep yearning to be free again. The pain of being enclosed was nearly unbearable. With some effort I pulled myself together and got up to feel if our washing was dry. Not yet. I sat down again and looked at the line with the other washing. Only three garments were hanging from the line: a bra, a singlet and a pair of panties. The underwear showed stains of menstruation. Strange, I thought, all the women had stopped menstruating shortly after arriving in Belsen. I never got my period any more and neither did Mum. Maybe it was not such a bad thing. After all, how in the world could we have managed without pads or soap to keep us clean? I had no idea how it could be achieved and deeply pitied the woman who had to cope with this problem in this situation. It was generally believed that the SS put camphor in our food, which stopped all sexual reactions in men and women.

The washing was dry. I took it off the line and went back to the barracks. Mum and I made up our beds with not-so-clean, but at least fresh sheets. We gave Dad his sheets in the evening.

One day, the camp telegraph let us know that high-ranking SS from Berlin were going to visit us. Frau Müller, our barracks elder, confirmed this later. The whole camp received a spring clean. Red Müller was the Scharführer in charge of the operation. Frau Müller advised us that an inspection of our barracks would take place in a few days. We were shown how our beds had to be made up each morning. They were to be smooth and flat at the top, not a ripple was to be shown in the blankets. We were not allowed to store or hide anything in our beds. For those who had a cupboard it was not hard, but we had problems. Our suitcases with our belongings were stored on the end of Mum's bed, where they had been under our constant surveillance. Now we had to put them under the bunk and at night, someone could steal them. I packed all our clothing in one suitcase, and another one with our soup bowls and other belongings. The barracks was scrubbed and cleaned from top to bottom. Those who did not go to work had to do the cleaning.

Our food miraculously began to improve. With our bread rations, we received a small square piece of butter, and a packet of Limburger cheese for the week. The cheese smelt terrible. We had never eaten it at home, but the fact that it was made in Holland somehow made me feel that we had not been forgotten. Amazing how this small packet of cheese seemed to give me comfort. Our midday soup also improved. It was thicker and even pieces of meat and potatoes could be found in it. We became cunning. We waited to collect our soup until the large forty-litre container that held the mixture was two-thirds empty, as at the bottom the soup was thicker. We had our midday soup with Dad in the dining room. He had been allowed back into our barracks after apologising to Frau Müller. How happy we were when we discovered a piece of meat in our soup. One day, I received what I thought was a very large piece of meat. Excitedly, I returned with the bowl to the table. Dad lifted the large piece from the bowl with a fork so he could divide it between us. We were horrified to see that it was not meat, but a very dirty cleaning cloth, which had been cooked with our soup. It had taken on the same brown colour as the soup, so there was no doubt it had been cooking for many hours. What should we do, we pondered. How could we eat this soup? How unhygienic! Half the people in the barracks were eating it at the moment. But the worst thing was that the volume of the soup left in the bowl had dropped considerably after removal of the cleaning cloth. I decided to go back to Frau Müller. I put the cloth back in the bowl and showed Frau Müller what was in the soup. She removed the cloth from the bowl and topped it up with some more soup.

'Don't worry,' she said. 'It won't kill you!'

I gave Dad half the contents of my bowl as I had promised Mum. Our eyes met across the table and we knew what the other was thinking. To stay alive, we were going to eat the soup. Our hunger had reduced us to this. I determinedly put the thought of the cleaning cloth and the consequences out of my mind. I picked up my spoon and started to eat.

It was about the middle of June when Scharführer Red Müller came for the first inspection of the barracks. The inspection took place while we were at roll-call. When we returned, the barracks elder informed us that everything was okay. We were relieved, and within a few days, the barracks looked a mess again and our cases were back on Mum's bed.

My father's youngest brother, Max, and his wife, Clara, had come with us to Belsen in the same transport. My Uncle Max had always been my favourite uncle. Clara was sleeping a bit further away from us near the wall of the dining room. We did not see much of them as Uncle Max was working in the kitchen, sometimes for eighteen hours at a time. They were well fed, those lucky kitchen workers. Clara worked with Mum in the peel kitchen, but she did not have to eat the raw carrots as Uncle Max stole plenty of food.

The days when Uncle Max was free and Clara came home from work they would have 'dinner' on top of their bed. They hooked a blanket to the rafters to give themselves privacy. From our bed we used to see them going behind their blankets, and we knew that they were eating and that they would not be so hungry. But they never offered any food to us. This is how it was in Belsen. People became very mean, only thinking of their own survival. They degenerated to the law of the jungle, or even worse, because even an animal would leave food for the next one after it had eaten enough. It had become obvious that Uncle Max and Clara had been avoiding us over the past months, scared that we would ask them for food. Max and Jacky complained bitterly about it, but Mum forbade them to go begging. They were still so young and could not understand how their uncle had changed.

Thousands and thousands of old shoes were brought in by truck and unloaded into a mountain next to our camp. My father was chosen for a new work detail: the shoe commando. He would go to work at six o'clock in the morning, come back for a lunch break and then go back to work until six in the evening. The only reason the workers had a lunch break was because the SS wanted a lunch break. Sometimes the SS made them work until eight o'clock; it depended on their moods. The work itself was not heavy, but very dirty. The workers had to separate the top leather from the soles with a sharp knife. Among the large command of two hundred men were academics from universities, businessmen from worldwide organisations, rabbis and engineers. To break the monotony of this mind-deadening work, the academics gave lectures on various subjects while they were working. The rabbis would also keep them busy with their knowledge. Chief Rabbi Dashberg was usually sitting close to Dad and they became quite friendly. They seemed to be an odd combination, as my father was an atheist.

The SS hated the few rabbis who were in our camp – their beards worked on the SS like a red rag to a bull. The SS took great pleasure in finding sadistic punishment for the rabbis, but nothing could shake the faith of these frail men.

* * *

By July 1944 an optimistic feeling was sweeping through our camp, matched by the lovely weather. We received some news of the outside world when new transports arrived from Westerbork. How totally isolated we were. Did people in Holland or anyone else in the rest of the world still remember us? Other nationalities would at times get a food parcel from the Red Cross, but those of us who came from Holland never received anything. I vowed that if I came through this terrible time, I would never support the Red Cross in Holland.

Max's twelfth birthday was on 22 July. For days he had been nagging Mum for permission to see Uncle Max on his birthday to ask for something to eat. At first Mum refused but them gave in.

'How can I deprive my child of a chance to get something to eat?' she said.

Although my hunger was as great as Max's and everyone else's, I could not agree. The thought of going to ask my once-favourite uncle for something he apparently was not willing to give voluntarily went against every fibre of my being. I would not reduce myself to begging for food yet.

Mum had managed to be free on the day of Max's birthday. During the lunch break, Max went over to Clara's bed, where Uncle Max was sleeping. Hesitantly, he called out. We were watching from a distance and saw the blanket being lifted and Uncle Max's head appear. After a few words, Max was invited up and disappeared behind the blanket. He remained there about ten minutes and when he climbed down again, he had in his hand a thick slice of white bread with butter and sugar. His face was shining with happiness. When he returned to our bed, he handed his present to Mum, offering to share it between us. Mum cut off a small piece for Jacky, and after my refusal of a share, she told Max to eat the lot as it was his birthday. With small bites, he relished this unexpected delicacy.

Perhaps Uncle Max's conscience was bothering him because the next day at lunchtime, he called Max over to Clara's bed and when he returned, there were two more slices of bread with butter and sugar for 'Hetty and Jacky'. I divided them between the five of us, keeping Mum's share until she returned from work that night. How good it tasted, when I sank my teeth into my share of this heavenly windfall! I am sure the finest cake from a baker could not have surpassed it.

We did not receive any more handouts from Uncle Max.

In August 1944 it was so hot that it was impossible to sleep. Despite the heat, we still had to attend agonising hours of roll-call. One day the SS left us standing there for eight hours. We had supposedly not cleaned our barracks properly and Red Müller was in a foul mood. Perhaps they were losing the war, and that would be the end of their thousand-year dream. Red Müller would storm into the barracks and scream like a maniac, pulling the blankets off beds that were not made up to standard. He would open the cupboards, and if he found bowls with any soup still left in them, which the owner had saved to eat later to stave off the hunger pangs, he would throw it through the barracks, shouting at the top of his voice. It was his usual practice to hold on to our bread rations for a day or two after such a performance. We had gone hungry for so long now that we got used to it. We became lethargic and our speech slowed down. People were dying every day.

Müller was a bully who delighted in screaming at the elderly people. These poor people, with fright showing on their faces and their legs trembling, knew his fury would be turned on them. He would hit them with his fist and punish them by making them stand for many hours at the gate with their caps in their hands in wind, rain or in the burning sun. He also confiscated their rations for two or sometimes four days. Müller was a sadistic monster.

Scharführer Hertzoch was in charge of the sewer, if one could call it that. He used to walk through the camp with a boy of about twelve years of age who carried a long stick and a bucket. Hertzoch ordered the boy to lift the lid of the inspection point, after which he would poke the stick in the hole and, if satisfied, would continue to the next inspection point. The 'Shit King', we called him. If a drain was blocked, you could hear him swearing. His face would turn red and the veins in his neck would stand out to the point of bursting. We were hoping they would, but – what a shame – they never did. At other times he was friendly and you could see him smiling and talking to children or elderly people. I had the feeling that he did not fit into the SS regime.

Our food did not arrive on time any more. The kitchen worked day and night to cope with the influx of people in Belsen. The carriers could not cope and sometimes our soup containers would not arrive until eight o'clock at night. Although only a small amount, the warm, inferior concoction would somehow sustain us for a while.

The weather was very hot. It was better outside the barracks than in, so we spent most of our time outside. Sitting outside could be done in comfort if a chair could be found, otherwise you just sat down on the dusty, dry ground. There was not a green leaf in sight. Grass did not grow and everything was covered in a dreary grey dust.

Dad heard through the camp telegraph that Uncle Max was in the bunker, not in the small bunker Dad had been kept in, but down where the camp section for the SS was.

'What happened?' I asked.

'I'm not sure,' Dad said, 'but I have been told that he stole some butter and they caught him.'

I could not sleep that night. What would happen to my uncle? I knew how cruel and vicious the SS were. The next two days were unbearable with no news, but on the third day, late in the afternoon, I saw Uncle Max entering our barracks. He looked pale and had lost weight. Dad, who had played hooky that day from work, was resting on Mum's bed. When I informed him that Uncle Max had returned, he immediately went over to find out what had happened. Both of them returned to our beds. Close up, Uncle Max looked terrible. Our eyes met and despite my resentment of him for being so mean, I threw my arms around his neck and kissed him. I was really very happy to see him again. For a moment, the old Uncle Max emerged. His eyes smiled into mine as he told me that I had grown. He then told us that he indeed was caught with one kilogram of butter, which he had tried to smuggle into our camp. For two days he was held in solitary confinement, with the SS coming in every couple of hours to give him a beating. It was his strong physique that had carried him through and he was lucky that he was not sent to Auschwitz. He was very, very tired, as he had had no food for two days.

'Better go and lie down and get some rest before Clara comes back from work. You need it,' Dad said.

Uncle Max agreed. He patted my head and walked toward Clara's bed. With some difficulty, he climbed on top and we saw him disappear behind the blanket. It was good that the family ties were restored, and when I went to sleep that night I thanked God that Uncle Max had been spared and that he had become one of our family again. The next day, Uncle Max was allocated to the shoe commando as he was not allowed to return to the kitchen. This gave the Scharführer in control of the shoe commando the opportunity to sing out 'the criminal brothers', as he called my father and uncle, and he gave them the extra hard, dirty jobs.

The heat was oppressive. The air in the barracks was stifling. No one could sleep at night. The water supply was cut off for long periods, so when the taps were running there was a tremendous rush as everyone wanted to fill up bottles or buckets. Some lucky ones were able to give themselves a quick wash.

There was a tap near the men's quarters on the Appelplatz. Gypsies who had come from Italy a few days earlier, and who had just returned from the gruelling work of digging up tree stumps without food or water, fought among themselves to get to the tap. It was there that I learned the meaning of 'aqua finito', which they kept on screaming to each other when the flow of the water stopped. The deliberate rationing of the water and the chaotic results amused the SS tremendously. They smiled and watched the human misery from a distance.

The heat also affected our sewerage system, which was not

constructed to cater for so many people. Hertzoch went berserk and meted out penalties left, right and centre. Whole barracks would lose their rations for two or more days.

During this heatwave, one evening Mum told me to come with her to the washhouse. Her face told me there was something terribly wrong. When we entered the washhouse, I saw my father standing in the only pair of trousers he possessed, covered in excrement from his shoes to his armpits. His face was not too clean either. He smelt a mile in the wind.

'What happened?' I gasped.

Dad told me that Red Müller had come to the shoe detail's barracks and demanded that four men clean out the latrines. Chief Rabbi Dashberg was chosen first. This was done to humiliate him. Next were 'the criminal brothers', and another man by the name of Myer made up the fourth. In private conversation, Myer's nickname was 'Hap-Myer'. He was a very nice person, a bit backward with a low IQ. He used to gulp in air before he spoke. He was as skinny as a stick, but he was a survivor. My father and the other three men were told to empty the enormous latrine with buckets.

'Was the Rabbi standing in the pit?' I asked

'No,' Dad said. 'We didn't let him do that. We handed the buckets up to him to cart away. Of course he got dirty, but we did not let him stand in the latrine pit.'

'All right, get those filthy clothes off,' Mum told Dad.

Luckily, the washhouse was empty except for the three of us. I discreetly turned my back to my father while he undressed. In the meantime, I filled the trough with water. It was a wonder that the water was on. Mum handed me Dad's trousers. Phew! What a smell! What a mess! Quickly, I dumped them in the water, which at once turned into a miniature latrine. I let the dirty water run out and repeated the process again and again. Dad's underwear and shirt got the same treatment. It was to no avail. I could not get those clothes clean again. How could I? There was no soap or detergent to help me. I asked Mum to give me the scrubbing brush, but this was not successful either. It remained a hard, dried mess, with the original colour unrecognisable. While Dad washed himself, Mum tried to clean his shoes with a scrubbing brush.

In the middle of our misery, I could not help but laugh when I saw Dad in his clean clothing. Mum had borrowed a pair of trousers for Dad from someone, but they were far too short. He looked ridiculous. But anything was better than the ones that were soaking in the wash trough. Mum and I discussed various ways of getting the trousers clean again, throwing them away was unacceptable. Clothing was unobtainable in Belsen, so we had to hang on to what we had or go naked. We decided to let all the clothes soak overnight in the water, and I would make another attempt to clean them in the morning. Of one thing we were sure: no one would steal them from the washhouse.

The next day after roll-call, I went back to the washhouse and rinsed the clothes again and again for about an hour. While I was doing this, a man entered looking for his wife. When he saw me labouring away at the trough, he asked me what I was doing. I told him what had happened while I continued to rinse and re-rinse the trousers as, by now, the shirt and underwear were reasonably clean, although they remained stained and smelly. After watching me for about ten minutes, the man said, 'You're a courageous girl,' and then left. I decided to leave the trousers soaking for another day, but took the shirt and underwear to the lines to dry.

For two more days, I soaked, rinsed and scrubbed the trousers, and when at long last I hung out them to dry, you could still smell the latrine. I hoped that the sun and air would take care of that problem. Despite their poor appearance, Dad was grateful when I handed him his trousers that night, so he could return the borrowed ones he was wearing. I hoped that Dad would never have to clean a latrine again. I did not think I could cope a second time.

Four

'What beasts they are!'

In September 1944 the hot days were over, thank God. The weather was beautiful. Every day transports would arrive in our camp. The dining room disappeared, and beds were placed in the area. A small corner stayed reserved for Frau Müller, and a long trestle table served as a counter from which we collected our daily rations.

The barracks across from ours was taken over by French women. Where they came from I had no idea. They were not the stereotypical petite brunettes from Paris. They were strong, tall women. In my opinion they looked like Amazons, although I had never seen an Amazon in my life. They did not interfere with us and kept to themselves. At night after work, they would group together outside the barracks and sing the Marseillaise and sentimental French songs. They also had no shame. They would take a bowl of water and squat over it and wash themselves between their legs outside their barracks in front of everybody, including men and children. There were usually two of them. While one squatted and washed herself, the other one would hold the towel for her. When one was ready, the other repeated the ritual.

During the first weeks in September, a small transport of women arrived from Westerbork and among them was Sonja. The reunion with Sonja was a high point in our dreary lives, and at the same time a sorrow, since we thought she was safe in Amsterdam. At last we found out what had happened to her after we left the station in Amsterdam, on our way to Westerbork. Apparently, they let her stand with her face to the wall in the station until ten o'clock in the evening, and after that she was given a sermon, a few whacks in the face by the SS and allowed to leave. She also told us that she had met my mother's brother and his family in Westerbork and, very sadly, they had been sent with the last transport to Auschwitz a few weeks ago. My mother was devastated. She asked Sonja all sorts of questions. What happened? They had been hiding in a farm in Drenthe for three years. They were so safe there! How did they get caught? Sonja did not know the answers. We all were very sad to hear this news. After Mum had a good cry, she said that perhaps they would be all right. Hope was shining in her eyes. We were not so sure, but we did not tell Mum this.

We were sitting around a table outside the barracks with Sonja. The conversation continued about old friends and relatives, when the sunlight caught the ring on Sonja's hand.

'That's a lovely ring, Sonja. Let's have a closer look,' Mum said. When Sonja stretched out her hand, Mum recognised it at once. 'It's my ring!'

'That's right,' Sonja said. 'I found it between the towels in your linen cupboard after the SS took you away, but if you want it, you can have it back,' and she removed the ring from her finger and handed it to Mum.

Mum's face lit up. This ring with five little diamonds in a row reminded her of happier times, when everything was normal in our lives. It was a precious memory of an earlier wedding anniversary with the whole family present. She slipped the ring on her finger, but it was too large, as Mum, like everyone else in our camp, had lost a lot of weight. She took it off again, afraid of losing it, and hid it in a pocket in her slacks.

That night, on top of our bed, Mum let me hold the ring for a moment. I admired the flashes of light which reflected from the small diamonds. I handed the ring back to Mum, who rolled it in a handkerchief and put it in her bra. It easily fitted, as Mum had lost so much weight that it now hung loosely. To make it look even, she took out another handkerchief and stuffed it in the other side. The safest place to keep something in the camp was on your body.

The lovely weather continued and on the days Mum did not have to work we would sit around the tables outside the barracks. As usual, Mum and I would do the washing early in the morning if there was water in the washhouse. From our position at the tables, we could observe the washing lines.

Elderly women and some old men sat around chatting with each other. They talked about the latest death of their friends and relatives. They talked about the war, sickness and, above all, food. They would talk about large cakes with fresh cream, juicy steaks and all the delicacies which took their fancy. And in our imagination, we could see, yes, even smell, the aromas of the food they described.

Among us was Sheila. She was not old, she was about thirty years of age. There was something strange about her. She claimed to be a clairvoyant. She could read the cards and was, as Mum later told me, a Jehovah's Witness. She flatly refused to work, for she said her God forbade her to work for the enemy. One day she asked Mum if she wanted her cards read. Mum agreed.

'But if it's something bad, don't tell me!' Mum said.

Sheila proceeded to lay the cards out on the table and pondered over them for a while. Then she lifted her head and looked Mum in the face. A light shone in her eyes as she told my mother: 'I will not tell you all I see but I will tell you this – all five of you will come safely through the war and come home again. I see,' she continued, 'that you will not stay home for long but you will travel over great waters to a faraway land.'

Although it was good to hear that we would survive, we did not take Sheila's predictions seriously.

Sheila was offended.

'I am telling you the truth. Do believe me. You will all come home,' she said.

One morning I was looking in the mirror presented to me in Westerbork while I was combing my long black hair. Since my mother had cut it in the train the night we were picked up, it had grown back to a beautiful length again. I smiled at myself in the mirror and noticed that a small hole had appeared in one of my front teeth. I decided to go and see the dentist. A small medical centre was set up near Albela's office. You could see a dentist there during certain hours. The medical centre was initially set up for the SS but at times the dentist was allowed to attend to us. I went there after roll-call, but was told by the nurse to come back after three o'clock that afternoon, as the dentist had not come back after roll-call yet. When I returned two people were there before me, so I had to wait. When my turn came, the nurse called me in. I entered the room and was met by a gentle old man of about sixty. He was just over five feet tall and his eyes reminded me of the rabbi who had blessed me in Westerbork. The room was completely fitted out as a first-class dental surgery. Everything was clean and shiny. The dentist wore a spotless white coat, and I imagined being back home. After he had seated me in the dental chair, the dentist asked me what my problem was.

'I have a hole in my front tooth,' I said.

'Let's have a look, young lady. Open your mouth.'

I opened my mouth and the dentist examined my tooth quickly.

'Well,' he said, 'you also have large holes in two of your molars. We shall soon fix them.'

After giving the nurse some instructions, he started drilling my molars – no anaesthetic was given. I grabbed hold of the arms of my chair so I could withstand the pain from the drilling. While he was drilling away, he told me he would fill the holes in my molars with white cement.

'This way,' he said, 'we can preserve them until we are home again.'

When he finished the molars he started on my front tooth, after which he applied a temporary filling. By the time that was finished, I had been in the chair for more than two hours and was glad it was over. I was told to come back in a week's time.

When I left the surgery, it was starting to get dark outside. The camp was deserted. I walked quickly towards our barracks. When I arrived, the family was seated on top of our beds. We were lucky to have top bunks. At least we had somewhere to sit. Sometimes there was a lot of bickering in the barracks between the people in the lower beds and those above them. The space between the bunks did not allow the person on the lower bunk to sit upright. This created jealousy, and at times many angry words could be heard when the person at the top climbed up or down.

'Where have you been?' Mum asked.

'I went to the dentist!' I told her. I opened my mouth to show her what he had done to my teeth.

'It looks lovely!' Mum said. 'Here, have some carrots and Max got you a cup of tea – a shame it's cold now.'

I quickly drank the cold tea. I gave the carrots to Max and Jacky as I was not allowed to eat anything until the filling hardened. Max and Jacky were very happy with this windfall and the carrots were consumed in seconds.

I returned to the dentist a week later at the time I had been told; five o'clock.

'Oh, there you are,' the dentist said when I entered the surgery, 'I've been waiting especially for you. I am not too well and as soon as I am finished with you I will lie down.'

I sat in the chair and the dentist quickly started to remove the temporary filling from my front tooth. When he completed the removal and prepared the tooth for its permanent filling, he instructed the nurse to prepare a mixture of ceramic glazing. The nurse did not respond.

'Why are you not doing what I told you to do?' he asked.

'The ceramic glazing is only for the SS. They will notice if you use some of it,' she answered.

'Do what you are told and be quick about it before the rest of the filling sets.' The dentist spoke softly but urgently.

Reluctantly, the nurse prepared the mixture and the dentist finished my front tooth expertly.

'Here, Hetty,' he said, 'look at yourself.'

He gave me the mirror. He had done a beautiful job. My teeth reflected in the mirror like white pearls.

'Now,' the dentist said, 'look after them as best you can. You're a very pretty girl. I could not put white cement in your front tooth. It would be a shame. So, my dear girl, go to your barracks. Remember no drinking or eating for four hours. Gosh, I'm very tired,' he finished.

I became concerned when I saw how ill he looked.

'Are you all right, sir?' I asked.

'Yes. But I think I'll go and lie down after you go.'

I bade the dapper, kindly man goodbye and thanked him once more before I left the surgery.

The next day, the news that the dentist had died in his sleep went through the camp. I was very upset by his passing. He really meant it when he said to me, 'I have been waiting for you,' and now I knew why he had not been concerned about the consequences of stealing white ceramic glazing for my tooth from the SS. He had known I would be his last patient.

At four o'clock every day, the dead bodies were collected for cremation in the small crematorium at the end of the camp. When the cart with the dentist's body passed through the gate, I was there to pay him my last respects and, because I could not follow the cart, I walked inside the fence as far as I could along the perimeter of our camp, which was parallel with road leading to the crematorium. When I could go no further, I watched the cart with his body disappear in the distance. My heart was crying as I had lost a kind friend. I remembered his kind eyes and gentle hands, his reassuring smile when sometimes he had to hurt me. 'Oh God, oh God,' I cried. He was a good man. He did not deserve to die yet or to have such an undignified end. My eyes were burning with tears as I slowly returned to the barracks.

Within the diamond group were two prominent families, the Aschers and the Soeps. In Amsterdam, Abraham Ascher had been the Jewish Council president and Abraham Soep had been a prominent councillor. The Jewish Council had been formed on 12 February 1941 at the request of the Germans, on the pretext that it would help the Jewish population in Holland. Instead the Germans had used the Council as a disguise to obtain an orderly deportation of the Jews to Germany.

It was about mid-October when Ascher and Soep were taken to SS headquarters early in the morning. For the whole day everybody was speculating about what was happening. Hour after hour rumours swept through the camp. The day dragged by slowly, and by the time the curfew came around Ascher and Soep had still not returned. The next day we heard that they had returned at about ten o'clock the night before. The camp telegraph reported that the SS had demanded that Ascher and Soep obtain a large consignment of diamonds from Amsterdam. The SS wanted to use these diamonds for processing at their newly built factory just outside the fence of our camp. We believed that Ascher and Soep made contact with the diamond merchants in Amsterdam but they would not comply. No one in their right mind would hand over diamonds to the enemy. The camp was buzzing with rumours.

The next day Ascher and Soep were again called to SS headquarters, from where they returned at about three o'clock. The camp telegraph reported the same story as the day before. No diamonds could be obtained from Amsterdam. From that day on, things changed for the diamond group. The double rations were cancelled and they also had to join the work details, except for the

Ascher and Soep families. It appeared that some private deal had
been negotiated for those two families.

* * *

In November 1944, a large tent was erected on the flat ground
close to the shoe pile, about fifty metres from our camp. Soon after,
we saw long columns of women passing our camp. They were
poorly dressed. Some had no shoes at all and had their feet covered
in dirty rags. Most wore some material to try to cover their bare
bodies. It was eerie to watch. Their feet made no noise and they
made no sound as they shuffled past. They were housed in the large
tent. A few days earlier, bales of straw had arrived for them to sleep
on. Many of them had dysentery, so one could imagine the indescribable conditions inside their tent after a few days.

Our men had been ordered to dig the latrines. The latrines were
in the open, but the women had degenerated to the point that they
did not care. I could observe all this with ease, as our barracks was
very close to the dividing fence between the barracks and their
tent. All the time we could hear them fighting and screaming
among themselves. Sometimes a kapo with a whip would enter the
tent and mete out a belting to those poor creatures in order to
restore some peace.

On the evening of the second day after their arrival, a group of
women had come up to our dividing fence to talk to some of our
people. We soon found out that there were some Dutch women
among them. My father and mother had gone to the fence out of
curiosity. After a while my mother came back to the barracks and
found me sitting on top of the bed. I had no inclination to go near

these women. The sight of them walking silently past our camp the day before had scared me to the depths of my soul.

'Aunty Beth is there, and Sonja's mother,' Mum said. 'Dad is talking to them right now. I have come back to take some clothing to them, they have nothing. Look in the suitcase, Hetty, see if we can spare something.'

I pulled out a red cardigan belonging to Mum and a flannel pyjama top of Dad's.

'That is about all we have that will fit them, Mum,' I said.

I found the black woollen jumper which I had packed away because of the lice.

'Do you think we could give them this jumper, Mum?' I asked. 'It's not very clean.'

'That's all right,' Mum said. 'They can change it for some food if they don't want to keep it. I will tell them, but considering the state they are in I suppose everything is welcome.'

I handed Mum the goods and she left in a hurry. As I slowly repacked our suitcase I heard Eva from a bed further on, calling my name.

'Hetty, can I come over?'

'Of course,' I said.

A few seconds later, Eva climbed onto our bed. Eva was a few years older than me. We had spoken briefly now and then in the barracks or at roll-call.

'I went to the fence with my mother, and those women told us that they had come from Auschwitz and that they were burning people there,' Eva said.

'What do you mean, burning people?' I asked.

'Well,' Eva said, 'they put them in an oven and burn them.'

87

'You are crazy,' I said. 'I don't believe it. This is like the story of Hansel and Gretel.'

Eva was adamant.

'I'm not making it up,' she said. 'It's really true!'

As I looked at Eva, trying to comprehend what she had just told me, her mother called her to return to her bed.

'See you later, Hetty,' Eva said, as she climbed down from our bed.

After Eva left I sat motionless, trying to digest what she had told me. Many questions went through my head. How could the SS have done it? No one would willingly let themselves be put in an oven, and, of course, the picture I conjured up in my mind was of a kitchen oven. Eva was absolutely mad, I decided.

Mum and Dad arrived back from the fence. The first question I asked Mum was: 'Is it true that they burned people in Auschwitz?'

Mum looked at Dad, unable to answer.

'Yes, Hetty,' Dad said.

'But how did they do it?' I asked.

'When the trains arrived in Auschwitz, mothers and children were separated from the fathers, and then they were taken to a building where they were told that they had to take a bath,' Dad replied. 'They were all given a towel and a piece of soap, but instead of water, gas came out of the showers. They gassed our people first and then they burned them in huge crematoriums.'

I was frozen like stone. I opened my mouth to say something but could not utter a word. A kaleidoscope of pictures went through my mind. I saw my lovely grandmother gasping for breath. I saw people rushing the doors and, in vain, trying to open them. When at long last the horrible reality sank further into my soul I knew that never, never again, would our lives be the same. I knew that there was no hope of ever seeing my grandparents again, nor any of our large family of about three hundred people. My mother was crying on my father's shoulder. She also knew there was no hope of ever seeing her parents again. Dad tried to comfort Mum as best as he could. His eyes were also burning with tears. How hopeless we felt. What could we do? We were helpless! I started to pray that God would give us strength, and asked him to help us to get out of this inhuman situation. My tears were running freely. Mum had recovered somewhat and stroked my hair to calm me down. Dad said he had to leave with Max as curfew was nearly here.

Long after the lights went out that night, you could hear people discussing the horrific news we had learned this evening. Like most of the people in our barracks, I did not sleep that night. Now I knew why I had not wanted to go to the fence to meet the women. I had sensed the evil spirits surrounding them while I had watched them shuffling past the day before. I had felt their pain and sorrow and now it scared me even more.

When Mum left at three o'clock I lay awake, staring into the darkness. How, if ever, are we going to get out of this place? I thought. Why is no one in this world helping us? I was glad when daylight broke and I decided to get dressed. I went to the toilets and gave my face and hands a wash. I had no towel with me and used the sleeve of my jumper to dry my face and hands. My slacks were not clean any more. On my return to the barracks Jacky was awake and I told him to get dressed and to go to the washhouse. I gave him a towel, which showed signs of wear. There was not much left of our clothing. Our shoes were worn out from standing in the rain during roll-call. I supposed we were lucky we still had something warm to wear compared with the women who had arrived from Auschwitz.

Life in our camp became very, very crowded. More and more barracks had been built on the Appelplatz. The new barracks looked dark and forbidding. There were hardly any windows in them and they were a lighter construction. Inside, the three-tiered bunks were placed very close together so more people could be housed in them.

A storm blew away the big tent in which the women of Auschwitz were housed. In the wind and pouring rain those poor women stood without any protection against nature's brute force. Most of them were without clothing or shoes and were soaked wet to the bone. They looked like white ghosts in the downpour. In the afternoon the shoe detail was sent back to our camp and the women were able to find shelter in the workplace. A few days later the women were moved to another part of Belsen. We were relieved that we could not hear their screams and ear-splitting noise any more.

The shoe detail had gone back to work again. It had not been operating for the short time that the women had used the barracks. We missed Dad as he had been with us during the days he did not work. The weather was bleak and the drizzly rain made the hours standing on roll-call more and more trying. At least our feet were dry, as Dad had smuggled out shoes for Max, Jacky and myself under his heavy coat. The shoes were made of heavy, oiled black leather and they had wooden soles. They resembled Dutch wooden clogs. Max and Jacky had no problem wearing them, but they hurt my sore foot. However, it was better than no shoes at all. Dad had taken an enormous risk in bringing the shoes through the gate as the SS kept a close eye on them. Many men were caught as they passed through the gate, which meant a beating and hours standing near the gate in rain and wind under the watchful eyes of the SS guards. Their food rations would be cancelled for days. Luckily, Dad had come through safely.

It was about the last week in November that Mum told us that for the next four weeks we could go to barracks 26 at four o'clock every day to drink a glass of milk. The sister of Frau Albela would give it to us. When I asked how that had come about, Mum told me that she had sold her diamond ring. She had received twenty very large potatoes, three jam jars of sugar and a jar of salt. While Mum was telling me the details of the transaction, she pulled a jar with sugar from our suitcase, shielding it with her body from prying eyes. Everybody was so hungry that, if it was known that you had some extra food, it might be stolen, so you either ate it or exchanged it for something else. We had not seen sugar for more than a year. Mum opened the jar and gave Jacky, then Max and myself a teaspoonful of sugar. I relished the sweetness as it slowly dissolved in my mouth.

'Every day you'll get a spoonful of sugar to keep up your strength,' Mum said.

She then showed us the enormous potatoes, each about twenty centimetres in length, which she had hidden between our clothes in our suitcase. But what could you do with raw potatoes? I took a knife and cut a big chunk from one of them, divided it into smaller parts and handed each of us a piece of raw potato. We were very hungry. We were constantly hungry and started to eat. But it was horrible and even with all my hunger I could not eat it. What could we do with these potatoes if we could not cook them? Mum closed the suitcase firmly and said, 'From now on, one of us must always guard the suitcase. Our bed must not be left alone at any time, not only to safeguard us against pilfering, but so that we are alert for when Red Müller comes for inspection. You organise the schedule, Hetty, so the three of you can take your turn.'

'Yes, Mum,' I said.

How happy we were. We felt like millionaires, and when Dad came home from work he was shown our treasures. Mum gave Dad a spoonful of sugar, although he protested and said that he wanted the sugar only to be for us children.

Dad told us that night that Red Müller had visited the shoe detail, and he and the Scharführer had given the men a hard time. When he spotted Uncle Max and Dad among the men, Müller screamed, 'There are the criminal brothers – stand up!' Uncle Max and Dad had scrambled onto their feet and stood to attention. Müller started with Uncle Max.

'You lazy shit pig. Can't you work any faster?' he bawled. 'Watch out. I will report you for sabotage. I will have you shot.'

To impress Müller, the Scharführer had hit Uncle Max over the head. Then Müller turned to Dad and noticed that Dad was wearing a woollen scarf around his neck to keep him warm.

'What is that for?' he shouted at Dad.

'I have a sore throat, Herr Ober Scharführer,' Dad answered.

'Is that so?' Müller said. 'I know a better way to use the scarf. Come over here,' Müller said to the Scharführer. 'Now, give me a hand and we will show this pig here (meaning my father) what we really believe his scarf is for.'

Müller grasped Dad's scarf, and gave one end to the Scharführer and between them, they lifted my father off the floor by his scarf, which became tighter and tighter around his neck.

'You see, criminal,' Müller screamed, 'that's what we do with pigs like you!'

Müller released his hold on the scarf and Dad dropped with a thud onto the floor. It was just in time as Dad was choking and had stars before his eyes. Müller left after this incident, but it had taken Dad about five minutes to regain his breath and to stop his heart from pumping.

'My God,' Mum said, 'hanging you with your own scarf. What beasts they are!'

We sat in stunned silence, looking at Dad. We had come very close to losing him.

'Better not wear your scarf any more,' I said to Dad. 'Or hide it under your shirt so they will not notice it as much.'

Terrible things were happening in our camp. In the past few days, people from other barracks were told to move out with all their belongings to other barracks. The order usually came when the work details had just returned late in the afternoon and everybody was very tired. The moves lasted until late into the night and this soul-destroying task had to be done without lights. The people were in a panic to find beds in the allocated barracks, which were those recently completed, ominous-looking barracks near the Appelplatz. As the beds were so close together, people pushed and struggled to find a bed in the dark, only to discover that there were no mattresses, or planks underneath to carry the mattress. It was bedlam. Our barracks had until now escaped the ruckus, but we knew our turn would come eventually.

It was Friday night, and cold and drizzly rain was falling when someone came into the barracks and urgently requested able men to come and help at the barracks for the old people. They had been ordered to move.

'How sadistic those bastards are!' Dad said, when he left with some other men for the hospital. Everybody was visibly upset.

When Belsen was new and our group had arrived in February, Albela had allowed, with permission from the SS camp doctor, two barracks to be used for the old and the frail. One of the barracks was for infectious diseases. The SS were very scared of infectious diseases as they could carry to their quarters. The old people had been looked after by a male nurse and a few women. A fence surrounded the hospital barracks and we were not allowed to come close to it. When someone got seriously sick they were taken to the hospital but they seldom returned from there. Daily you could see one or two bodies being taken from the hospital to go on the lonely journey to the crematorium. I remembered the lovely young woman with a beautiful baby. I had loved that baby and for many hours I had played with him. The woman got sick quite early after our arrival and died two days later in the hospital. Some women in the barracks had looked after the baby, but then he got sick and his father took him to the hospital and stayed with him to care for him. I was told later that the baby had also died, but his father stayed on in the hospital as a male nurse. Sometimes I had seen the father behind the hospital fence. It was not hard to recognise him as he had a bright red beard, which he grew after the death of his wife and son.

Dad was away for hours. In fact, he did not come back that night. He returned to his own barracks after he left the hospital.

The next day, Dad told us about the appalling conditions of the newly designated barracks for the old and the sick. It had been the same story as before – not enough mattresses. They had to leave some very frightened and exhausted elderly people lying on the cold floor. In the end, they had not moved some very sick people from the hospital. There was no room anymore. We were very depressed when we heard the sad story, but out of something bad came something good; for us, at least. In the old people's barracks, stoves were burning to give some warmth. Dad had made arrangements with the male nurse, who was still living in the hospital, to cook some of our potatoes. The price was five large potatoes for the cook. The next day, Dad did not go to work. When it was time to leave for work in the morning he hid himself in the ladies' washhouse. He came to my bed at about half past seven. I was awake and dressed, ready for roll-call.

'What are you doing here, Dad?' I asked, surprised to see him.

'I am staying in,' he said. 'It was about one o'clock when I got to bed last night but I could not sleep. I could not get those poor bewildered old people out of my head.'

'Won't they miss you?' I asked.

'I don't think so,' Dad answered. 'Things are very chaotic at the moment with people going from barracks to barracks, and all the new SS guards we have lately are not familiar with the faces in the work details yet.'

The new SS guards had come with the recent transports from Auschwitz. We observed that the Russian camp across the main road opposite our camp had many more inhabitants than before.

The Russian POWs had disappeared a while ago – where to, we did not know, and we could only pray for their safety. My thoughts

95

had wandered and I came back to the present when I heard Dad say, 'I'll have a sleep in your bed, Hetty. I am very tired.'

'What about roll-call?' I asked. 'The figures won't be right if you play hooky!'

'Don't worry,' Dad said. 'I have spoken to the barracks elder. She knows I helped the old people last night and has agreed to list me as a sick person in the barracks for the roll-call.'

'That's okay then,' I said.

I did not want to think about what would happen at the Appelplatz if there was someone missing from roll-call.

'Don't worry, darling,' Dad said, 'I have it all arranged. Now you'd better get ready and go to roll-call. The boys have left already. I'll see you when you get back.'

I climbed down from our bunk, and Dad slept fully clothed with the blanket covering his head completely so that no one could see that a man was asleep in the female barracks. Even before I left the barracks, Dad was asleep. Poor Dad, I thought, he is so exhausted from hard work and lack of food. I lifted my eyes to the grey clouds and prayed that soon someone from somewhere would come to help us.

It was about half past eleven that morning when we returned from roll-call. Dad woke up when he heard our voices.

'They have kept you at roll-call for a long time again. Come up on the bed and get warm under the blanket for a while until the soup arrives,' he said.

The three of us climbed up. We took our shoes off before we snuggled under the blanket. We could not leave our shoes on the floor as they would be stolen immediately, so in order to keep them we had to take them off on top of the bed and keep them close to our bodies. By now hygiene took second place – survival came first.

Five

'God will look after us.'

At the beginning of December 1944 we had to move to another barracks. Everyone packed their meagre belongings together, and slowly the barracks in which we had lived for ten months emptied. It was very unsettling. The barracks had become our home, our bed so familiar. We had slept, eaten and talked, sitting close together as a family unit. Now there was this uncertainty again, that feeling we had experienced so many times at home in Amsterdam when the SS had gone from door to door to bring people out of their houses. We heard the knocks on other doors and were relieved when the sound of heavy boots passed our home without stopping. Here in Belsen it was no different. Uprooting people en masse was a cunning and sadistic technique that created panic in our hearts and had a great psychological impact.

Mum, Dad, Jacky and Max had gone to investigate the new barracks and to find us a bed. I was left behind to guard the suitcases and our blankets, which were already rolled up in a bundle. While I was sitting on top of our bed, I surveyed the now near-empty barracks. Here and there some discarded or forgotten possessions were lying around. They won't be there for long, I thought, someone will have a use for them. A bit further down the aisles an elderly couple was getting ready to leave, the man telling the woman to hurry up otherwise they would not find a bed. The woman was crying and her movements were slow and difficult.

'Come on!' the man urged her. 'Here, let me carry this case, and maybe that will be easier.'

With sad eyes I watched them leave the barracks. She will not live much longer, I thought. What a shame, she was such a pretty old lady. When we arrived about ten months ago, she always had such a friendly smile, and now she was skinny and old and worn out from being systematically deprived of sustaining food.

Mum and Dad arrived back after about two hours.

'For goodness sake! What took you so long?' I asked.

'Be quiet! I have a surprise for you,' Mum said.

Mum and Dad climbed up. Mum opened a bundle wrapped in some old cloth.

'Here, you may eat it all,' she said, as she handed me one of the large potatoes cooked in its skin and still boiling hot.

'How did you do this?' I asked.

'Well,' Dad answered, 'it was really your mother's idea to take advantage of the chaos in our camp at the moment, so we went to the hospital with the potatoes, and, as everyone was moving around with bundles and suitcases, no one noticed anything.'

While the potatoes were being cooked in the hospital, they had gone to find beds in the new barracks. They had also found two mattresses, and they had to find some planks for underneath as well. Max and Jacky had stayed behind to guard the beds. Mum and Dad had returned to the hospital to collect the potatoes. While Mum and Dad were telling me the story, I had peeled away the skin of half the potato and broken a piece away. I started to eat it slowly as it was still piping hot. Mum and Dad also ate their potatoes with some salt which Mum had retrieved from our suitcase. No further words were said as the three of us ate on top of our bed in the now-deserted barracks. But what was that? I looked up at Mum in surprise. I had only finished half the potato when I could not eat another bite. I was full! My stomach could not handle any more food. I could have sworn I could have eaten a whole cow, I was so hungry when I started.

'I cannot eat any more,' I told Mum.

'Go slowly,' Mum urged, 'your stomach has shrunk. Better keep the rest for breakfast.' She opened the old cloth which still held two potatoes for Max and Jacky.

'There,' Mum said, 'put it back in here, it will keep till tomorrow.' I put my half a potato with the other two, after which Mum carefully wrapped them and put them in the suitcase.

'Well,' she enquired, 'was it good?'

Was it good? Of course it had been good. For the first time in many months my stomach was full and I was not hungry. Mum and Dad finished their potatoes soon after.

'We better be going, it's getting late,' Dad said.

We climbed down from our bed for the last time. Dad took the two suitcases and Mum and I each carried a bundle of blankets.

It was dark when we left the barracks. The weather was mild for the time of the year. There were still a few people shuffling around but most were already in their barracks. We crossed the Appelplatz. When we arrived in our new barracks it was not as bad as I had imagined. Some people were burning a candle, which they must have brought from home a long time ago. It gave them a dim light and it helped us find our beds. Max and Jacky were glad to see us as they had been a bit scared in the new surroundings. Mum gave them each a potato before we made up our bed as well as possible under the circumstances. The sight of the potato soon stopped any complaints from the boys about making them wait so long. But even before Max could finish his potato Dad told him they had to leave in time for the curfew. We kissed each other goodnight and Dad left with Max.

Mum had managed to get a top bunk again with Jacky on the bed below us. Jacky had to share a bed with another woman as there was a shortage. In the lower bed slept two sisters. Soon we were told that all the lights had to be out. The barracks was in total darkness. Mum had fallen asleep as soon as her head hit the pillow, but I could not sleep. I was staring into the darkness and listening to the sounds of so many people resting in an exhausted sleep in this creepy place. I turned on my side and looked through the window next to our bed. I could see the deserted Appelplatz dimly lit from the big light on the gate, the barracks throwing their shadow on the ground. I do not even know where the toilets are, I thought. Better not think about it, I told myself, otherwise I will have to go. I leant over the side of the bunk and, as my eyes had become accustomed to the dark, I could see Jacky sleeping peacefully on the bed below. I must have dozed, as I woke up when Mum gently untangled herself from the blanket to go to work. We all had gone to sleep fully dressed. Being in an unfamiliar place we felt safer with our clothes on.

'Mum,' I whispered, 'where are the toilets?'

Mum told me how to get there, gave me a kiss and was off to work. It was still dark outside and looking out the window, I could see about forty women standing in formation on the dimly lit Appelplatz with the SS counting heads before they marched out of the gate.

Max came early in the morning and told us to give him our beakers so he could get some of that brown sloppy coffee for Jacky and myself. It did not take him long to return. He handed the beakers up to me, having difficulty not spilling the coffee, as our bed was much higher than in the previous barracks. Max quickly climbed on top and snuggled under the blanket with us. Jacky had come up from the bed below earlier. The closeness of our bodies radiated heat and kept us warm. It was lovely to feel warm. Jacky and I were sipping the warm drink while we observed our surroundings. In the light of the morning we did not see many familiar faces from the previous barracks. To our surprise we noticed that men were also sleeping in the barracks. How that had come about we did not know, and frankly we did not care much. Women were not prudish any more, and dressed and undressed and washed themselves, sometimes naked, in front of strangers. Who cared? Who would want to look at those skinny women? The only thought which drove everybody on was food to stay alive. The three of us stayed in the barracks all day. We only left it for three hours to stand on roll-call. Before we went to the Appelplatz we had covered the suitcase containing our precious sugar with a blanket, making sure that our bed was made according to SS standards.

The hours went by slowly, as we waited for our parents' return. In the morning I ate the rest of my potato after giving Max and Jacky a small piece from it. They had eaten theirs last night but somehow I could not eat alone. We did not feel at home yet in this new barracks, as we did not know many of the people. It housed twice as many people as the previous one. Max got us our soup at lunchtime and, as usual, we saved a bowlful for Dad. He was ever so hungry when he came home from work. When it was time, the boys went to meet him near the gate. Dad would always ask if Mum was back, as for the past few months the hours she had to work were longer and longer. There were only two kitchens in the camp to cater for the tremendous influx of people in Belsen. Mum got home about an hour later than Dad. It had been a long, long day for her. Max and Dad had gone to meet her, and when they entered the barracks I was so very happy to see her again. They all climbed onto our bed. It was more difficult now as it was one bed higher and there was not much room to sit. Most of the other people also sat on their bunks, and when you climbed up or down you would unintentionally step on the person below.

After Mum and Dad had rested a bit they decided to go to the hospital to have some more potatoes cooked. When they returned they told us that the potatoes would be ready for us to pick up the next night. When Max had collected the soup at lunchtime, he had also collected our bread rations, so a thin slice of dark dry bread was our meagre meal that night, supplemented by a few pieces of carrot Mum had smuggled in her boots. Mum was very tired so Dad and Max left early. This way we could all have an early night.

The next day was the same routine. We soon found out that there was no washhouse near the barracks, only a tap outside. Jacky and I went there in the morning to wash our faces and hands, while Max guarded the bed. Roll-call took two hours. We were glad to be inside again after it was over. At lunchtime, we were given bread rations for three days. This brought another worry; where to hide it so it did not get stolen. The only place we had was in the suitcase, and that is where I put it. After lunch Max and Jacky left the barracks in search of food. They took a bowl with them. The boys both had a special spoon and table knife. It had a silver-coloured handle and the cutting blade was made of sweeping steel. They used it to scrape out the empty food containers before they were collected. Sometimes Max came back with half a bowl of soup but there were times when the food he scraped off the side of the food containers was contaminated with worms and mould. When Max was not sure of the risk involved, or if it looked as if rust particles were in the food, he always asked me for my opinion. I told him not to eat it because it was dangerous. He looked so disappointed. At times he worked so hard to acquire only a thin layer of food on the bottom of his bowl. He would reluctantly throw it away. With the boys gone, I was obliged to stay on our bed to watch over our suitcases.

One of the sisters on the lower bunk started a conversation with me. Her sister was not feeling well and was lying in bed. They told me that their respective husbands had been picked up in a raid in Amsterdam two years ago and they did not know what had happened to them. The sisters had been living together after that had happened, and now they were here together.

The boys returned after about an hour. They had not had much success and I told them to eat what they had in the bowl. Mum came home early that day and after giving us some pieces of carrot, she said she would go to the hospital to collect our last potatoes. Max and Jacky went with her. Soon after they left, Dad arrived, looking worried.

'Where is everybody? No one was at the gate to meet me!' he said. I explained that Mum and the boys had gone to pick up the potatoes.

His face cleared.

'Yes!' he said, 'I don't think I will eat this now. This water (indicating the soup, if you could call it that,) will fill me up and then I won't be able to eat the potato. You know what? I will exchange it for something. I know a man who has some razor blades. I will see him straight away. Hand me the bowl, Hetty.'

Dad climbed down again. When he reached the floor, I handed him the bowl with the cold soup. I had used my headscarf to cover it. Dad left with the bowl and I settled down to watch and wait again. About half an hour later Dad returned with two razor blades and, soon after, Mum and the boys arrived. Mum and Max were carrying our precious potatoes. When everybody had climbed up, Mum opened the wrapping and we counted eight potatoes. Mum told Dad that she had to give another two potatoes to the cook. Soon we were all eating our precious meal. I had immediately cut my potato into halves as I knew that a whole potato was too much for me. It was wonderful to be able to eat so much that you were not hungry any more. After we were finished, Mum gave Dad another potato to eat in the morning before he went to work, and the rest she put in the suitcase.

We sat together for a while, Dad telling us about a workmate who had been caught that night. He had dropped a stolen shoe as he was walking through the gate. We felt very sorry for this man as it was quite nippy outside, so the hours standing at the gate would not be easy for him. After about an hour, we all felt very drowsy – the result of having a full stomach.

Dad decided to call it a day and, after kissing us goodnight, he left with Max, but not before Mum told Max that it was her free day tomorrow and he had to come here before it was time for roll-call, so he could share in our special breakfast. We were a united family and received strength from each other in these horrendous circumstances.

The next morning I woke up at seven o'clock. I had had a long deep sleep. Mum was watching me and gave me a big smile and a good morning kiss.

'Have you been awake a long time, Mum?' I asked.

'About an hour. Would you like your breakfast?'

'No, Mum,' I said. 'I'll keep it for later. Where is Jacky?'

'He has gone with Max to look for food. They won't be long as we have to go to roll-call.'

'Well, I'm ready,' I said. 'I'm dressed.' We were still sleeping in our clothes.

'Comb your hair a bit and you'll look fine,' Mum said.

I started to look for a comb in the suitcase. It was about half past seven when we were told that there would not be a roll-call today. That was good news, but usually when there was no roll-call, they had something more sinister in store for us. Mum decided to investigate what we could expect.

'Mum, I have been in the barracks for two days guarding the suitcase. Could Max and Jacky stay for a while to guard it? I would like to get some fresh air,' I said.

'Of course!' Mum said. 'When the boys get back you may tell them that I said so. I am going now. I won't be long.'

She climbed down and soon, through the window, I saw her crossing the Appelplatz towards our old barracks. When Max and Jacky returned to the barracks I told them that Mum wanted them to stay in and guard the suitcase, to which they both immediately agreed. So I climbed down from our bed and headed outside, where there were some groups of women standing around talking to each other. I did not take much notice of them and turned the corner of the barracks, when I saw Mum coming towards me. She appeared nervous and shaky.

'What's the matter, Mum?' I asked when she was close enough.

'Something terrible is going to happen!' she said.

'What?'

For a moment Mum could not answer. I could see she was very upset.

'What is it?' I urged her.

'They say that the diamond group is going on a penalty transport today,' Mum said.

For a moment I was stunned. Then the realisation settled in that our names had been added to the group about six months ago.

'Oh, no! But perhaps they will exclude us and maybe there is no truth in the rumour.'

'No,' Mum said, 'it's true. There!' She pointed to the gate. 'The guards are bringing the men back from the work details. It's true all right.'

I panicked. I took hold of Mum's arm.

'What are we going to do?'

Mum put her arms around me.

'Hush. Stay calm, then you can think more clearly. Somehow we will manage. We aren't going, but Dad is. They are only sending the men away.'

By now, the whole camp was in commotion, the news having spread like wildfire. Max came outside and saw my distressed face, and by now Mum could not hold back tears. He ran to Mum and buried his face in her chest with his arms tightly around her.

'What are we going to do?' he cried.

Mum stroked his hair while trying to compose herself.

'Look, there's Dad,' I said. He was marching in with about ten other men brought back from the shoe detail. As if in a dream, I watched the small group of men downing their hats, faces turned right, in salute to the SS guard at the gate as they entered the camp. Dad spotted us at once and hurried toward us. No words were needed as Dad's eyes met Mum's. The misery their eyes mirrored was unbearable. Dad's arms went around Mum. They stood very still, embracing each other without a word, the pain of the impending separation written on their faces. When at long last Dad released Mum, he kissed Max and me and said to Max, 'Come with me to our barracks to pick up our suitcase and bedding. From now on you will sleep with Mum, as you cannot stay on your own up there after I am gone. Let's go! They have given us an hour.'

Max and Dad left, and Mum and I entered the barracks to wait for them to return. Mum told Jacky the bad news while I could not sit still. I opened the suitcase to pull out three rations of bread to give Dad to take with him. I found a reasonably clean handkerchief in which I rolled the bread. So this is why they gave us a three-day bread ration, I thought. How cunning they are. They had it all arranged, the filthy swines.

It did not take long for Dad to return with Max. Dad carried his suitcase and Max carried a blanket and a sheet, whose colour could not be established any more as it had not been washed for weeks. As usual, everything took place on top of our bed. There Dad opened the suitcase and took out a singlet, a shirt, underpants, two pairs of socks and his razor, with the two razor blades he had received only yesterday in exchange for the soup.

'Jacky,' Dad said, 'give me your little carrying bag. I can carry it better than a near-empty suitcase.' Jacky emptied his bag and handed it to Dad. Dad also put the three rations of bread into the bag. Mum wanted to give him a jar of sugar, but Dad steadfastly refused.

'It's for my children. I won't take it!' he said.

No matter how Mum pleaded, he would not change his mind. The time when Dad had to go grew nearer. One by one he embraced the three of us and told us to be good and to look after Mum. We all scrambled down to the floor to escort Dad to the gate. As we were leaving the barracks, lots of women and men came up to Dad and wished him well.

Outside, I noticed how grey the sky was. Everything looked grey. About four hundred men with their families had gathered near the gate and our family joined them. A hush settled over the Appelplatz. Most people had done their crying in private, I thought. At the moment of departure it appeared that an inner strength within this group gathered near the gate had come to the surface. Although everyone was anguished with the knowledge that they may never see their loved ones again, with only a few exceptions, they made an effort to look cheerful in order to give each other the courage to face the uncertain future.

We were standing close together in these final moments when the SS guard called the names of the men who had to come forward. Just outside the gate, they lined up five abreast. The first few names had been called in alphabetical order. When they came to the gate, they were told to leave their luggage behind. When we saw that, Dad opened his little bag, took out the bread rations and put them into the pocket of his coat. He then took out his razor and the two blades, which he had previously rolled in a piece of paper, and put them into the other pocket of his coat. He handed Mum the carrying bag and said, 'I will eat the bread, and if they do not take away the razor and blades, then I can exchange them for food.' By now, half the group had gone through the gate and part of the group had marched off. Once the men had left, their wives and children cried bitterly. They did not have to pretend any more.

Dad turned to Mum and said, 'Darling, take good care of yourself and the children, but most of all, stay alive. I will see you again soon. I am sure that the war will soon be over. I will find you.'

Mum could not speak; her eyes were burning with tears. Jacky and Max were crying. Dad kissed Mum and held her close, then Dad kissed the boys and told them to be good for Mum. At last he turned to me, and his warm brown eyes looked into mine.

'Hetty,' he said, 'you are the oldest. Look after your mother for me, and the boys.'

I nodded. I could not speak and he kissed me goodbye. Then his name was called. There was nothing we could do. He had to leave us now. A final kiss for Mum and he walked away from us towards the gate where his name was ticked off against the list by the SS officer. We saw Dad going through the gate to join the other men already standing there. Uncle Max was among them. Dad had been one of the last ones to go.

Every wife and child tried to get a last glimpse of their dear one and we vied for a position along the fence. The order was shouted and the men started to move. The men looked as grey as the weather except for their eyes.

'Goodbye! Goodbye!' We called and waved to all the men who were forced to leave us, until they disappeared into the distance.

Slowly the Appelplatz emptied. Women and children collected the luggage left behind by their respective husbands and fathers. We had nothing to collect. Silently, we walked towards our barracks. No one spoke. Each of us was busy with their own thoughts. In my imagination, I followed Dad on the road to the station where they would board the train, but to where? An immeasurable distance without horizon appeared in my mind. I could not see anything. It was void. Dad, where are you? My heart was calling out to him, but no answer came back. In despair I returned to the barracks, yet no tears would come. After climbing onto our bed, I dared to look at Mum for the first time. In her eyes I could see the pain from Dad's departure. What could I say? I felt her pain, but I knew I had to say something.

'Mum,' I said, 'Dad will be all right.'

'You think so?' Mum answered. Like a frightened child, she was asking for reassurance.

'I am sure of it,' I told her. 'You must not let it get you down. We will see him again soon. He said so and I know it! You know he is always optimistic. He is a survivor.' From somewhere the words came to me, and I was glad that Mum took comfort from my words. Strangely, my own words also comforted me.

Mum lifted her head and saw the two boys who had sat silently while I had talked to her. She embraced them both as one and said, 'We have to do it together now Dad is gone.'

The boys nodded their heads.

'Well,' Mum said, 'we'd better make arrangements so Max can share our bed tonight.' Mum opened the second suitcase and emptied it of the few belongings. She told Max to put the empty suitcase under the bunk on the floor. Nobody would steal the suitcase as we had nowhere to go. Mum put everything in the other suitcase and then moved it into an upright position on the end of our bed so that Max could sleep on our foot end. Somehow, we would manage.

Later that day, we shared the last potatoes and ate some of our bread ration. At times, Mum stared in front of her and we knew where her mind had wandered. We all felt desolate and depressed, and I am sure we all were glad that it was time to go to sleep. We each found new positions as Max was sharing the bed now. Max slept at once. Mum lay awake for some time, but then I could hear her steady breathing and I knew she was asleep. I lay awake for many hours thinking of Dad and I prayed to God to look after my father.

After Mum left for work in the morning, Max lay next to me. We slept until half past six and woke up because Jacky had told us that the coffee had arrived. As usual Max got the coffee. He took a bowl as this was easier to carry than three mugs. We drank the warm brown water to get warm.

'Where do you think Dad is now?'

'I don't know,' I answered.

Silence fell between us. I took out a bread ration from the suitcase; it was brown and dry. I cut off three very thin slices from the daily ration of about six centimetres by three centimetres. This had to last us until the soup arrived. Just as we prepared to go to roll-call we were told that there would be no roll-call this morning, so the three of us remained sitting on top of our bed.

It was 5 December 1944, St Nicholas Day, the day when all children in Holland are spoiled with sweets and presents.

It was about nine o'clock when Mum walked into the barracks.

'What's the matter, Mum? Why have you come back from work?' I asked.

'We are going on a transport!' Mum said.

'What? Where are we going?' I was shocked, and a feeling of impending catastrophe took hold of me. The eyes of the boys reflected their shock.

'We must pack our things now. We have to be ready at eleven o'clock,' Mum said.

Mum's quiet words subdued the panic. How strong she is, I thought. She knows she must stay calm for our sakes.

'God will look after us, believe me!' Mum said, looking at me.

I was not so sure. How could God allow people to know such suffering as we had experienced?

Mum told Max to get the suitcase off the floor and to hand it up to her. I helped her to fold up the blankets and sheets. It didn't take long to fold two blankets and sheets into one suitcase, and the third blanket easily fitted into the other, with the meagre remains of our clothing. She carefully placed our jars of sugar and the salt in between the folds of the blankets. It had taken us no more than twenty minutes to be ready. She sent Max and Jacky away to wash their hands and faces, and told them to use the toilets as well. When Max and Jacky returned, Mum and I left to do the same. We returned about ten minutes later. By now it was nearly ten o'clock and we had one more hour to wait before going to the gate. We sat on our bed. We did not say much. Now and then someone would come up to us and wish us well. The woman from the lower bunk told us that after we were gone, she and her sister would take our bed.

'Of course,' Mum said.

We were torn between hope and despair. Perhaps we were going to a better camp. Where were we going? I did not want to think about the possibility that we could be sent to a worse place.

It was now half past ten.

'We'd better go outside, then we can see what is happening,' Mum said.

Mum and I climbed down, and the boys handed the suitcases to us. While the boys climbed down, the woman from the lower bed climbed up to claim possession of our bed before anyone else could. Mum and I carried the suitcases as we walked towards the exit. Max and Jacky followed. We did not go to the gate immediately, but stayed near the barracks. We could observe from this position what was taking place on the Appelplatz and the gates. Lots of women with their luggage and their children had already assembled on the Appelplatz with their friends or family, who had come to say a final farewell.

At ten minutes to eleven, Albela came to the gate and we could see Mr Weiss as well. Three SS officers arrived five minutes later, alighting from the truck parked on the road outside the gate. We could see one of the SS speaking with Albela, who nodded his head, and he gave the list which the SS had handed him to one of his lieutenants. Mr Weiss was present to translate, as not many women could understand German. More and more well-wishers had filled the Appelplatz, so our view of the gate was obscured. We noticed that some of the women had moved towards the gate. We could not see the children as adults blocked our view. Suddenly we could hear a commotion and struggling at the gate. A woman started to scream hysterically, 'My baby, my baby, I want my baby!' Another woman cried, 'No! 'No!' We could hear the SS yell, 'Move on! Move on!'

'My God, we have to leave the children behind. They are not allowing them to come with us,' Mum said.

I was numb with horror and could not bring out one word.

'Quick, Hetty, get back into the barracks with the suitcase, we have no time to lose!' Mum commanded.

I walked into the barracks with Mum following me. The barracks was deserted as everybody was watching at the gate. Just inside the door, Mum told me to open the suitcase as she opened the other one. In a few quick movements, she separated one blanket and her clothing into one of the suitcases. She also took one jar which was half full of sugar and put it in her case.

'Now, Hetty, I want you and the boys to eat a spoonful of sugar now and then, but be very careful with it, because you can exchange it for bread or something you need. Promise me you will do this,' she said.

'Yes, Mum,' I said, and I could feel the tremendous responsibility which now rested on my shoulders.

'Hetty, look after the boys for me,' Mum said again. 'Especially take care of Jacky, he's been sickly the past few years.'

'Yes, Mum,' I promised. We both knew that our last minutes of being together were quickly ticking away.

'Oh,' Mum said, 'I nearly forgot. Here is the steel nit comb.' She pulled it out of the pocket of her coat. 'Keep your hair clean, and the boys' too.'

I nodded and put the comb in my pocket. During all these months in the camp, Mum had kept our hair free of lice. Mum took me in her arms and kissed me again and again. I clung to her as I knew she had to go soon. No tears had come to either of us. Our eyes were dry but our hearts were bleeding.

'Come,' Mum said, 'I must say goodbye to the boys.'

We picked up our suitcases and went outside and found the boys, where Mum had told them to stay put.

Mum embraced the boys, who were crying bitterly.

'Hush, you both must be big men now and listen to Hetty. She will look after you now. You must stay together and come back to Amsterdam to the Pomstra family after the war is over. Now don't forget, my darlings,' Mum said, kissing them again and again.

'Are you going to bring Mum to the gate?' she said, as she slowly straightened up.

She picked up her suitcase and with the boys clinging to her coat, we slowly walked to the gate. When we were about five metres from the gate, Mr Weiss gently removed the boys from Mum's coat. Mum turned to give me a last kiss, bending down to the boys to do the same. The boys were now clinging to me, crying out their sorrow. I could not hold back my own tears any more as I watched Mum climbing onto the back of the truck with her suitcase, assisted by some of the other women. It was like a nightmare seeing Mum go in the same manner as Dad had gone the day before.

We ran towards the fence so as not to miss the last seconds of seeing our mother. We waved and called our goodbyes. Everybody was crying and our hearts were breaking. When the truck started to move, Mum called out, 'Be good, my children, goodbye!'

Six

'Jewish children?'

When the truck had disappeared into the distance, I turned around and noticed, for the first time, that about forty children were grouped near the fence. Their ages ran from ten months to seventeen years although most of them were under ten years of age. A few women from the hospital were caring for the babies and the very small children.

'Are we going back to the barracks now?' I asked, turning to Mr Weiss, who had followed us to the fence.

'No, Hetty,' Mr Weiss said, 'a truck is coming for all the children in a moment. You are all going away.'

Hope flickered in my heart that we would follow Mum, but that was not to be.

We were standing around or sitting on our suitcases. Our tears had dried, but all the children, including myself, were in a state of shock. The cruelty of it all had left its mark. Some women were walking up and down with crying babies, little children were walking aimlessly around in the area to which we were confined, crying out for their mothers. From somewhere a few bottles of milk arrived for the crying babies. The women carers fed them.

Although we were still within the perimeter of our camp, just outside the fence two armed guards were watching us. Mr Weiss had come over to us a few times but could only stay for a short while. His presence instilled some calm, but each time he left, the children cried and cried. At last, at about four o'clock the truck arrived to take us away. Mr Weiss and some other men were allowed to help us onto the trucks. They lifted up the children one by one, but the babies were handed over to me and one other girl. We were the oldest of the children.

With sad eyes, Mr Weiss and the few men waved us goodbye as the truck started to move. The children had stopped crying. The ride in the truck took their attention away from their misery. Our camp lay behind us and we passed the Häftling camp. Those poor creatures were still standing on their Appelplatz. They must have been there for eight hours by now.

The trucks passed the food store and we could see Chris, the fat SS officer in charge, standing at the door. Two pretty women from our camp, who were working at the storeroom, were standing next to him. I was glad to see familiar faces and I waved at them. We went through the gate and into the camp reserved for the SS. The trucks slowed down and stopped in front of a building with big double doors. We were told to alight. The older boys helped the little ones down from the trucks. I handed Max the baby I was holding and then came down myself. I turned and helped little girls and boys off the truck.

We were herded into the building, which turned out to be the SS garage. When we entered, we saw the luggage our mothers had taken with them and understood that they must have been ordered to leave it behind in the garage. Soon the children had identified their personal luggage and taken possession of it. After finding out the name of the baby, I told Eva, the tallest girl, and some other children, to find his mother's suitcase, as we desperately needed to change his nappy. We made a little corner with a blanket so we could put the baby down, and Max was relieved when I removed the baby from his arms. It was amazing how quickly the children found the suitcase, and when Eva opened it, we were happy to find a clean change for the baby. Eva offered to change the baby so I could attend to a second one. The children quickly brought me the suitcase which belonged to the second baby. This baby was about ten months old, but not so very small. Two girls of about ten told me that they could change the baby. I let them do it as there were other things to attend to. The little ones of walking age all had wet pants and were crying their eyes out. Again, I enlisted the seven- or eight-year-olds to find suitcases, after I found out the names of the tiny ones. It took some sorting out and it took a while to change them all. When I went through the suitcases left behind by the mothers, I felt like an interloper into the private belongings of other people, but I told myself that the mothers would be happy that their children were being taken care of. I made sure that all belongings, such as soiled clothing, were returned to the right suitcases.

We had been in the garage for at least two hours. Nobody guarded us and we had been left to our own devices. Everybody was very tired. We had been on our feet since early in the morning without any food or drink. It was very cold outside and the light was fading fast. Stars appeared and the moon was rising. As darkness settled in the garage, most of the children were terrified in the unfamiliar surroundings, especially as their mothers were not here to comfort them. They were cold and hungry. Pandemonium broke out. A chorus of crying voices screamed in fright and horror. A boy named Iesy I had once encountered in Amsterdam suggested that we should all cry out in unison. As we were so desperate we tried to do it and on the count of three we all screamed in the hope that someone would hear us. We kept it up until our voices began to fail us.

By now it was very dark in the garage. The only light was from the moonlight, which filtered in through the open door. Nobody came near us. We huddled together and felt lost and forlorn. Through the darkness I felt my way to the door and looked out. There was no one in sight, the road was deserted. Some lights were burning in the SS quarters. The children kept on screaming, it was ear-splitting. This was not just crying any more, it was the sound of desperation. We had lost our fathers and our mothers in a matter of two days and now, after having been left alone for hours in the garage, we believed that we had been forgotten by the world.

I was sitting on one of our suitcases when two shadowy figures appeared in the doorway. A torch was lit and shone into the garage. One of the two walked in and switched on the lights. What a sorry sight we must have been. About forty children were huddled together in the corner with tired, tear-stained faces. As I was the nearest one, the guards asked me where we came from. I told him that we had come from Sternlager at about four o'clock that afternoon. The two men conversed with each other, and then one left. The man who stayed with us in the garage did not wear the uniform of the SS, his uniform was green. He looked about fifty years old and held his rifle in readiness. When the light had been switched on, the crying stopped for a little while, and during the lull we heard a St Nicholas party in progress in the SS barracks. The SS were singing St Nicholas songs at the top of their voices.

The crying and screaming started again; when one child stopped another would start. They were bewildered and without hope. I approached the guard and politely asked him what the time was. He told me it was a quarter past nine. He asked me if I could stop the children from crying. My German was very limited, so it took me some time to understand what he was saying. I told him in broken German sign language that they were very hungry and tired.

The guard looked ill at ease amid this misery. After he understood what I had tried to tell him he nodded his head and said, 'Don't go away! I will come back!' He then left the garage. I did not understand what he meant by 'Don't go away.' Where would I go?

I walked back to where the small children were sitting huddled together on the floor. Their eyes swollen from crying, they were totally exhausted by their ordeal. The worst of the wailing had quietened down. They were spent. Some of the little ones were even asleep on the cold concrete floor. They were worn out and, mercifully, sleep had taken over. I told some of the older boys to get some blankets which I had noticed rolled in bundles between the suitcases. I covered the little ones with these blankets as the night was really cold. I told the other children not to cry any more but try to sleep and tomorrow when it was light again, we would try to find out where Mummy was. With the help of the bigger children, we tried to make them comfortable and cover them up as well as possible.

I also told the older children to make themselves comfortable by sitting on the suitcases. Everybody was so very tired from the long, long hours on our feet, the traumatic upheaval we had experienced, as well as having had nothing to eat all day. It became quiet now. Most of the little ones were sleeping. By now the older ones were talking to each other in low tones, all afraid to go to sleep. I was tired but not sleepy.

About an hour after the guard had left us, he returned with two male prisoners who each carried a large carton. At the same time, a car arrived. Two men entered the garage with their arms full of blankets. I recognised the men from our camp. When Mr Weiss had found out that we were being held in the SS garage, they arranged for the blankets to be delivered to us. How they had been able to arrange this was a mystery to me, but we were very glad as now the older children could have some covers as well. When the four men left, the guard called me over and pointed to the two cartons standing on the floor. He nodded his head in approval, motioning me to look into the boxes. I hesitated. I did not trust him. I walked slowly towards the two cartons and then looked at the guard again. He did not say a word but made a movement with his head, indicating for me to look into the boxes. Ever so slowly, I opened the first box, still not trusting the guard's meaning. I removed a paper cover and then I could not believe my eyes. Under the paper, I found thick slices of white bread sandwiches filled with thick butter and sugar. I lifted my eyes to look at the guard, too afraid to touch anything. He nodded approval and then turned away, making out he saw nothing.

I called out to Max and some of the older boys and girls who were still awake. They came towards me and, whispering, I told them of the heavenly gift the guard had brought us. We looked at the guard who had turned his back to us and, ever so carefully, we each took a sandwich from the box. I told some of the boys to take a sandwich to all the other children who were still awake but were bedded down for the night. I also told them to be as quiet as possible so as not to attract attention from someone passing by. We were so hungry, what a party we had! Fresh white bread with butter and sugar. For ten months we had eaten only dry brown bread a quarter of the size of one of these thick slices – our rations for twenty-four hours – and now, we had this huge amount. I looked into the second box, which was also filled to the top with those beautiful sandwiches. I contemplated waking the sleeping children to let them have their share, but decided against it. To sleep meant forgetfulness and the sandwiches would keep until they woke up. Max and Iesy came back for a second sandwich along with Bram, a boy of sixteen or seventeen, their hunger was insatiable. I let them have one but told them that, although there were plenty more, we had better keep something for the next day. Looking at the faces of the children while they were eating, I told myself that from this moment on I would believe in St Nicholas. He indeed makes children happy on his birthday. I closed the lid of the box after I had eaten my delicious sandwich and joined the group of older children.

It was now half past eleven. The chilly outside air penetrated the garage. Trucks could be heard coming down the road. They stopped in front of the garage, then two SS officers and a female guard entered. Most of the children who had been asleep woke up; a few kept sleeping from sheer exhaustion. We were told to move onto the trucks. The children, so rudely awakened, started to cry again. I went on the first truck with a lot of little children and Max and Jacky. I carried our suitcase, and Max carried the suitcase that Mum had left behind. The last to board our truck was Bram, his sister Bella, and Iesy. Bram and Iesy each carried a box of sand-wiches. In the hurry I had forgotten about them as my attention had been taken by the little ones. The female guard came with us on the truck.

The truck drove fast. We had no idea where we were going. The night was jet black, the moon had disappeared behind the clouds. It was midnight. Nobody spoke, even the crying had stopped. I noticed that we left the camp through the main gate and that we were on the road towards Celle, but then the truck turned left and it seemed like we were driving aimlessly around in circles through the heather. For hours we drove like this. What evil plans did they have for us? The moon had come from behind the clouds and through the open rear end of the truck I could see the vast expanse of the Lüneburg Heath. There was no one in sight and no sound to be heard, only the engines of the trucks breaking the deathly silence. Then the trucks stopped. The female guard left the back of our truck and the driver from the second truck came over to our driver. We could hear them discussing something. Our driver seemed very upset as we could hear him say, 'Nein, nein,' a few times but we could not follow the conversation. What were they talking about? Were they going to kill us? We were silent, feeling the danger around us. After about ten minutes of arguing, the female guard climbed back in our truck and we started to drive again. I realised that we were driving back in the direction of the camp, and as we entered Belsen again I saw that we were going towards the Sternlager, but the truck continued along the road and then near the end made a left turn. After about two minutes it stopped and we were told to alight. We were pulled out of the truck by the female guard before two tall, strong women prisoners arrived to take over from her. They were dressed in prison clothes with scarves around their heads. On seeing those scary skinny women, the children started to cry again.

The little ones were scared out of their minds and screamed in panic. Some of them clamped on to me, preventing me from moving. I told them not to be afraid, that I was with them. It took a few minutes to calm them down. Still holding tightly on to my coat, they allowed me some movement. The second truck arrived and its lights lit up the area. When our truck started to move away, one of the women prisoners went up to the driver and asked what they should do with the children. 'I don't care,' he said. 'They can burn in hell.'

The trucks drove away and we were left standing close together in the darkness. The children were terrified and began wailing again. After my eyes became accustomed to the darkness I could see the vague outline of a barracks in front of us. A woman prisoner told us to enter the building, which looked ominous in the dark. Slowly, we moved forward. When we came to the door, another woman prisoner with a scarf around her head to hide its baldness told us something in a language we could not understand and pointed in the direction we had to go. I felt very scared, but did not dare show it for the little ones' sakes. When we entered the building my heart skipped a beat. There was what appeared to be a very long corridor. It was pitch-dark, and at the end of it stood an old woman holding up a kerosene lamp. If ever there was an image of a wicked witch, then this woman was certainly it. The sight of her scared the children again and they buried their faces in my coat, preventing me from taking another step. The figure at the end of the corridor did not move. She was standing deathly still holding up the lamp, which cast her shadow behind her. I realised we had to move forward. The children were hanging on to me like a dead weight. I raised my voice and told them very firmly to come with me, and that they did not have to be afraid. They had the choice of coming with me or I would leave them alone. It had the desired effect, they loosened their grip to allow me to move forward. I freed my hand from the little one who had been holding it tightly and allowed her to hold on to my coat. With my freed hand, I shoved the little ones behind me to protect them as much as possible with my body. Slowly we moved towards the figure. As we came closer I realised she was standing in a doorway. A faint light spilled out from the opening. Now that we had come very close to her, she pointed to the doorway without saying a word. Trying to keep as much distance between us and the witch (I was convinced by now that she was a witch), we stepped into the room.

What a relief! The room was clean and had about ten double bunks where we could sleep. The beds took up about half the room and the other half was an empty space. Two chairs were standing against the wall, a bare bulb hanging from the ceiling spread sparse light, but enough for us to see everything. The children were also relieved and let go of my coat. Some had already moved towards the beds. I dropped my suitcase on the floor when I heard more screaming in the corridor. The children from the second truck had just seen the witch. I quickly returned to the corridor, so the terrified children could see me. I told them to come in, everything was okay. Soon all the children were assembled in the room. Eva and another girl had carried the babies. They put the babies on a bed. In the meantime, female prisoners carried in our suitcases and other belongings and stacked them in the middle of the open area of the room. Then they left and we were alone. Iesy and Bram were still holding our precious boxes of sandwiches. I told them to put them on the chair and asked if there were any children who had not yet had a sandwich. Iesy gave those who had not eaten a sandwich from the half-empty box.

Eva and I took control. We told everybody to find a bed and go to sleep. Those who were too small to climb up were assisted by the bigger boys. Amazingly, both babies were asleep although they had had nothing to eat. We had given them some water earlier, and that may have filled their tummies up. Then some little boy said, 'I have to go to the toilet!' We looked at each other. In our misery, we had overlooked that fact. What to do? Going outside into the long dark corridor was out of the question. We did not have any idea where we were or where to find the latrines. My eyes fell on a large green cooking pan in the luggage. One of the mothers must have brought it from Amsterdam. By the looks of it, it must have been used for a very large family. I told one of the boys to get the cooking pan, which had a lid. We placed it in the far corner of the room and I told the little boy to use it. After that, I got everyone out of bed again to use the pan. In the process, we found that some of the children had wet their pants already. It had been such a long day. Eva and I slipped those children out of their wet clothing and, after they did their business, we put them back to bed with bare bottoms, covering them with the blankets which had been brought to us in the garage. Thank God no one had wet their bed yet.

We were all on the point of collapse, so I suggested we should go to sleep. All the beds except the one nearest to the door were occupied. In some beds, four children were sleeping, two on each end. The bigger children had sorted their beds out and chosen their own partners. I had chosen the double top bed which I shared with Max, Jacky and a nine-year old boy called Louky. I was the last to climb onto the bed. I left the light on, so that if someone woke up to use the pan they could see where they were going and I also felt safer that way. I must have fallen asleep as soon as I lay down. It was three o'clock in the morning.

I was awoken by Emile, who called me to tell me the pan was full. Light was filtering through the window. It was a wintry grey morning. Most of the children were still asleep from sheer exhaustion. Emile told me that he had opened the unlocked door on the far end of the room.

'It takes you outside,' he said.

I woke Max and Louky and told them to take the cooking pan outside and empty it.

'Try not to make too much noise to wake the children,' I said.

Max and Louky were still sleep-weary when they climbed down to do what I had asked them. It was amazing how all the children accepted my authority. I suppose I represented the mother they had just lost. They had unreservedly put their trust in me and without hesitation I had taken it upon myself to look after them as best as I could.

Emile opened the door for Max and Louky as they carried out the pan and the three of them disappeared out of sight. They soon returned with the empty pan, just in time, as the children woke up and there was a big demand for the pan.

The babies woke up and started to cry. They were very, very hungry. By now, we had found some small pots and containers in the suitcases, and I sent Emile outside to find a tap to fill containers with water. We also found some small bowls. I put some of the white bread with sugar and butter in two bowls and, with the water Emile brought me, I managed to soften the bread into some sort of porridge for the babies. Eva and another girl had found some clean clothing for the babies and had changed them by the time I had the porridge ready. There were plenty of helpers ready to feed the babies. Some of the older girls enjoyed doing it.

For breakfast, with Iesy's help, we gave each child half a sandwich. The other half, we told them, they could have at night. Cold water was the only drink we had. Silence fell as everyone enjoyed their sandwich. We left the children to do their own thing. Emile went outside with another boy to do some exploring and to find a toilet block. They soon came back, as it was very cold outside. They had found a latrine not far from our barracks. The biggest children could manage this, but not the little ones, so we decided they should use the cooking pan during the day as well. As we were using every inch of the open space in the room now that everyone was up and about, we put the cooking pan on top of an empty bed.

Iesy, Eva, Louky, Bram, Max and I decided to discuss our position. We sat on top of my bed. The double bunk allowed us to sit in a circle. We were with forty-four children and we were the oldest, so we had to take care of the little ones. Iesy suggested that we go through all the luggage to see if there was some food in it, and if we found anything, to put it all together. We agreed. The boys climbed down to go through the luggage. Eva went down to attend to the children, who, as young as they were, knew or sensed the predicament we were in. They did not cry any more as they felt secure within our group. We had a roof over our heads, we had beds and there was enough food for today. Soon, some younger boys started to help with the search through the suitcases. When they found something, they brought it to me on the bed. When the last suitcase was searched, we took stock: two packets of biscuits as hard as rocks, half a packet of sweet biscuits, a half-empty small tin of tea, half a small tin of milk chocolate powder, a very small bag of soap powder and a near-empty small tin of milk powder.

The boys came up onto the bed to survey the goods. It was obvious that none of the food could sustain us except for the few biscuits and the little bit of milk powder for the babies. It would not still our hunger in the days to come. I put it all in our suitcase and took it into my control. I told the boys to stack the luggage against the wall in the far end corner of the room. They were glad to have something to do and they made a good job of it. This way, we had some more space and an open area.

The day dragged by. No one came near us and we did not mind. It was as if we were in a world of our own. We had a chance to recover from the trauma of the day before. When daylight started to fade, I handed out, with the help of Iesy and Eva, the other half of the sandwiches. For the babies I made porridge again, like I had done in the morning. We still had about three-quarters of a box of sandwiches left for the next day. To keep them safe, the box of sandwiches was placed on top of my bed. Everybody went to bed early and it was not long before we were all asleep.

After breakfast the next day some of the boys had gone outside to explore the surroundings. It was very quiet in this part of the camp. When the boys came back they said there were a few more barracks in this section of the camp, but most of them were empty and no one was around. Iesy and Max had been in a barracks full of women lying on beds. They told us that they looked very scary, with skinny faces and their eyes deeply sunken in their sockets. I told Max and Iesy not to go to that barracks again as the women could have some awful illness.

I had not ventured outside yet, as the little children needed me. They looked so forlorn and although the crying in unison had stopped, now and then a little one would cry for his or her mummy. The ten-month-old baby called Phillipje was very quiet. He would just lie there and stare into space. Now and then a smile touched his little mouth when I spoke gently to him, or tickled him under his chin. He emanated sadness and must have missed his mummy. He was not active and I had not seen him sit up yet. He was not skinny, so his mother must have been able to feed him somehow. I was glad in one way that he was a good baby. This allowed me to give my time to the other children. The other baby was, I thought, about twelve months old, but I could not be sure. She was a girl and no one knew her name. And then there was little Robby, who was about three years old. He had such a pretty face, blond hair and blue eyes. He did not say one word, even when he was spoken to. He looked so lost and lonely, poor little Robby. I sometimes gave him a cuddle, but never a smile came to his eyes. It was as if he had built a wall around himself, which was hard to penetrate. I decided that I would keep a special eye on him and one day I might gain his confidence. Slowly I got to know the names of most of the children.

You cannot keep young girls and boys indoors for ever, and groups of three or four would go outside and return a while later. They reported that the latrine was brand new, so it appeared that we were the first inhabitants in this part of the camp. Later in the afternoon I had to go out myself and one of the boys showed me the way. It was so peaceful here, not a sound could be heard. The sky was light grey, the air crisp but not cold. I was glad to be out in the open air for those few minutes and I filled my lungs with it. When I returned to the barracks I asked if anyone had come to see us. The answer was negative. I could not understand why no one came to see us or brought us food. Someone wanted to forget about us, I thought, but I kept this thought to myself. No use worrying the others with it.

It was about four o'clock when all the children returned from outside. There was nothing much they could tell me, but they had discovered that the building where the shoe detail worked was situated between our old camp and the one we were in now. This at least established our position. They also reported that they had found the gate to the main road, which was open, with no one there to guard it. They had not ventured outside the gate although no one was in sight there either. Thank God, I thought, and I told them that it had been a wise decision not to go outside the gates.

Night was falling. Someone switched on the light and Iesy went and retrieved the box of sandwiches from the top of my bed and put it on top of the chairs in the middle of the room. Everybody lined up in a queue, which slowly passed Iesy and me as we handed each child the last half of the white bread sandwiches left in the box. When we finished, there were four halves left. Iesy and I decided to keep these to feed the babies the next day. Some of the children were sitting on the floor eating their evening meal and others were sitting on their beds. This time Eva had made the porridge and when some girls had finished their meal, they volunteered to feed the babies. For a while we were sitting around talking to each other. A few little girls were sitting close to me and I gave them a hug. Eva was reading a story from a book she had found in the luggage to a group of children who were listening intently. How idyllic it looks, I thought. One would think we were on holiday. Through the windows I saw that night had begun. It was pitch-dark outside, not a star could be found in the sky.

'I think it's time to go to sleep,' I told everybody. 'It's getting cold, so get under your blankets.'

No one undressed. We slept in our clothing except for the babies, who had been changed after their meal. We had to find a way to wash the babies' things, as soon we would have nothing to change them into. One empty suitcase was used to store the soiled baby goods. But I will resolve that problem somehow tomorrow, I thought, as I also climbed up on my bed.

Soon the children were asleep except for Iesy and me. We sat on the end of my bed talking in whispers. Iesy was intelligent and in him I found support. He was about thirteen years old, a year younger than myself. I told Iesy of my concern that no one had come to see us and that no food whatsoever was brought to us. We felt trapped. Could we go through the gates to get help? We really did not know what to do.

'If no one comes tomorrow, I'll call out to the guard in the tower and tell him we are alone here,' I said to Iesy.

Iesy thought it much too dangerous and advised me against it.

'I understand that,' I said, 'but what are we going to do? All the sandwiches are finished and we have nothing to eat tomorrow!'

We talked and talked about ways to get out of our predicament, but we could not see a solution. It was getting late and Iesy suggested we try to get some sleep.

Iesy was just moving away to his bed when the door opened and

Max, Hetty and Jack, President Brandt School, 1941.

Left: Herman, Hetty's childhood sweetheart who died in Treblinka.
Right: Sonia Santiel, Hetty's school friend. She was among the first
to be sent to Auschwitz, where she died.

Clockwise from top left: Uncle Max Werkendam who died on 30 May 1945 in the recuperation camp after the liberation; Leni and Maurice, school photo, 1941; Louky, aged eight, immediately after the war; Robby, 1946.

Barrack 211, the Children's House.

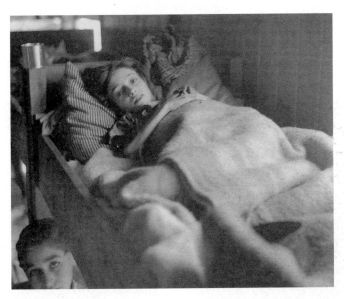

Leni, the day after liberation. Her arm shows the emaciation of her body. Jacky is sitting in the lower bunk.

The mass grave in front of the Children's House. Hetty's bed was behind the open window, second from the left.

(Courtesy of the British Imperial War Archives.)

The SS removing the dead, with the liberated prisoners looking on.

(Courtesy of the British Imperial War Archives.)

Irma Grese and Josef Kramer, the Beasts of Belsen, stripped of their uniforms and awaiting trial at Nuremberg, 1945

(Courtesy of the British Imperial War Archives.)

SS *Aufseherins* after their arrests. They had not gone hungry. The white armbands are a sign of surrender to the British Army.

(Courtesy of the British Imperial War Archives.)

Right: Dick Williams, the first British soldier to enter Belsen.

Below: The liberators took the children on a picnic on the Luneberger Heath, May 1945.

(Courtesy of Stanley H. Winfield, a liberator from Canada.)

Above: Sister Hermina hands out chocolates to the children while Sister Hella looks on, May 1945. *Below:* Sister Luba pushes Mieke on the swing which the British soldiers built for the children, May 1945.

(Both courtesy of the British Imperial War Archives.)

Above: The fiftieth anniversary reunion in Amsterdam, 15 April 1995. Luba and her 'children'. Hetty is directly to the right of Sister Luba.

Right: Sister Luba, The Angel of Belsen, after being awarded a Silver Medal for Humanitarian Services by Queen Beatrix of the Netherlands, 15 April 1995.

The Jewish Monument erected by
ex-prisoners at Bergen-Belsen on 15 April 1946.
'Earth conceal not the blood shed on thee.'
(Courtesy of PA Photos.)

two women entered. They were the first people to come and see us in two days. The shorter of the two was a strong woman: her blue blouse strained over her breast and her short sleeves revealed strong arms. Neither of them showed signs of hunger or starvation, indeed they appeared well fed. My instincts, although I had never encountered anyone like them before, told me that these two women were 'Prominents'. Prominents had special privileges, granted by the SS, as they kept the prisoners in their control. They were not dressed like other prisoners. They both wore black skirts and leather boots. Their high cheekbones showed them to be of Polish or Russian descent. For a moment, the two women observed the surroundings and then the short one spoke to me in Polish. When she saw that I could not understand it, she asked in German, 'Jewish children?'

For a moment I hesitated before nodding. The woman became agitated and spoke urgently to the second woman. What they were talking about, I did not know. The woman said, 'Hunger,' and made a movement with her hand towards her mouth to make sure I understood. I thought it advisable not to tell her that we had had sandwiches tonight, but I thought of tomorrow and nodded.

'I'll come back,' she said and then she left with the other woman. I was still staring at the door as it had all happened so quickly.

Iesy climbed back onto my bed.

'What was that?' he asked.

I told him what had happened.

'What do you think of it?' he asked.

'I don't know. I don't like that she asked me if the children were Jewish!'

Iesy nodded.

133

'I hope we don't have to move tonight, the children are sleeping so nicely,' I said.

'We had better go to sleep. Sitting up is not helping us. Tomorrow, we'll see what happens,' Iesy said.

Iesy went back to his bed carefully, so he would not wake up his bedmate, and I decided to do the same, and try to get some sleep. As I lay down next to Max, under the blanket, I was thinking about the two women. I was amazed that they did not feel the cold. They both wore only cotton blouses with short sleeves, and yet they looked strong and healthy. They still had their hair and each wore a headscarf in the manner of a Russian peasant. I had no doubt that the shorter woman was the boss.

I woke to hear footsteps coming down the corridor. Immediately I sat upright, my whole body tense, afraid of what might happen next. I could hear voices. The footsteps came nearer and then the door was opened. The two women had returned and, behind them, four women prisoners carried two twenty-litre food containers. The short woman told the prisoners to place the food containers in the middle of the room. She then ordered them to leave. From the top of my bed, I watched with great relief. When I heard them coming down the corridor, I was worried that we might have to move again. The two women, after having observed the sleeping children, also started to leave. At the door, the shorter woman looked up at me and said, 'Start eating.'

The noise created by the arrival of the food had woken up a few children. Iesy, Max and Emile had left their beds already to investigate the food containers. I climbed down to have a look. Iesy tried to open the lid of one of the containers but without success. The catch stayed firmly shut. By now, Bram had joined us. He took hold of the levers but only managed to lift the lid a little bit, not high enough to release the spring, so the lid would stay open. Bram let go.

'All right,' I said, 'when Bram tries to lift the handle again, you, Iesy and Max, put your hands on the levers to stop them from springing back. I will count to three and together you will pull it up.'

Max and Iesy placed themselves in position. Bram put his hand on the lever and said, 'Are you ready?'

'Yes!' Max and Iesy said.

Bram started to pull with all his might. When the levers came up enough to allow Max and Iesy to place a hand around them, I started to count, 'One ... two ... three.' The boys started to force the lever up with all the strength they possessed. Their faces were contorted with the pressure. They were not very strong. Ten months of slow starvation had taken its toll. Slowly the lever came up until, with a mighty click, it released its hold on the containers. Out of breath but excited by their victory, it took them only a second to release the second lever, as the pressure had been released when the first lever was opened.

By now, more children had awoken and come out of their beds to find out what was happening. Iesy lifted the lid. A beautiful aroma penetrated our nostrils. Inside the container was a thick creamy potato soup. We could not believe our good luck. In no time everybody who was up and about produced a soup bowl and helped themselves to a generous portion of soup. We sat on the floor, close to the containers, as if afraid that it would disappear. It tasted so good! No one spoke as we relished this delicious food, a food we could only have dreamed about during the past ten months. Through the steam rising from his soup bowl Iesy's eyes met mine; we knew we did not have to worry about how to feed the children for the next two days.

When some of the boys wanted to help themselves to a second serving I told them not to do this as 'too much of a good thing could make you sick'. I also suggested that everybody went back to bed. Bram placed the lid on the container but did not close the clips, to make it easier to get it open in the morning. Iesy put a small suitcase on the lid to keep it down firmly so the soup would stay warm. After that, everybody went to bed and within seconds we were all asleep.

The next morning I woke up to find that the suitcase on my bed was open. That seemed strange as I was sure I had closed the lid the night before. I went through the contents of the suitcase: no sugar had been taken and the jars were still there. On further investigation, I found that half the sweet biscuits were missing from the packet. I called Iesy and Max over to discuss the matter. I was very angry, and in my anger I raised my voice while asking Max and Iesy who they thought could have done this. Neither had any idea who could have done such a cowardly act. Most of us were not hungry the night before, so who could it be? If we were to survive, we could not tolerate pilfering. Louky, who had climbed up on the bed, interrupted our conversation.

'Hetty, a little boy said that Emile did it!'

I remembered that Emile had done something like this before. I had to be sure so I told Louky to bring this little boy to me. Louky climbed down and returned with the boy. From the top of my bed I asked the little boy, whose name I did not know, 'Tell me! How do you know that Emile stole the biscuits?'

'I saw him eat the biscuits early this morning,' the little boy answered.

'Are you sure?' I asked him again.

'Yes, I am sure,' he replied.

'It's true,' a little girl said. She had been standing close to Louky and the boy, and had followed what was being said with interest.

'If you make these accusations, you have to be very sure of it,' I said, turning to the girl.

'Well,' the little girl said, 'it is true because I saw it too! He ate three biscuits and he was sitting in that corner.' She pointed to the end of the last row of the beds and I realised that the place she was pointing to was out of view from my position.

'Where is Emile? I want to speak to him,' I said to Louky.

'I believe he went outside a while ago,' he said.

'Go and find him, and take Jacky with you,' I told him.

Jacky and Louky left through the back door.

'What are we going to do with Emile? He seems to be incorrigible,' I said to Iesy and Max.

'Wait until we hear what Emile has to say,' Iesy said.

'You're right,' I said. 'We'll listen to what he has to say.'

The other children in the room were well aware of what was happening. They were wise at an early age, these children, and most of them had learned to deal with the hard times and crises which took place from day to day since they had arrived in Belsen. The happy mood which had prevailed because they were going to get a good breakfast of potato soup now turned into a depressing atmosphere. In all this unpleasant mess, I had forgotten to feed the kids. I came down from the bed and told everybody to line up to receive their soup. It was heartwarming to see their faces. Iesy moved the suitcase from the top of the container and opened the lid. The soup was still warm. The children were holding up their bowls and Eva was filling them up as they passed by, one by one. Soon everybody had been served. Iesy and I were the last.

I was just sitting down on a suitcase to eat my soup when Louky and Jacky returned with Emile. Not wanting to spoil the happy mood and also wanting to delay the unpleasantness I knew would follow, I told the three boys to get their bowls and help themselves to a good portion of soup, which they did without delay. When everyone was finished, we stacked the bowls and I told three girls and three boys to take them to the tap outside and wash the bowls and spoons. Two other boys wanted to go as well, so I told them to help carry some of the bowls to the tap. The weather was nice and the sun was shining. The chilly air of dawn was gone.

'Leave the back door open when you go out,' I told the small group, as they prepared to leave with the bowls. So, I thought, these children are out of the way. I quickly got Iesy, Max, Louky, Bram and Eva together and we all climbed onto my bed. We sat in circle and we all looked very serious, as the responsibility of dealing with this matter now rested on our young shoulders. I called Emile to come up. Emile sat opposite us. While he was settling down, I studied his face. Emile was quite a good-looking boy. He had nice black hair and, surprisingly, made a very decent impression, but there was something about him which made him appear distant and impenetrable. I told Emile that biscuits were missing from the suitcase and that it was alleged that he had stolen them during the night. To our surprise, Emile immediately admitted that he had done it. He showed no remorse, only a deadpan look. I asked him why he had done it, but he just shrugged his shoulders, indicating he had no answer.

'You know what you have done is very serious?' Iesy asked.

Emile did not answer, but looked straight ahead. We did not know what to say, so I said, 'You'd better get down, Emile! But don't go away!'

Emile climbed down and the five of us turned to each other and started to discuss the situation in low voices. What could we do? I was very angry as I remembered that Emile had done this earlier in the Albela camp, and Max and Jacky had been blamed before they had caught him. We could not let Emile get away with it scot-free as this would not be a good example for the other children. I believed that whatever punishment we meted out, we would never cure Emile of his affliction.

Different methods were proposed, but were rejected until Iesy said, 'What about if we let Emile empty the pan every morning for a week? This is an unpleasant task and it may teach him a lesson.'

We all agreed this was the best idea. Louky called Emile to come up again and he was informed of our decision. I asked Emile if he agreed and he said, 'Yes.' After this, our 'court' broke up and Bram, Emile, Max, Louky and Eva went below. Iesy and I sat a while longer discussing what had happened. We decided to keep a close eye on Emile in the future.

It was about eleven o'clock in the morning when the door opened and the two women who had visited us before, and brought us the potato soup, entered our room accompanied by two other women. We immediately noticed an air of authority. Later we found out that one woman was second in charge to the camp elder of all the prisoners. She was a mature prisoner who had been in Auschwitz for many years. She was a prominent and a kapo.

Kapos were feared for their brutal treatment of prisoners. The other woman was a doctor.

The children, who had until this moment been happily chatting away, fell silent. As young as they were, they recognised danger in a flash. I was just washing little Johnny's face when they came in, and I pulled Johnny close to me for protection, but the women did not take much notice of us. After a fleeting glance, the tall woman started to talk to the other one in Polish, which we could not understand. I could see the short woman pointing at us and talking persuasively with the kapo. I also noticed she was very respectful to her. After about five minutes' discussion, they started to leave. During the time they were there, the short woman never looked my way, nor did she address any question to me. Just as they were passing through the door, the short woman turned to me and said, 'Do you need more soup?'

Without hesitation, I said, 'Yes.'

'I will bring it later,' the woman said.

After they left, it took us a few minutes to be ourselves again, and we were glad they had gone.

'What do you think about that?' Iesy asked me.

'I don't know,' I answered, 'I only hope we don't have to move again.'

The back door was open and we could see a column of women prisoners walking past towards the empty barracks.

'It looks like the empty barracks will be occupied,' Iesy said. 'I'll go out and see what's happening.'

'You do that,' I said. 'I'll stay with the children. If you see any of them outside, tell them to come back. Anything can happen outside and we had better stay in. We seem to be the protégés of prominents in the camp.' Iesy left with Louky and Max after these words of caution.

At about three o'clock most of the children had returned to our room. After doing a headcount, I was missing three children. The weather had turned bleak, the sky was deep grey and the clouds were hanging very low. I felt ill at ease that three of the children had not returned. After asking around, I was told that Erika and another girl were believed to be in the toilet, as they were seen there last. I sent two boys to find them and told them to return to our room immediately. They returned about ten minutes later with the girls. I gave Erika and the other girl a scolding and told them not to stay away for long periods of time, as I wanted to be sure they were safe. They promised not to do this again. Now only Jacky was missing and nobody knew where he was. How could I have been so stupid not to have given him more attention, I asked myself. I promised Mum I would look after him.

Jacky was a quiet boy, a bit of a wanderer. Even back home he would disappear for hours, and he often used to worry our lovely Oma with his absence. But to our great relief, he always returned safe and sound. I remembered the day when the street organ had played in our street – Jacky was only four years old, and when the organ moved on from street to street, he followed it for hours, not returning until about half past five that day. The spanking he got from our always gentle Oma only relieved her anxiety but taught Jacky nothing. The other time I clearly remembered was when he borrowed my brand-new bicycle to take it for a spin around the block. He did not return for five hours, and I had never seen our Oma in such a state. She imagined Jacky lying injured on the road and every other terrible thing, and she kept on saying, 'What will

I tell your mother?' I was in an upset state as well but my concern was centred around my beautiful bike. Jacky was too small to reach the saddle and he was standing on the pedals in order to ride the bike. He barely rose above the handlebars. As the afternoon wore on, the more concerned we became. At about five o'clock when dusk was settling in, Jacky returned. Needless to say, he was in all kinds of trouble from us.

I came back to the present and decided that I would wait another half an hour before I allowed myself to panic. Just then, the door opened from the corridor. Two women carrying a container of food walked in. After placing it next to the other, one woman made a gesture, asking me if she could take the old containers back. I pointed to one container and made a movement with my hand to tell her to leave it where it was. She understood and picked up the empty container, and they both left. Soon after, Jacky returned. I gave him a good scolding, although I knew it was useless.

Eva and Iesy got out the bowls and I served the children their evening meal. By now the soup was lukewarm but that did not bother us. After dinner, the bowls were stacked in a corner. We would wash them in the morning. It was too dark to go outside now. Everybody prepared to go to sleep. It was still early in the evening but there was nothing else to do other than just hang around on the cold floor. The baby had been attended to and was sound asleep. I also decided to go to sleep. How safe we felt in this room, I thought, as I crawled under the blanket with my clothing on. Maybe it was our guardian angel, this woman whose name I did not even know. Deep in my heart, I was really scared of her. I had no doubt that she could be very tough. Her authority showed in her mannerisms, during the few times she had come to see us. I must find out her name, I thought, as I slowly drifted into sleep.

I woke up the next morning just as the dawn was lifting, looked out of the window and saw that the grey low-hanging clouds were still there. Max stirred next to me and slowly woke up, then Jacky and Louky.

Max sat up in a flash and said, 'Emile has to take the pan out.'

That's right. Jacky and Louky were clearly awake now and were looking around the room to see if Emile was up, but he was still fast asleep. Iesy, who was also awake by now, told Louky to wake Emile and tell him to take the pan out. With heavy, sleepy eyes, Emile got out of bed and began the operation. From the top of the bed Max and Jacky carefully lowered the nearly full pan to Emile, who waited below with arms and hands stretched into the air to receive the pan. Expecting problems, I went down to direct 'Operation Panlift' from the floor. I cautioned Max and Jacky to be careful as I did not want a mess on the floor. Looking at Emile as he stood there, I did not think he could carry the weight of the pan on his own and I could foresee a disaster. He had his hands on the handles.

'Okay?' Max asked.

'Yes,' Emile said.

At this, Max released his grip but a fraction earlier than Jacky. The result was devastating. The pan unbalanced slightly, spilling some of the contents over Emile and on the floor. Despite the mishap, Emile kept hold of the pan, preventing the rest of the contents from spilling out. He staggered back, still holding the pan.

'Put it down!' I yelled at Emile.

With a bang, Emile dropped the pan on the floor, spilling more in the process.

'Louky, go with Emile to empty the pan,' I said.

Now that the weight was divided betwen two boys, the danger of spilling more had passed. Someone held open the back door to let Emile and Louky out, and we noticed that during the night it had snowed. The pristine white of the snow contrasted sharply with the grey clouds. It was dead still outside, not a sound could be heard. As a result of the drama with the pan, all the children had woken up, and they got excited when they saw the snow and wanted to go outside and play in it. I told them to have their breakfast first and then they could play for a while.

Louky and Emile returned with the empty pan, which had been rinsed under the tap at the end of our barracks. I sent Emile back to the tap with a piece of old towel to wash his face and wipe down his jumper, the only one he possessed. Eva took some of the children with her to wash the dirty bowls. While everybody was out I tried to clean up the mess on the floor with some rags I found in one of the cases. When everyone had returned, we all had breakfast. After that I told the boys and girls to go and wash the bowls again, so they would be clean for dinner. When they returned, I allowed all the children to play outside in the snow. It was a pleasure to see their clear eyes and rosy cheeks when they came in an hour later.

The day passed uneventfully and soon the evening meal was served. We had not been this well fed for the past ten months and I sent up a silent prayer of thanks. We had been left alone. No one had come that day. We had good food and good shelter.

During the day I told Iesy that someone needed to help Emile with the pan the next morning. We chose Louky because he seemed to get along well with Emile. We also decided that Bram, who was the tallest, should receive the pan from the top of the bed and place it on the floor, then Emile and Louky could take it outside. Louky was a nice boy, ten years old, with a lovely disposition, and he always had a friendly smile. He immediately agreed to help. In the morning the business with the pan started all over again, but this time no unpleasant accidents happened.

Seven

'Just be good to my brothers.'

One day followed the next and we settled into a routine. Those who were allocated to do certain chores could now do them without supervision, and we had plenty to eat, thanks to a regular supply from that woman. The constant quest for food to sustain our survival was removed. The children had accepted, as only children do, that they could not be with their mothers. Instead, they had adopted me as a substitute. Whenever a mishap occurred, they came to me for comfort. Whenever there was a problem, I had to sort things out. They trusted me implicitly and I did my best not to let them down.

We had not seen anybody for days. It looked as if the SS had forgotten our existence. Then on the ninth day after our arrival, the two women returned to advise us that early the next morning all children up to and including the age of thirteen were going to a new barracks, where they would be cared for by them. They told me that all luggage would be collected, and needed to be ready by eight o'clock the next day. This created an upheaval. The children became scared again. They had only just settled in and were beginning to feel secure. All day they came to me for reassurance, but when they found out that I could not come with them, as I was fourteen years old, they really panicked. I tried to pacify them as much as I could, and showed them a happy face, but inside I was not so happy, as Max and Jacky had to go with them. I hid my anxiety from the children but discussed the position with Eva, as her little sister had to go as well. Iesy and Louky also had to go and I was desolate. Eva and I decided to sort out the children's belongings and put them back into the right suitcases ready for their departure the next morning. This kept us busy until halfway through the afternoon. The suitcases were stacked neatly in the middle of the room ready to be taken away. Eva and I did not trust the two women and kept some clothing stored in cases which had been placed in a corner in the top of my double bed and covered with a blanket to hide them. This meant that Louky and Jacky had to sleep on another bed that night. We went to bed early, worn out by the emotion of the day.

Surprisingly, the children slept well, which was not the case for me. For hours I stared out of the window across from my bed. The darkness of the night reflected my feelings. No stars were shining. A reflection of light may have given me some hope for the future. The uncertainty of our existence overwhelmed me as the hours dragged by. Max stirred next to me and opened his eyes.

'Can't you sleep?' he whispered.

'No,' I replied. 'Promise me, Max, that you'll look after Jacky, as I'll not be able to do it.'

Max nodded. He got hold of my hand on top of the blanket.

'I promise,' he said, 'now try to get some sleep. You must be strong for tomorrow.'

I managed to smile at him, realising that he must be worried about me staying behind.

'I will try,' I said. 'Now you go to sleep again.'

Max turned over onto his side and, within seconds, was sleeping peacefully. Sleep would not come for me and I was glad when first light arrived. Carefully, trying not to wake Max, I slithered out of bed and walked to the back door. I went outside, closing the door gently behind me. I could see the sky lightening in the east, and the contours of the fence and watchtowers became visible. It was so quiet outside. Only the sounds of the guards and the dogs broke the silence as they patrolled the outside of the fence. I leaned with my back against the wall of the barracks and took deep breaths of the cold fresh air into my lungs. I lifted my head to the heavens and prayed that God would look after my two brothers and all the children who were going to leave in a few hours' time. Tears were running down my face. I felt so helpless. The door right next to me opened. Emile came out. He was usually an early riser. He was startled to encounter me so early in the morning. His appearance made me get a grip on myself.

'Where are you going?' I asked.

He hesitated, but then replied, 'To the washhouse,' which meant to the toilet block.

'Don't be long,' I told him, 'We're having an early breakfast.'

'Okay,' he said, as he walked past me.

I stood looking after him for a while. What a strange boy he is, I thought. What is he doing up so early in the morning? What is he up to now? The door opened again. This time it was Louky.

'Oh there you are!' he said. 'Everybody is looking for you and some of the children want their breakfast already.'

I quickly wiped my eyes with the back of my hands to make sure no traces of tears showed on my face so as not to upset the children. When I came back inside, everybody was up. Eva had dressed the little ones who were sitting neatly in a row on the floor. Eva had been wise enough to put a blanket underneath them, as the floor was very cold in the mornings. I told Iesy and Bram to open the container of food which had arrived yesterday. What a surprise! It contained rice cooked in milk with lots of sugar in it. This put our departure out of our minds for the moment, we were so delighted with this beautiful food. Soon, everybody had been served and when someone wanted a second helping, I let them have it.

After the bowls had been washed, we used the sandwich box to pack them. The children were ready and an uneasy silence had fallen between us now that their departure was near. I moved slowly past the row of children on the floor and, kneeling down with each child, I told them to be good and to listen to the sisters. I had adopted that name for the two women to make them sound more friendly. I told the children not to be afraid, as the sisters would give them food and they would not be hungry any more.

'Will you come to see us soon, Hetty?' one little girl asked.

'Of course!' I promised as I hugged her.

The last precious hour seemed to have gone by fast, as all of a sudden, the two women and the four female prisoners were there. Because I had prepared the children for this moment, they remained calm and, as I had hoped, they showed no panic. I told the children to form themselves into a line and to go with the women. Eva decided to go with them some of the way. Iesy came over to me and hugged me. He was always so demonstrative.

'Look after yourself, Hetty,' he said, and kissed me on both cheeks.

I nodded. My throat was closed. I could not answer immediately, but I somehow managed to say, 'Take care of the children, they trust you.'

'I will,' Iesy answered.

He let go of me. One by one, the children left the room. Only Max and Jacky remained. I embraced them both and kissed them goodbye. I walked them to the door. Jacky held tightly to my arm, and while loosening his hold gently, I told him that he was grown up now and must look after himself.

'Keep yourself warm, darling, and stay close to Max. He is your brother, stay close to each other.'

A final kiss for both of them, and I told them to hurry after the children.

'I will come to see you,' I called after them.

Max and Jacky turned once to wave goodbye from a distance and I waved back with a smile on my face, but when I went back inside, the tears came freely. I was at the end of my strength. I climbed on top of my bed and cried until I had no more tears left. I felt lost and alone. The room was empty except for some of the suitcases which still had to be collected by the female prisoners. Eva and Bram, who had gone with the children, had not returned yet. A hundred thousand thoughts crowded my head. Where was my father? Where was my mother? And now my brothers were gone. I felt abandoned. The stillness of the room was ominous. I looked at all the empty beds and started to cry again.

The four women returned for the last of the luggage. They looked terrible in their grey striped dresses. Their cheeks were hollow and their eyes were sitting deep in their sockets. They scared me. Their claw-like hands carried the cases. They were so thin. Where did they get the strength from to work so hard, I wondered? Outside the door I could see a kapo who told them to hurry up and, like zombies, they responded. They also took the containers of food and the clean pan. I was glad I had stayed behind, otherwise they would have taken the cases on my bed as well. After they left I crawled under my blanket and tried to get some rest. I had no wish to go outside. Slowly, I became warmer until, mercifully, I fell asleep.

It was late in the afternoon when I woke up as Eva returned to the room. She told me that the children had been taken to a barracks at the far end of our camp and the two women were looking after them.

'How far is it?' I asked.

'Not far. About five minutes away, past the hospital,' Eva told me.

'Is there a hospital?'

'Yes,' Eva said 'and they told me it has a complete operating room as well.'

I was amazed at this news.

'Eva,' I said, 'I would like to go to the toilet. Will you go with me before it gets dark?'

'Okay,' Eva replied. 'Let's go now.'

I put on my coat and climbed down. Eva was already waiting for me outside. She was much taller than I was and still looked robust and strong. I felt safe with her around me. As we arrived at the toilet block, Eva pointed in the direction that the children had been taken, but all I could see in the failing light was a grey, deserted road disappearing into the distance. I could just make out a few barracks on the right side of the road.

'Is it there?' I asked.

'No, that's the hospital.'

We returned to our room as it was getting dark outside. The fresh air had done me good, and the sleep during the day had renewed my resilience. I told Eva that we should eat one of the biscuits, as there was nothing else to eat. Eva came up on the bed with me and helped to take my suitcase out from under the blanket. We took one biscuit each and kept one out for Bram for when he returned. The biscuit was old and hard but it had to do.

'Tomorrow I will go out and try to find us something to eat. There is no one at the gate. I will walk to the kitchen and see what I can organise,' Eva said, yawning.

'Do you think that's wise?' I asked.

'Maybe not,' Eva answered, 'but I think I'll give it a try.'

Soon after, Eva went to bed. She plonked herself down, shoes and all. It had been a hard day for her.

'See you in the morning, goodnight.'

Eva turned on her side and slept within a minute. As there was nothing else to do, I crawled under my blanket again. Even when I could not sleep, at least I could keep warm. I pulled the blanket tightly around me. The room was colder than before, the natural body heat of so many children had made the temperature more bearable in the room. I missed them and I wondered how they were sleeping now.

Bram entered the room.

'For goodness' sake! Where have you been all day?' I asked.

'Visiting,' he said

'Visiting?' I asked. 'Where did you go?'

'Just up the road in one of the barracks there are a lot of women,' Bram told me. 'Most of them have no hair and their eyes are very big, scary really, and some of them are having a baby soon.'

'What are you talking about?' I asked.

'The women in that barracks are under treatment by the SS doctor,' he said. 'That's the group we saw passing a few days ago.'

'Did you have something to eat?' I changed the subject.

'No,' Bram said.

'Here, Eva and I saved a biscuit for you.'

Bram ate the biscuit and went to bed. Before long, he was sound asleep.

I lay awake for some time. The room was very still and again and again my eyes wandered over the empty beds, while I debated whether I should go to see the children tomorrow and whether I would be allowed to do this. I felt scared and insecure. During the past few days, it had become clear to me that, although life in the previous camp was not so good, we did have some protection through Albela and the elders. This section of Belsen had different rules. It was run by very cruel kapos and only the strong and the devious would survive. I must try to get some sleep, I told myself.

'Hetty, wake up.'

I opened my eyes and saw Eva standing below my bed.

'I'm going now,' she said. 'I'll see you when I get back.'

'Okay, be careful.'

By now, I was wide awake. Bram also emerged from his bed. Until now I had not taken much notice of Bram, as I had been busy with the younger children. He was tall for his age, his cheeks were hollow and he had high cheekbones and a pointy chin, which made his face look like a triangle. He avoided eye contact when I spoke to him. He was a bit strange and I felt that I had no connection with him.

'I wonder how Bella is,' Bram said, looking around the room.

I saw a sad look in his face. Perhaps I am misjudging him, I thought. He does care for his sister. Soon Bram left, and I was alone. After a few hours, I decided to go for a walk. I had not ventured further than the toilet block before now. Before I left, I covered the suitcases with blankets, hoping nobody would enter the room and see them. I knew I took a risk leaving the sugar jars unguarded, but I could not stay inside all the time.

The weather was gloomy. Grey, low-hanging clouds did not let the sunshine through. Our section of the camp looked deserted. When I passed the toilet block, I saw a woman using the outside tap. On my approach, she lifted her head. I had stopped with the intention of having a chat, but she went back to her chore and ignored me. I decided to continue my walk. I followed the road in the direction Eva had shown me the night before, which led to the hospital.

There was not a sound, it was eerie. It was as if I was all alone in the world. I came to the building which I thought was the hospital. I stood for a while looking at it. Clean red bricks, high windows and no sign of life. Where was everybody? I started to feel very uncomfortable. Then a door opened and a tall SS officer came out of the building with a woman who was immaculately dressed in a dark blue suit. The two were in deep conversation and did not notice me. I decided it was better to move on.

As I walked further along the road, two women appeared from behind the trees and walked towards me. They walked arm in arm as though they were on a Sunday stroll. As they drew near, one of the women pointed at me.

'That's Maurice's daughter,' she said.

Then I recognised them: Aunty Beth and Sonja's mother.

'How are you, darling?' Sonja's mother asked. 'What are you doing here?'

I told them how Mum and Dad had been sent away and Max and Jacky had gone to another barracks yesterday.

'Do you know which barracks the children are in?' I asked.

'Yes,' Sonja's mother said, 'it's there behind the trees. Have you got something to eat for us, Hetty?' she asked.

'No,' I answered.

'What about some salt? Have you got some salt?' Sonja's mother asked.

For a moment I hesitated as I looked at them. Aunty Beth was not in a good state. She was so skinny and had not said a word.

'Wait here,' I told Sonja's mother. 'I'll get you some salt.'

I walked quickly back to our room. With some effort, I extracted my suitcase from the others and opened it. I found the jar of salt, shook some out onto a piece of paper and then folded the paper the same way I had seen Dad make small parcels of diamonds. This way, not a grain of salt would be lost. When I was finished, I closed the lid and left my suitcase where it was on the bed, as I did not have the strength to put it back between the other cases. The aunties were waiting for me where I had left them. I handed the packet with salt over to Sonja's mother, who quickly hid it inside her dress. She thanked me very much and then walked away with Aunt Beth. It was the last time I saw Sonja's mother.

I continued my walk. Around the corner from the cluster of trees I saw three barracks. I stood still. Which of the barracks would be the children's? Nothing I could see gave me any indication that the children were there. I approached slowly. The first barracks was deserted so I advanced to the second one and peeped through the window. This was it. I saw most of the children sitting around a long table. Some others were sitting in the middle of the room on the floor, a few little ones were crying their eyes out. The short woman went over to a crying child, but when she was bending down to the child, it started to cry even more loudly. On straightening up, the woman saw me peering through the window. She asked through the glass what I was doing there. I told her, 'Brother, brother.' She opened the door for me and asked me to come in.

Once inside, I surveyed the room. The bunks for the children were placed in two rows, along the length of the right wall. A corner on the left near the door was divided off with two bunks and to my dismay some of our blankets had been used to shut off the corner for privacy. As soon as I entered, a horde of children encircled me and grabbed hold of me. They were so happy to see me! All the children who had been crying stopped and nearly pushed each other over in order to touch me. They were hanging on to my arms and all talking at once. I told everyone to sit around the tables and I would tell them a story. For two hours I kept them busy and made them feel good.

I decided not to overstay my welcome and made a move to go, but not before I had a private talk with Max and Jacky. I asked them to show me where they were sleeping and they took me to their bed. I inspected the blanket on their bed, it was not ours but at least it kept them warm at night.

'How are the women treating you?' I asked Max.

'They are okay,' he said, 'but we are not allowed to make any noise as we are close to the watchtower.'

Jacky, who had not spoken a lot, suddenly said, 'You think we will see Mum and Dad again one day?'

'Of course, darling.'

I put my arm around him to reassure him. For a while we talked and then I really had to go. I waved to all the children and then walked towards the door. By now I had found out that the short woman was called Luba and the other Hermina. When I opened the door to leave, Sister Luba came over and asked for my name.

'Hetty,' I told her. 'Can I come back tomorrow?' I asked in broken German, at the same time using my hand, pointing at myself and making a movement towards the room. Sister Luba understood my body language and said yes.

I walked slowly back to my room. It was late in the afternoon. It was not cold, or, at least I did not feel it. I was so happy that I was allowed to see Max and Jacky and all the children. I was not so happy that the Sisters had used our blankets to shut off their sleeping quarters. During my brief stop with Sister Luba at the door, I had been able to glance into their sleeping quarters and had noticed that a woollen travel rug was lying on the floor, used as a carpet in an effort to make the area more homely. But what could I do about it?

While all these thoughts had been going through my mind, I had nearly covered the distance back to the barracks. I had not met anyone on the road. It was a great improvement on our old camp, as it had become overcrowded, and what was even better was there was no roll-call. What date was it today? I had lost track but thought it was 16 December 1944.

Eva was already back in our room. She was happy to see me.

'Where have you been?' she asked.

'I have been to see the children. They are all right. How did it go today?' I asked. 'Did you get us something to eat?'

'No,' Eva said. 'I have taken two biscuits I was so hungry.'

'So am I,' I said, as I climbed up. 'I will have some as well.'

Silently Eva looked up at me as I ate two small biscuits.

'Things are looking grim,' I said. 'There are only about three biscuits left. What are we going to do?'

I had not eaten all day except for those two biscuits. The only drink I had had was cold water.

'I don't know. I hope they will not let us starve to death. I found out that the women in the barracks near the hospital do not have food either,' Eva said.

We were both silent, busy with our own thoughts.

'We had better go to sleep,' I said. 'When we sleep, we don't feel so hungry.'

When I woke up the next morning, Eva and Bram had gone. I stayed in bed as there was nothing to do, but after a while mother nature was calling. I put on my coat before I went outside. I took a red scarf as well, which I tied around my head to keep my ears warm, and a towel so I could wash my face and hands at the outside tap. The weather was very mild, and although the snow had not yet melted, there was no cold wind like the ones we had experienced at times at the Appelplatz in the Albela camp.

The short walk to the toilet block refreshed me. My stomach was empty and hurt at times, reminding me that for the last couple of days I had not had much to eat. When I get back to the room, I will eat a spoonful of sugar and this will help me, I decided. Somehow, I have to get Max and Jacky out of the barracks so I can give them some sugar as well. The water from the tap was very cold. My hands felt like iceblocks after I had washed them and splashed my face with water. After a while, feeling returned to my hands, and my face tingled with the stimulated blood circulation created by the ice-cold water. I went back to the room and found the jar of sugar. I took one teaspoon of sugar and hid the jar under my clothing in the suitcase again.

The time went by slowly. After a few hours, I could stand it no longer and decided to go and see the children. It was still early in the morning.

I wonder if she will let me in, I thought, as I walked towards the children's barracks. When I arrived, I knocked at the window. A little girl opened the door for me. I entered, a little apprehensively. Sister Luba was occupied with Phillipje and Sister Hermina was tidying up. It was then that I noticed that some of the children had no shoes on, and some little ones no trousers. Automatically, I started to dress the little ones and put on shoes and socks where needed. I organised some of the children to do some of the chores they had done earlier, such as straightening their beds, picking up discarded or dirty clothing and putting them in a heap to be sorted out later. Max and Jacky were very happy I was there, and they helped to achieve some order in the room.

Iesy was in bed with a sore throat. His eyes were shining and he had a fever. He had caught a cold, so I told him to stay in bed to keep warm. Poor Iesy, he was a sorry sight.

After a few hours I realised that no one had had anything to eat and some children asked me for food. I asked Sister Luba if she had anything to eat for the children and she told me that the lady doctor had gone out to see if this could be organised. I returned to the children and told them to be patient and sit around the table in readiness. They did what was asked of them and I joined them at the table. I kept them busy by playing simple guessing games and telling them a story, but as time ticked by their attention waned and I could see them becoming very lethargic. I asked Sister Luba's permission for the children to play outside for a while so they could get some fresh air. Permission was given, so I told the children to dress warmly and put on their coats and scarves or caps. I went outside with them. Some of the girls stayed close to me. As we walked around the area in front of the barracks, the other boys and girls were running around, glad to be outside for the first time in three days.

After about twenty minutes, I told everybody to go back inside and put their coats away. When we entered, Sister Luba told us to sit at the tables. I realised that while we had been outside the doctor had brought us some food. After I had organised the children around the table, I made a move to leave. I felt I had no right to stay to share their food as I did not belong with them, although I was very, very hungry. I said goodbye to the children and hugged Max and Jacky before I walked towards the door. Before I reached the door Sister Luba waylaid me and asked, 'Don't you want to eat?'

I hesitated and answered, 'But it's your food!'

Sister Luba took my arm and guided me back to the chair I had vacated.

'Sit,' she said.

The children were delighted to have me back to share some of the food with them. I felt embarrassed but also very happy. I had only had a few biscuits to eat in the past three days.

The meal did not take long. Each child got a slice of brown bread with jam and a beaker of warm tea. Slowly I ate my bread, trying not to upset my stomach. My stomach played tricks on me. After it had been empty for so long, it did not want to accept food when I ate something quickly. I suppose it was not used to food any more.

When we were all finished and the table was cleaned, I decided to go back to my room and have a little rest. I felt very tired all of a sudden. I said my farewells to Max and Jacky and told them I would be back in the morning.

Returning to my room, I climbed up to my bed. The room was empty. Eva and Bram were out somewhere. I pulled my blanket off the suitcases to see if the sugar was still there. It was, so I decided to go to sleep. I slept right through the night and woke up at first light.

I had not heard Bram and Eva return and they were both still asleep. I wondered what they were doing all day. I knew what I was going to do. As soon as it was possible, I would go to the children. I went about midmorning and helped with the chores as I had done the day before. When it was time to eat, it was natural that I also got my share. At times during the day I had caught Sister Luba watching me, but she never said anything to me. That was all right by me as I was still scared of her, and I kept my distance as much as possible. But when I was about to leave, Sister Luba stopped me at the door and asked me if I knew where she could get some sugar. Through her connections in the kitchen she wanted to have a cake baked for the lady doctor whose birthday it was the next day.

Which child has blabbed? was the first thought that flashed through my mind. Somebody had told her about my sugar. What should I do? My brothers' lives depended on this woman. I made a snap decision.

'I have some sugar,' I told Sister Luba. 'I will bring it to you.'

I walked quickly to my room, cursing the one who had given the information away. I took a full jar of sugar out of the suitcase and hid it under my coat, holding it with one hand. I walked back, hoping that nobody would notice the treasure I was carrying. I was aware how vulnerable I was to a robbery attempt, but my return to the children's barracks went uneventfully. When I entered, Sister Luba was at the door and invited me into the private area where she and the lady doctor were sleeping. Once inside, I pulled the jar from under my coat. Sister Luba produced a white coffee cup from somewhere. I opened the lid of the jar and poured the sugar into the cup. When the cup was half-full I slowed the flow of sugar with the intention of stopping, but Sister Luba pushed the rim of the cup onto the jar, indicating that she wanted more. With a bleeding heart, I saw the volume of sugar decrease in the jar, as more and more sugar poured into the cup. When the cup was nearly full, Sister Luba indicated that was enough. I stopped and screwed the lid on tight. There was only a third of the sugar left in the jar.

Sister Luba asked me what I wanted in exchange for the sugar.

'Nothing. Just be good to my brothers,' I said.

She looked at me with disbelief when I said that I did not want anything in return. She thanked me profusely and said that she would tell the doctor that I had given her the sugar.

Before I left I went to see Max and Jacky and gave them each a spoonful of sugar to eat. I also gave Iesy a teaspoon of sugar as he was still sick in bed. He had seen me give the sugar to Max and Jacky and my conscience would not allow me not to let him share a little bit.

The next day, when I arrived to see the children at about eleven o'clock in the morning, Sister Luba called me into her private cubicle.

She showed me a plate with three small cakes and said she would divide them between the children. Later in the afternoon she gave each child a minuscule piece of cake. It was so lovely, even though it was so small, but it was not enough to still our hunger. In the past few days, there seemed to have been a problem obtaining food for the children. We had been spoilt before, with potato soup and rice, but no food had arrived for us recently except for some loaves of bread, and we received only half a slice of bread for our meal during the day. The children became listless again and a lot of them got sick with heavy colds.

The weather had become colder and there was no heating in the room. Max had to stay in bed for two days with a high fever. I found some aspirin in my suitcase and gave them to him, which soon reduced the fever. We wore nearly all the clothes we possessed to keep warm inside the room: two jumpers, double socks and our overcoats. I kept my red silk headscarf on day and night to keep my ears warm.

It must have been Christmas, as we heard the guards in the watch-tower singing Christmas carols one day. The food supply in the children's barracks dwindled until one morning a few boxes of big carrots arrived. The raw carrots were horrible but at least we could fill our stomachs with something. My jaws ached from trying to chew the carrot pieces, which then would cramp in my empty stomach. I had to choose between going hungry and the pain, I chose the former. Every day I gave Max and Jacky a teaspoon of sugar from a small jar I carried in my coat pocket. There was less than a third of the sugar left in the jar hidden in my suitcase.

I had become a regular part of the group of children, staying with them all day and only going to my barracks to sleep. I had not seen much of Eva and Bram lately but I did not care. Our barracks was on the edge of the concentration camp, far removed from the misery which took place in the other sections. Our section was quiet and no atrocities took place. You hardly saw a person outside the hospital and no sound could be heard coming from within. I had no inclination to investigate inside the hospital, and I always hurried past on my way to and from the children's barracks.

Christmas had gone and it was New Year – the first day of 1945. I knew this because the guard who patrolled the camp with two ferocious-looking dogs had called out his New Year greetings to the guards in the watchtower. What would the future hold for us? I wondered. Perhaps this year we will be freed. Hope rekindled in my heart and I sent up a prayer while I walked towards the children's barracks. I spoke to my mum and my dad, hoping that they would be able to hear me.

That morning I asked the children to sing with me and they did. We sang all the simple songs we had learned at school. When one song was finished, somebody would start on another one and we all joined in. It was the first time that I saw Sister Luba smile, and when we were out of breath and our strength gone, Sister Luba and Sister Hermina sang two beautiful Russian songs.

Later that afternoon a container of food organised by the doctor arrived. The doctor came at the same time as the food, and I realised that this was the same woman I had seen coming out of the hospital with the SS officer. She was just over five feet tall and had short, dark curly hair. She was wearing the same blue suit. Sister Luba called me over and introduced me to the doctor, telling her that I had supplied the sugar for her birthday cake. The doctor thanked me and then turned back to Sister Luba and talked in Polish. I managed to walk back to the table without them noticing. After about thirty minutes the doctor left and things went back to normal.

Eight

'How old are you?'

On 4 January 1945, early in the morning, all hell broke loose in our section of the camp. We could hear screaming and running feet. Our door was forcibly opened and a female SS guard screamed, 'Everyone out and bring your luggage.' Bram and Eva lost no time in going outside with their suitcase, leaving me alone in the room. There was no way that I could carry all the suitcases assembled on my bed. I was desperate and contemplating what I should do when a female guard walked in to inspect the room. I sat on my bed, unable to move. Her eyes met mine and I was sure that, next, her whip would land on me but, for some reason, she made out that she had not seen me. As she turned towards the door to leave, another guard entered and started to talk very animatedly about an experience they both had apparently had the night before. As if it were a dream, I could see that the first guard was manoeuvring her position so that the second one had her back to me. Slowly I slithered under my blanket, trying to make myself invisible, when one of the children, Maxy K., walked in, calling out my name at the top of his voice. He walked straight past the two guards towards my bed, all the time calling out my name.

There was no way out. I had to sit up. With one eye on the two guards I asked Maxy what he wanted.

'You have to come straight away to Sister Luba,' he said.

'Why? Are you sure it is me?'

I still did not trust Sister Luba.

'Yes,' Maxy said. 'She told me to get the girl with the red headscarf. You must come now!'

With a bouncing heart I slid down from the bed. Maxy was pulling on the sleeve of my coat and for a moment I hesitated to walk past the two guards. I mustered all my courage and swiftly walked past them while they were still in deep conversation. I sighed with relief when Maxy and I reached the outside, and we ran all the way towards the children's barracks. When we ran past the hospital, we could see the sick people being herded outside, accompanied by lots of yelling and the use of the whips. I recognised a woman who was the wife of a business associate of my father. She was expecting a baby and looked very tired. They were being lined up by the kapos.

When Maxy and I arrived, short of breath, at the children's barracks, Sister Luba and the doctor were standing at the door. Sister Luba told me that our camp was being evacuated, but the children were allowed to stay. The doctor wanted to ask Commandant Kramer if I could live with the children. She took my hand and we walked back to the area where the sick people were being lined up. As we came closer, I could see a tall man dressed in a black uniform standing alone. He was immaculately groomed, his jet-black hair was combed back and his black boots were so shiny that the light reflected off them. We stopped at a respectful distance, at least twenty metres away from him, and stood mouse-still. If he noticed our approach, he gave no inkling of it.

While we were waiting to be noticed, I had the opportunity to observe him. He was six feet tall, his hair was cut short at the back, he had a fat neck like a bulldog, and he constantly hit one of his boots with a short whip. He stood there like Caesar, overseeing the lining up of the sick people. For the benefit of the Commandant, the guards and kapos acted more cruelly towards the poor creatures.

The doctor and I remained still, not moving a muscle. The minutes felt like hours, until Commandant Kramer turned towards us. He said one word to the doctor, ignoring me, 'Jawohl!' The word was a command which stood no nonsense.

'Sir, may I take the little one with me as well?' the doctor asked.

Only then did he turn his eyes to me and I came face to face with the Beast of Belsen. The evil authority showed on his arrogant face. He had black bushy eyebrows and dark brown piercing eyes, which inspected me from top to toe. After he had scrutinised me, he nodded his approval to the doctor and barked, 'Get going!'

Before he could change his mind, the doctor and I ran for our lives back to the children and the waiting Sister Luba. When the doctor told Sister Luba that I could stay, she put her arms around me and said, 'I have now paid for the sugar.'

That cup of sugar saved my life. The section of the camp where I had been living was evacuated that day to another part of Belsen.

In the afternoon, when peace was restored in our section of the camp, I went back to my old room with a small group of children and Sister Hermina, and we carried all the suitcases which had been stored on my bed to the children's barracks. I handed over everything except my own suitcase to Sister Luba. I also kept my blanket which I put on the bed. I had to share with Max. How happy everybody was that I now belonged to the children's house of Belsen.

I had been in the children's house for a few days and life started to fall into a routine. As soon as I woke up in the morning I helped the little ones to get dressed warmly in a few layers of clothing, and if they had an overcoat I would dress them in this as well. In fact, we were all dressed up as if we were outside. It was bitterly cold and fresh snow had fallen soon after the New Year. As I looked through the fencing, the world outside the camp was white as far as the eyes could see, with no sign of life. The air was crisp and clear in the mornings when I took the children outside. It was never more than ten minutes before the cold became to much for us. When we came back inside we huddled together to keep warm. The hours dragged and boredom set in. The children became lethargic. There was very little to eat.

Our barracks was the only occupied building in this section of Belsen, which was right at the very end of the camp along the fenced perimeter. The doctor moved somewhere closer to the SS camp, and whatever her support had been when she slept in our barracks, this disappeared when she left. Sister Luba had to find us some food every day. Some days she would be away for hours, sometimes returning with no food, other times bringing us beautiful potato soup and bread. We were so far away from the main part of the camp that the kitchen forgot to cater for us. Things started to look pretty bleak when we had to live on one thin slice of bread for the whole day. Soon the little ones started to cry because they were so hungry. I tried to keep them occupied by telling them stories or by putting them to bed telling them to be still as the guards outside did not want to hear the noise.

Sister Luba left early in the morning to get food for us. In the meantime, Sister Hermina looked after the two babies and I looked after the smaller children. After the doctor left, Sister Luba acquired a few helpers to assist Sister Hermina in her absence. Iesy, Max and Jacky and a few other children were sick with severe colds. I gave Max and Jacky a spoonful of sugar when no one was around, so they would have some energy to fight the cold. I could not ignore Iesy as he watched me give the sugar to Max and Jacky, so I gave him a spoonful as well.

A strong bond grew between Iesy and myself. As the oldest of the children we started to discuss our problems and tried to solve them as well as we could. The very first time I had encountered Iesy was in Amsterdam, Christmas 1942. I had gone with Max and Jacky to a small private theatre to see an amateur play, Aladdin's Wonderlamp. Iesy played the role of the king's evil adviser like a born actor. I was very impressed at the time and had enquired about his name. Now, as I stood next to his bed in Belsen, I told him how much I had enjoyed Aladdin and the part he had played. I suggested that we organise a play for the children.

Two days later Iesy was able to get out of bed, and we started to make a plan to entertain the children. I had been in school plays, although it seemed like a hundred years ago. Soon some of the children became aware of the pending entertainment and their spirits lifted in anticipation. Their lethargy disappeared and they were distracted from their hunger pains. A proper play was out of the question, and even a variety show was too much, so Iesy said, 'Let's put the tables together to make a stage and we will go from there.'

Willing hands put the tables together, and in a short time the chairs were arranged in rows in front. Iesy climbed onto the tables and told everybody to sit down, including Sister Hermina and the helpers, Sister Hella and her mother. Those without chairs sat on the floor.

Iesy started to sing. His voice was not schooled but soon everybody was singing along with tunes from happier times in Holland. After about an hour we all were exhausted from singing, but everyone agreed that it had been a nice show.

After two weeks of misery, existing on hardly anything to eat in the unbearable cold, Sister Luba told us that we had to move to another part of Belsen. She had organised about ten helpers to assist with the children and the luggage. Early in the morning they left with most of the children, and I was left behind with a few small children guarding some of our small possessions. Dusk had arrived when Sister Hermina and some of the helpers returned to get me and the children. It was about time! We had had nothing more than a raw carrot to eat for the whole day. There was nothing to drink, not even water, and it had been a trying experience looking after the little ones on my own.

Sister Hermina carried a little girl, and I held on tightly to two other little ones as we walked back over the long main road which divided the camp in two. When we had passed the vegetable kitchen where our mother used to work, Sister Hermina motioned for us to turn left, and there behind the kitchen was a gate in the fence. As we came closer, a woman who had no hair and looked awful opened the gate and let us in. Sister Hermina said something to her in Polish as we filed past. Darkness was falling quickly now and we hurried the rest of the way. I noticed a dark-looking building on the left of the road which showed no signs of life. The door stood wide open but we could see nothing inside. About ten minutes later, we went through the gates into a compound and entered our new barracks.

Sister Luba and her helpers had created a dormitory and a room where we could eat. How she had managed it, I do not know. The beds were only two-storey bunks and the room looked very clean. All the beds had been made in readiness for the night. The children who had arrived earlier during the day were very happy to see me and showed me my bed. It was the top bunk, in the far left corner of the room in front of the window. A double row of beds was in the middle and one more row of bunks along the opposite wall. I shared my bed with Phoebe, a nice girl who used to live not far away from us in Amsterdam. At the end of the bed, mounted on the wall, were two small wooden shelves with a small curtain over them. I put my meagre belongings into the locker. I still had some sugar left and some tea in a blue tin. I hid both under the remains of my clothing.

Soon after I arrived, everybody was called to the 'dining room'. The few beds in this room had been moved aside along the walls. A bare bulb dimly lit the room and everyone sat around the long table. This was our first meal in our new barracks. Everyone was given a slice of bread with jam and a mug of black tea; this was our main meal for the day. It did not take long for 'dinner' to finish and everybody returned to the dormitory to get into bed. We all slept very soundly that night. Two women kept watch over us during the night, and a light at the far end of the room was on during the dark hours. Sister Luba had organised it well and after a few days we all felt at home.

I did not have to dress the little ones any more as the helpers did this in the morning, but most of us went to bed fully dressed anyway. To keep warm was of prime importance. We sometimes washed our faces and hands with a wet cloth in the morning. This same cloth was used by all of us in turn, so many of us never bothered. If we smelt bad, we did not notice it. We had become used to it, I suppose.

We had strict instructions not to leave the compound, and to make sure we did not leave, Sister Luba posted a helper on the gate who stopped anyone from leaving or entering without permission.

Breakfast was usually at eight o'clock in the morning. Seated around the long table, we would be given a half slice of bread with jam and a beaker of tea or water. Our food rations had become more regular as we were incorporated into the hospital section and no longer on the outskirts of the camp. When breakfast was over, the children were allowed to play outside within the compound. We were not allowed back in the dining room until it was cleaned. So the children who wanted to play went outside and the others trooped back into the dormitory. The end of the dormitory had about eight empty bunks, so it soon became the headquarters for Iesy, Max, Jacky, Louky, Maurice, Gerry and me. We would sit on top of the beds for hours and talk about Amsterdam and our families, but the ever-present topic was food. The yearning for good, wholesome, life-sustaining food was felt by all of us as a constant pain.

When we squatted on top of the bunks it was usual for Iesy to do most of the talking. His imagination knew no bounds and he always found willing ears in us. Iesy would tell us about the Portuguese synagogue in Amsterdam, which he said was under protection from the Germans as a monument. I could recall the German guards outside the synagogue but I had believed that this was to prevent the Portuguese Jews from going to their services. He told us how he had attended the services on Friday night with his father and uncle, and the deep satisfaction he got from his religion. One morning Iesy told us that the building further up the road was the morgue.

'How do you know that?' Max asked. 'Have you been outside the gate?'

'I sneaked out when there was no one on the gate,' Iesy said. 'Anyway, that's where they bring the dead bodies.'

That was the building I noticed the night that Sister Hermina brought me down from the old barracks. No wonder I felt funny when we passed it.

'I have been thinking that if the SS are going to kill us I am not going to stand still to let them do it. I am going to run away,' Iesy said.

'Where to?' Louky asked.

'I don't know, but I am not going to let them put me in the morgue,' Iesy replied.

No one spoke as we contemplated the horrible fate Iesy had portrayed. After a short time Gerry and Jacky said they would also run if they could. I said nothing. Where would we run to? There was no way out. That night I had nightmares where the SS chased me relentlessly through the camp.

The days became weeks and the cold weather did not abate. We were indeed very lucky that we did not have to attend roll-call. The morgue just up the road was full and the bodies started to pile up outside the building. From our compound you could just see it. The mound became bigger and bigger as the days went by.

Life in our new barracks became more organised. One of the helpers, Sister Hella, was a beautiful young Polish woman with golden blond hair. Her mother was also a helper. She was a small, scrawny woman with sharp, chiselled features and a scarf constantly around her head. She was assigned to keep the floor in the dining room clean, so she always held a broom in her hand. She was not a friendly person, and when the children sometimes wanted to warm their hands near the stove burning in the middle of the room, she would shout, 'Stay away from the stove,' and threaten the children with the broom. When this happened, the children would run to me for protection, complaining that 'the Witch', as she was nicknamed, would not allow them near the stove to get warm. I told them to be good and stay clear of the stove as it was reasonably warm in the dining room. Usually I told them to sit around the table and I would tell them a story. I had the respect of all the children and they accepted my guidance. They came to me with their worries and problems. Young and old understood without being taught that we had to stick together and help each other when necessary in order to survive.

Our barracks was surrounded by a wire fence. The entrance was a gate on to a small courtyard which led to the barracks. The children were allowed to play outside during the day, but were forbidden to go outside the gate. Sister Luba had made this very clear and no one dared disobey her. She was a good woman but she stood no nonsense. We had to be good and do what we were told.

Sister Luba had dark brown eyes and a small mouth. Her eyes, although demanding, were kind, but when she was angry her mouth would set in a narrow line and God help the luckless who got the lash of her tongue. She did not suffer fools gladly. When Sister Luba was not in a good mood, we stayed out of her way.

A small group of women helped with the daily chores such as dressing the little ones and helping them on and off the potty. We did not see much of Sister Luba, as every morning in the very early hours she went to the kitchen to see if she could get something for us to eat. She took with her two strong Polish women who had to carry the food containers on the long road back from the kitchen to our barracks. Sometimes she returned empty-handed, only to go back to the kitchen a few hours later. When this was the case, Sister Luba usually took Iesy and Max with her, or at other times, Iesy and Louky, in an effort to attract pity for the little ones in her quest for food.

The first few weeks of the new year were good for us. Sister Luba was able to get food for us in the morning and in the afternoon. How wonderful it was to have breakfast, sometimes with porridge or rice, and another meal at night. We, who had gone hungry for ten long months in the Albela camp where we lived on carrots and parsnips floating in brown warm water, could not believe our luck. The hollow cheeks of the children started to fill out a bit and at times laughter could be heard. But time still dragged.

Although the children's house was isolated from the main camp, news of immense brutality and suffering filtered through to our barracks. We heard of prisoners standing on roll-call for hours on end in this freezing weather. We knew all too well what it meant, as we had shared the same experience many times in the Albela camp. Thanks to Sister Luba and God above, we did not have to stand on roll-call outside every morning. We were counted in the barracks by two of Sister Luba's helpers.

Then, one very cold and windy afternoon in about the third week of January, we were told to come to roll-call in the open area. It was in front of a two-storey wooden house surrounded by trees. We dressed as warmly as possible, remembering that roll-call could last for many hours. Everybody who was lodged in our barracks, number 211, had to be present, including the babies, the sick and the helpers.

The wind was howling through the trees as we stood huddled together, shivering with cold. Inhabitants from other barracks were standing nearby. They had been there long before us. We waited. It became clear that this was not a usual roll-call where we had to line up in rows of five and stand to attention. It had been called to register every person in this part of camp number 2, ironically named the hospital section. After about an hour it was our turn. By now the other groups had left for their respective barracks.

While we were waiting we had been told that this registration was being done in order to have a number tattooed on our forearm in the same manner as the Auschwitz inmates had been tattooed. One by one we were ordered to come forward towards administrators sitting at trestle tables, watched by female guards. When my turn came I went forward with Jacky and Max beside me. A hard-faced woman asked for my name, date of birth and the city from which I had come. After she wrote all this information on a sheet of paper she told me that my number from that moment on was 10564 and, until I was tattooed, I had to wear 'No. 10564' written on some white cloth and sewn on the front of my coat or jumper, or on whatever I wore, so it was clearly visible. My coat had to have a red stripe painted on the back to indicate that I was a prisoner. My coat would be collected at a later date so that the red stripe could be painted on it. The whole miserable exercise distressed the children enormously, who were all terrified that a number had to be tattooed on their arms.

The administrators made good progress with the older children who knew their names, but when the little ones from babies to five-year-olds had to supply this information, the persistent questions started them crying, and the older children were not allowed to come to their assistance. The administrators realised they were getting nowhere and, after some consultation with the female guards, our group was allowed to return to our barracks, after standing in the freezing cold for more than three hours. Sister Luba was instructed to make up the list with the help of the older children so it could be collected in a few days' time. Mercifully, there were no more roll-calls.

It was about the last week in January when Sister Luba told me to accompany her on one of her trips for food. We left after eight o'clock and walked the entire length of the camp towards the SS section. We left the women's camp and came to an area where we had had a shower about a year before. The whole Albela camp at that time had to shower in an effort to kill the lice which had infested everyone. I could see the red brick building. It had been at about ten o'clock at night and my mother was still at work. It had been the first time that I had been separated from Max and Jacky, as they had had to shower with the men. It was a large room with a concrete floor with many shower heads and all our clothing was fumigated while our group of about fifty women showered.

Sister Luba was unaware of my thoughts, and she walked a steady pace. We crossed the perimeter of our camp without being stopped by anybody. It was very quiet here. The noise of the women's camp faded into the background. Sister Luba and I walked in silence to the last gate before we turned back in the direction of the main camp. We walked on the great dividing road through the SS section, and as we neared the gate to the entrance of the concentration camp, there was a guardhouse with three SS guards inside, just as I remembered it from that second day of February 1944 when I first came to Bergen-Belsen.

Sister Luba gave her number, which had been tattooed on her arm in Auschwitz, and the reason we were walking about to the SS guard. She smiled at the SS guard while she was talking and he responded with a friendly face. He told her she could enter the camp with *die Kleine* – this being me. It was apparent that Sister Luba had a magic smile to which the SS guards responded favourably, and that they knew about her work at the children's house. Sister Luba had taken us into her care nearly two months before, and on some days she had to come through this gate twice to find food for us from the kitchens. What courage this little woman had, to mesmerise these evil men.

'Danke,' Sister Luba said, pulling me away from the guardhouse after she received permission to go through. She held my hand firmly in hers as we walked into the main camp and towards the food storage place. When we arrived at the store, the first thing I saw was the two women from the Albela camp who worked in the store. They were very surprised to see me and asked a lot of questions that I could not answer all at once. While we were talking, Fritz, the Scharführer in charge of the food store, came over, and the woman explained to Fritz that I was one of the 'orphans' left behind on St Nicholas night. Fritz turned to one of the women and told her to get me a salami. One of them gave me a salami, saying, 'Cover it with your coat so that no one can see it.'

In the meantime, the other woman returned with a second salami.

'Here,' she said, 'take this one too. Quickly, cover it up before the guard sees it.'

I took the second salami from her but I had a problem holding on to them under the cover of my overcoat. The salamis were quite heavy and I was not very strong any more, but I was determined to get the salamis back to the children. Sister Luba could not help me carry them as she was not wearing an overcoat. In the freezing cold she was still only wearing a blue cotton blouse with short sleeves and black skirt. I struggled the long, long way back to our barracks while the weight of the salamis became heavier and heavier. I was exhausted, but rewarded by the smiling faces of the children when they were told they would be given bread with salami for dinner.

After this experience I decided that there must be an easier way of carrying a salami without detection. A few days later I had an idea. The slacks that Sonja had sent me had very wide legs, so I cut open the bottom of the pockets and extended the lengths of the pocket by sewing one of my father's socks on the end of it. This created a pocket about the length of a salami. By sliding the salami (if I ever managed to get another one) into the long pocket it could hang unseen inside my slacks. As it was such a perfect hiding place, I also sewed whatever spare socks I could find into Max, Jacky, Iesy and Louky's trousers.

Sister Luba was now well known in the camp as our protector. She had gathered around her a group of women who were all dedicated to her work. There was no doubt that Sister Luba was the driving force, while Sister Hermina was second in charge and took command when Sister Luba was away on her food-finding efforts.

It became 'fashionable' for the prominents to wear skirts made from chequered material. Where they obtained it from, God only knew, but you could see the prominents wearing it whenever you encountered them in the camp. Soon Sister Luba and Sister Hermina acquired similar skirts. Sister Luba had found another tailor, Maria from Paris (the first one was Sister Hella). She repaired our clothing and this way she earned her shelter and food. She was always very nice to me whenever I met her in the dining room. I was well aware she was so friendly to me because I was Sister Luba's favourite girl.

Our whole life centred around Sister Luba. She gave us the security we so desperately needed. She would always leave early in the morning to organise food for us, and the children would wait at the gate of our compound for her return. When they spotted her coming down the road they would run into the barracks, calling out, 'Sister Luba is coming, Sister Luba is coming.'

One night when we all were in bed, we heard a lot of walking down the corridor of our barracks. I decided to investigate what was going on. When I cautiously opened the door of our dormitory I saw a few prisoners carting stacks of bread loaves into Sister Luba's room. When I went to the door of the room I could see it was stacked with hundreds of bread loaves. When Sister Luba saw me she put a finger to her lips, silently telling me not to ask questions. When the prisoners left, Sister Luba told me that a young SS officer had helped to organise the bread for the children.

The next day the SS officer came to our barracks and we saw our benefactor. He was young, perhaps twenty-five years old, six feet tall, with black hair, and his name was Maximillian. It soon became apparent that he had taken a liking to Sister Hella. He made many visits to our barracks, mostly at night, when he had organised bread or flour to be delivered.

It was about the second week in February 1945 when I heard wailing coming from the dining room. I ran towards the noise as quickly as my legs would carry me. In the dining room Sister Luba and two other sisters were crying. Sister Luba kept repeating, 'Something terrible has happened.'

'What has happened?' I asked no one in particular.

But no one answered and the commotion became worse as the children started to cry from fright and bewilderment at seeing Sister Luba behave in such an unusual way. It was pandemonium so I tried to calm the children. After about fifteen minutes the noise subsided and Sister Luba saw me standing with the children. What a sight she was; her face streaked with tears and her eyes red and swollen. This frightened me and when I went to her she put her head on my shoulder and cried.

'Oh God, Phillipje is dead,' she kept saying.

I went numb with shock. I knew that Phillipje was sick because the lady doctor had come to our barracks with Kurt the SS doctor a few days ago. I had seen them examine Phillipje and then move him to the hospital for a middle ear operation. Phillipje was returned to our dormitory about eight o'clock that night. The day before it had looked as if he was making a good recovery, and now he was dead. I felt a deep sorrow in my heart. I wondered if Phillipje really had had the will to live. He had been such a quiet baby. Unless propped up, he would not sit up by himself. He had seldom cried. I believed that Phillipje was missing his mother so much that he did not want to live. Of course, the poor baby never had the nourishment needed to grow. I was crying now with the rest.

When things quietened down, Sister Luba told Sister Hermina to help her take Phillipje away to the morgue. They both went to the dormitory and I followed but stayed at a distance from Phillipje's bed. I saw Sister Luba very gently roll Phillipje in a blue baby blanket. Sister Hermina picked up the small bundle and, with Sister Luba following her and crying all the time, they passed me on the way out. I had a glimpse of the blue bundle but it felt unreal. It was as if Phillipje was not in the blanket at all. Maybe his little soul had already left his body and was now searching for his mummy.

'Rest in peace,' I murmured as Sister Luba and Sister Hermina left the barracks for the morgue.

It was the first death within our group and our spirits were very low during the next few days.

One night, three Polish children arrived from Ravensbrück. Their heads were shaven but they looked healthy. They were the first children of a different nationality to join our group: two girls and a boy. We understood that the oldest girl was called Mala and was about the same age as me. We could not communicate with them so they stayed in the dining room where they could talk to Sister Hermina, Sister Hella and the Witch, all of whom could speak Polish.

Because of the bad weather all the children were confined to barracks, making the dormitory and dining room very crowded. Yet no one argued with each other or squabbled. We all knew that in order to survive we had to be good to each other. Within all this misery, somehow we developed a solidarity and commitment to each other other. There was nothing to do, so most of the children were hanging around or lying on their beds. We were very bored. As I looked around the dormitory, it occurred to me that this was not good. Our minds had to stay active in order to stay healthy. Leni was already very sick and did not move from her bed any more. Some of the children were always standing near Leni's bed, talking to her to cheer her up. Leni was a lovely girl, who never complained and always spoke to you with a friendly smile. We had no way to make her better, no matter how much we loved her.

I realised something had to be done and I suggested to Iesy that we should make another attempt to put on some sort of show for the children. Iesy agreed to give it another go, and I told the children in the dormitory about the plan. Magically, the lethargy was gone and everybody had ideas. I intended to do a rhythmic dance I had learned in Amsterdam during gymnastics. Because we had no music, a few of the children had to sing the Blue Danube Waltz. We started rehearsing in the small clear area near the door of the dormitory. It sounded terrible at first, but after a few false starts they got the hang of it. I rehearsed the dance as well as I could, while Iesy organised some sketches with a few older boys. We were very serious about it all, and, most importantly, it gave us something to do, which took away the boredom.

The day of the show arrived. Just like our previous show we put all the tables in the dining room together for the stage. With the help of a few sisters we were able to string a rope (I have no idea where they found the rope) across the room to hold up two blankets, which served as the stage curtains. Four boys were nominated to open and close the curtains as required. Every chair was taken in our improvised theatre, and when the curtains opened I could not believe my eyes, as there in the first row was the camp elder, Frau Stania, and four female guards to see the show. I whispered to the 'actors' to do their very best so we would not embarrass Sister Luba. Then I was on. While the children sang 'Die Danube so blau so blau so blau', I performed the routine I had danced so many times in Amsterdam.

The show lasted an hour and was a great success. Of course, we were very clumsy at times with no props or costumes, but the audience was lenient and applauded at the right times. When the show was nearing its end the guards left with the camp elder. Sister Luba accompanied them to the door and let out a big sigh of relief when they left. She lost no time in telling us how proud she was of us, and we could see that she was happy that everything had turned out so well.

The success of the show resulted in the female guards becoming more aware of the children's house. A few days afterwards, two guards entered our dormitory in the afternoon. All the children in the room stopped whatever they were doing and nobody spoke. No one moved a muscle as the guards slowly walked among us. One guard took a liking to Max and asked for his name in a friendly way. Although Max was very skinny, he was still good looking with black hair and blue eyes.

The guard started a conversation with Max while I watched them from the top of my bunk. She told Max that she had seen the show and was sorry that we had no music. Max agreed with her and said, 'If I had a mouth organ I could play it.'

'I will get you a mouth organ,' she told Max.

After the guards left, Max came over to me. 'Did you hear, Hetty? She is going to get me a mouth organ.'

'I would not get my hopes too high, Max. You cannot trust them,' I said.

The amazing part about this encounter was that Max had spoken in Dutch and the guard had spoken in German, yet they both seemed to have understood each other.

Two days later the same guards walked into the dormitory in the afternoon. The children froze and became quiet, but the friendliness of the two women quickly relaxed them so they continued what they were doing. One guard, who had told us that her name was Hilde, was the one who liked Max. She sought him out immediately and handed him a small parcel. When he opened it there were two pairs of socks and, unbelievably, a beautiful mouth organ. Max's whole face radiated with happiness. Soon he was able to extract a simple tune from the organ, and the guard smiled as she watched him while she sat opposite Leni's bed on the lower bunk. As usual I was sitting on top of my bed and observed the scene from above. Was it really possible that a SS woman could have a heart? I thought. No, I decided, I will be on guard as I do not trust them. I called Max to my bed and I whispered to be careful. He nodded. Because Max had received a gift, the other children came closer to the guard, who appeared to be enjoying the attention. When the guards left, they told us they would soon be back.

Obtaining food became difficult during the month of February 1945, and Sister Luba had a hard time getting enough for us. It was bitterly cold and when she returned from one of her fruitless journeys, she often became despondent and tired. At these times I noticed that the Witch was really a good woman. She would remove Sister Luba's boots, massage her tired feet and order Sister Hella to get her a dish with hot water so she could bathe Sister Luba's feet. I watched Sister Luba relax and regain her strength while she poured her heart out in Polish to the Witch, who, in a gentle voice, would calm her down until she was ready to go out again.

After one such occasion Sister Luba wanted me to accompany her to look for food. As we had done so many times before, we walked the long way through the camp to the kitchen. This time we targeted kitchen number one. This kitchen supplied the men's camp and a Polish kapo was in charge. Sister Luba talked to this man, her face lit up by her dazzling smile. I could not understand exactly what was being said, but I surmised that he told her to wait and be patient for a while. At that moment the Scharführer came running down from the far end of the kitchen calling out that he had cut himself with a knife. Sister Luba sprang into action, telling the Scharführer that she was a nurse and could help him. He told her to follow him into his office so she could give him first aid. I was left standing near the entrance of the kitchen and from there could see what was happening inside. The steam of the enormous steel cookers was escaping into the kitchen so it was very hot and hazy inside. The prisoners worked at high speed and a lot of orders were given, none of which I could understand. I waited a long time, perhaps more than a half an hour, before Sister Luba returned with the Scharführer, whose hand was now bandaged. As they re-entered the kitchen he told the kapo to let Sister Luba have sufficient food for the children's house, and that from now on she could come back every day to kitchen number one.

Sister Luba was assigned four prisoners to carry the containers with food to the children's house. From that day on getting food for us became a little easier. I heard later that this Polish kapo had quite a liking for Sister Luba and he had even told her that one day when the war was over he would like to marry her.

On 24 February 1945 I turned fifteen. Sister Luba was informed that it was my birthday by some of the children and in the morning she embraced me and wished me many happy returns.

When I told her I was fifteen years old, she said, 'Do not disclose your age to the SS as they will classify you as an adult and that could have some unfortunate results for a pretty girl like you. Remember this, Hetty.'

I nodded my head. My knowledge of German was improving by the day.

'Tell me,' Sister Luba asked, 'have you got heath?' I did not understand what she was saying so she repeated the question. Then in a flash of insight I understood, she wanted to know if my periods had started already.

'Yes,' I told her.

She then wanted to know if I still had them now. I shook my head. This seemed to upset Sister Luba and she took my hand and said, 'Do you want them back? I can get you something from the lady doctor.'

'Oh, no,' I said in my broken German, 'I do not want that at all.'

I could just imagine the mess it would make for me in these circumstances. Reluctantly, Sister Luba agreed.

That day Sister Luba took me with her to get some food for us. She thought that, as it was my birthday, Fritz in the food store might give me a birthday present. She was right. When I returned late that afternoon with Sister Luba, I showed the children the beautiful salami Fritz had given me. I had carried it without difficulty in the big pocket of my slacks. Although the salami had been given to me for my birthday, it never occurred to me to keep it for myself. Everything, no matter who found it or 'organised' it, we all shared and shared alike.

Later that day I was told to come to the dining room. When I arrived I saw that we had visitors, namely, the camp elder, Frau Stania, and her second in charge. Sister Luba appeared tense but managed to smile.

'Hetty, Frau Stania has come to take you for a walk with her, so go and get your coat and comb your hair,' she said.

Sister Luba warned me with her eyes not to ask any questions. So I did as she asked and then returned to the dining room where the two women stood waiting for me. Frau Stania took me by the hand and said, 'Come along' and the three of us left the barracks. Once outside we turned towards the end of the camp where the crematorium was. The weather was mild and the sun was shining. We passed the barracks called *das Revier* (sick bay), that was where you were sent if you were dying and there was no hope of recovery. This was what the barracks was meant for early in January, but now all the barracks were sick bays and the crematorium could no longer cope.

No sound was heard coming from the sick bay as we walked past. When we had left the children's house, the elder asked my name but did not speak to me any more, although she gently held my hand. After a few minutes' walk we arrived at the fence near a watchtower. The second in charge called something to the guard in the tower. I could not follow what she was saying but the guard nodded his approval. The second in charge then produced a key and opened the gate in the fence, and we moved outside the perimeter of the camp. It certainly felt strange to be leaving the camp. After walking about twenty metres, the camp elder sat down on a cluster of heather. She motioned for me to sit near her and then resumed her conversation with her second in charge.

Frau Stania seemed to have completely forgotten that I was present, and I had a good opportunity to observe her. She was a tall woman, her jet-black hair hanging down in curls. The high cheekbones told me that she was Polish or Russian. Her skin was white and her dark eyes were intelligent. She was a very beautiful woman. How could such a beautiful lady do such a cruel job, I wondered. On the other hand, the second in charge definitely looked the part. She was a tall, strong woman with dark blond hair. She had the high cheekbones of the Slavic race, her eyes were a pale grey colour and her mouth looked cruel. Both women were dressed in the chequered skirts of the prominents. They also wore the leather knee-high boots similar to those worn by the female guards. You could see yourself in the leather, it was so shiny. As if she could feel my scrutiny, Frau Stania turned to me and said, 'How old are you, Hetty?'

Sister Luba's warnings went through my head so I lied and said, 'I turned thirteen today.'

'Oh, it's your birthday today, how nice,' she said.

I nodded. After this short exchange she returned her attention to her second in charge. It was difficult to converse with Frau Stania as she spoke German and Polish, and I could only really speak Dutch.

Left to myself, I examined my surroundings. Behind me, a small red brick building stood in a clearing surrounded by a seven-foot high fence. With a shock I realised that this was the crematorium where those two nice boys were chosen to work about a year ago. But no one was about at the moment. It looked empty and no smoke came from the chimney. There were no corpses lying in the clearing around the building. I turned my head away. It depressed me.

I spotted some empty sardine tins lying on the ground so I got up and retrieved two of them. The elder had not even noticed that I had walked a few metres away. I returned to my seat and started to fill the small tins with sand. Then I selected a few small heather plants from near where I sat and created a miniature plant decoration which would have adorned any home. It was nice to create something dainty and delicate among all this misery.

Suddenly Frau Stania remembered my presence and looked at me. I showed her what I had made and she said, 'Nice.' I handed her one of my creations, saying, 'This is for you.'

She looked at it and after some hesitation she told the second in charge to carry it as we were ready to go. I pointed to the second tin with the plants and asked, 'Sister Luba?' Frau Stania nodded so I picked it up and carefully carried it.

When we arrived at the children's house, Frau Stania said a friendly goodbye to me, which her eyes told was sincere. The second in charge was not so friendly, her eyes told me that she was glad to be rid of me. I thanked them both for taking me out and quickly skipped into our barracks to find Sister Luba to give her the plant decoration. Sister Luba was very happy to see me again. She was worried about why the camp elder had personally requested that I join her on her walk. The hours I had been away had been a great strain for her. That evening she handed me an extra slice of bread as a birthday present, which I promptly shared with Max and Jacky.

We all had a slice of bread and salami that night and the children sang Happy Birthday to me. Erica came forward with a poem she had written for me in Dutch. It went like this:

Happy birthday to you.
I give you this bread without butter as I have none,
but I am sure you will be able to eat.
I hope that your sixteenth birthday you celebrate in Amsterdam
with your parents and your brothers Jacky and Max.

Erica handed me her slice of bread – her evening meal – but I would not accept it and told her to eat it herself. The very fact that she wanted to give me her bread showed that I was loved, and she appreciated that I took care of her. I gave her a big kiss and all the children clapped their hands to show their appreciation. We all went to bed that night in a happy frame of mind, and when Sister Mala told us to go to sleep as the lights had to be turned down we all obeyed immediately.

The next day a parcel was delivered for me from the camp elder. When I opened it, it contained a grey and white chequered skirt and a nice woollen jumper. It was the right size and fitted me perfectly. Sister Luba was beaming, she was so proud of me. I had pulled the heartstrings of the camp elder and this could only help Sister Luba in her quest to get food for us.

Life in the entire camp became unsustainable. The cold weather, the lack of food, the roll-calls and the indescribable overcrowding in the barracks resulted in many deaths. Here in the women's camp, the mountain of dead bodies grew and grew, and when we looked out from our windows the corpses stretched as far as the eye could see. Although the odour of decaying corpses must have been horrific, we could not smell it any more.

For about a month two women had kept watch over us during the night. This had been the case since Phillipje was sick and they had stayed on mainly to look after the toddlers. It was also comforting for the bigger children to wake up in the night, see the low light and hear the soft conversation between the two sisters. I experienced this feeling of comfort many times when I woke from a restless sleep. I rarely slept peacefully as my mind was always on the alert for danger during the night.

During the last days of February 1945 we heard through the camp telegraph that some of the men from the diamond transport, which had left on 4 December 1944, had returned to Belsen and were in the Häftling camp. We wondered if our father was with those who had returned, so when the female guards came to see us again, Max asked Hilde if she could find out if our father was in the men's camp. Max called me over and said, 'Hetty, Frau Hilde wants to know more details about Dad. She wants to know his birth date.'

After some hesitation I told her, '22 April 1902.'

Max had already told her Dad's name. She promised she would make enquiries but I could see in her eyes that she was cunning and false, and after she left I told Max to be very careful.

Frau Hilde visited the barracks on her own one afternoon. To the smaller children she was now familiar and they crowded around her. They had no idea of the danger she represented, and I believe she used this method to extract information from the unsuspecting children about Sister Luba. She wanted to know if we had enough to eat and so on. She told me to sit next to her on the lower bunk, so I did what she asked. After I sat down, she turned to me and asked, 'How old are you?'

'Thirteen,' I lied, with Sister Luba's warning still imprinted on my mind.

I do not know if the female guard knew I was lying, as it would have been a simple task for her to check the records. It was Max who spared me further questions. 'Frau Hilde,' he said, 'do you think it would be possible to get a cream cake? I would like that very much.'

My God, I thought, what courage to ask for something like this, but Frau Hilde told Max that she would try and then she pulled Max close to her, put one hand over his genitals and gave him a big hug. Max tried to free himself from her embrace, and seeing our astonishment the guard quickly released him and got up to leave.

'See you soon,' she told Max and she was gone.

Max was slightly shaken by the experience, but soon recovered. Frau Hilde returned two days later and gave Max a little box. When he opened it he found two cream cakes and a ham and salami sandwich inside. Max handed the box over to me and thanked Frau Hilde for her gift. She patted his head and was gone a few minutes later. The small box with its precious contents was handed to Sister Luba, who cut the cake and the sandwich into minuscule parts so that every child could have a piece. The tiny morsels tasted delicious and I doubt if any of us could have managed to eat a full cream cake as our stomachs were not used to this kind of food any more.

Before Frau Hilde left, Max had asked her again if she had found out anything about our father and she told him that she was making enquiries. If we had been older and wiser we would have refrained from making such request to an SS woman as it endangered our father's anonymity within the camp. Max's request to find our father would bring him to the attention of the SS which could be fatal, but in our innocence we did not think of this.

The day after my birthday it occurred to me that we did not know when Sister Luba's birthday was, so when she returned from the kitchen I asked her. It took some time to find out, as apparently birthdays in Russia and Poland are defined differently. In Holland our birthday is on the day we are born. In Russia or Poland a birthday is on the person's name date, that means there is a saint or an event after which they have been named. Anyway, after lots of discussion and trying to follow the cultural reasons, we believed that her birthday was on 5 March.

This did not leave me much time to organise something special. In fact, I had only nine days. I decided to consult Inge and Gretel, two Dutch women of German origin who sometimes came to see us. Gretel worked at the SS doctors' dispensary, and was able to get her hands on the medicines Sister Luba needed if some of us were sick. Inge and Gretel had no free entrance into our barracks so I instructed our gatekeeper to let them in whenever they came to visit us. When Inge and Gretel arrived in the afternoon I told them that I needed their help. I told Inge that I needed a present for Sister Luba's birthday, something really pretty if possible. The second request was for Inge to write a verse or poem in German which I could recite on Sister Luba's birthday. Inge said she would give it a try and I promised her food if she could do it. This conversation took place in our compound late in the afternoon out of earshot of any small talkative mouth who could reveal the surprise to Sister Luba. Inge and Gretel did not come back until four days later. On a not-so-white piece of paper, Inge had composed a poem for Sister Luba's birthday. She had included all Sister Luba's virtues as I had listed them.

After Inge had translated the meaning of certain words so I could understand them all, I was quite happy with the result. I then asked Inge about a present for Sister Luba and she showed me a beautiful black and white pure silk scarf with the Dutch trademark 'De Bonnetterie'. I was thrilled that she had been able to find such a thing of beauty in Belsen, let alone something from 'Maison de Bonnetterie' in Amsterdam, where only the wealthy could afford this exclusive shop. I asked Inge where she had been able to find such a beautiful shawl.

'From one of the old ladies of the Sternlager, she still had it in her suitcase,' Inge answered.

'How much does she want for it?' I asked.

'She wants one and a half bread loaves for it,' Inge said.

'And what do you both want for the poem?' I asked Inge.

Inge looked at Gretel, and then she said, 'We would like to have half a loaf of bread for it.'

I pondered over this for a while. There was no doubt about it – I wanted this beautiful shawl for Sister Luba, and the poem was important too.

'Okay, I will get you the two loaves of bread, but it has to be in slices. I cannot get hold of a whole loaf for you,' I told them.

Inge and Gretel agreed to the conditions.

'Now,' I said, 'I believe that one loaf has seventeen slices, correct?'

Inge agreed.

'So two loaves makes thirty-four slices of bread?'

Inge and Gretel nodded.

'I will pay you in two parts, thirty-four half slices on one night and thirty-four half slices on the second night.'

Inge agreed. With that settled, I asked Inge to bring me the completed poem tomorrow so that I could have some time to memorise it before Sister Luba's birthday. Inge promised to come back the next day and to write the poem in block letters, as she had noticed that I could not follow her handwriting very well. As I watched Inge and Gretel walking down the road it occurred to me that I did not even know where their barracks were. I had no idea and did not care but I was surely glad that they had come into our lives.

I went back into our barracks and sought out Iesy to tell him about my plan.

'I have to get two bread loaves together in order to get this beautiful shawl, and to pay Inge and Gretel for the poem,' I said.

Iesy did not answer at once and I could see that he was thinking this would be difficult to achieve. People were killed over one slice of bread and we had to get thirty-four slices together. But somehow we had to do it. Sister Luba was very special to us.

'The only way I can see how to do it is if each of us gives up half of the slice of bread we get for our evening meal for two nights. What do you think about it, Iesy?'

Iesy looked very serious.

'That's a lot to ask. We have not been getting a lot of food for the past few days,' he said.

'I know it will be a real sacrifice for all of us but I cannot see any other way to achieve it, short of breaking into the storeroom,' I said.

Iesy was quiet for a while and then he suggested that we should ask the others if they would agree. I turned to a few children who had been standing close by and told them to fetch everybody into the dormitory. Soon everybody except for the very small were standing around me. I told them about Sister Luba's birthday plans and what was needed from them.

'It's your bread ration and if you don't wish to give away half of it for two nights you don't have to do it,' I said.

But everybody agreed to it, and this act alone showed how much the children loved and cared for Sister Luba. So it was settled that the next night and the night after I would collect the half slices of bread.

The next morning when Inge and Gretel returned with the completed poem I told them to come that night at about five thirty to collect the first half of the bread.

During that day I studied and rehearsed the poem to memorise it. I also decided to make a presentation box for the beautiful shawl. Somehow I got hold of some cardboard, cut out two heart shapes and covered them with some pretty material from a summer dress I still possessed. It was too cold to wear the dress anyway. I managed to create a very beautiful box with a lid that could open and close. It took me two days to complete it but I believed that the final result was worth the effort.

The bread collection that night went very smoothly. I found two reasonably clean tea towels in my locker and I decided to use one for each night. The first night I collected the bread during dinner without the sister in charge noticing a thing. There was a second door leading into the corridor at the end of the dining room which was seldom used. I decided to leave through this door to prevent detection by the sharp eyes of Sister Luba. I ran down the corridor with the bread towards where Inge and Gretel were waiting near the gate of the compound. I handed Inge the parcel and she gave me the shawl wrapped in a piece of paper. Inge and Gretel quickly left as it was getting dark and Belsen was no place to be walking around at night. I went back inside and hid the precious shawl in my locker.

The next night the children again parted with half their evening ration. Although they were very, very hungry, their love for Sister Luba was stronger than their hunger. Sister Luba meant everything to us. She was our mother in Belsen, our trust in her had no bounds, our love for her was unconditional. She was the angel who took care of us.

The morning of 5 March 1945 arrived. Early in the morning we washed our faces, cleaned our hands and combed our hair, the older children taking care of the little ones. Everybody was lined up for my final inspection before we left for the dining room. When we entered the room we did not sit down as usual but formed a double row with the little ones up front facing the door. Sister Luba, who had been informed the night before that her presence was required, entered the room and spontaneously the children sang the Dutch birthday song 'She Will Live Long, Hurrah'. Sister Luba was so surprised and her face lit up in a happy smile. The children had kept this secret well.

After the song we told Sister Luba to sit down in the specially decorated chair and then I recited:

Schwester Luba, Diesen Namen wohl genannt,
mit Achtung und Liebe ist sie bekannt.
Sie schafft von früh bis abends spät,
sie ist es, die sich in unserer Mitte dreht.

Der Tag hat noch nicht angefangen,
Wo ist Schwester Luba? Zu der Küche ist sie schön gegangen.
Für ihre Kinder schafft sie den Morgenbrei,
das ist ihr bestimmt nicht einerlei.
Die Kinder warten mit grosser Frage,
was bringt Schwester Luba heute für uns zu Tage?
Ganz hoch beglückt kommt sie zurück, wenn sie aus der Küche

Kartoffelsuppe mit Speck hat heraus gekriegt.
Alle am Platze alle sind froh, denn das Essen macht das Leben
*   erträglich noch so.*
Keine Mühe, kein Gang ist Schwester Luba zu viel,
Sie hat nur einen Gedanken zu erreichen ihr Ziel.
Und dieses galt ihren Kinder die ihr sind anvertraut, sie schützt mit
*   beiden Händen jedes einzelne Haupt.*
War der Iesy krank viele Wochen schwer, gönnte die Luba sich gar
*   keine Ruhe mehr.*
Ihr Sinn und Gedanke galt dem kranken Kinde, wie konnte
*   Schwester Luba es besser geschwinde.*
Und endlich mit Geduld und Macht, bekam der Iesy wieder Kraft.
So hat die Luba immer ein Sorgenkind und weiss auch immer Rat
*   geschwind.*
Die Leni ist krank und recht schwer, Luba läuft traurig hin und
*   her, und abends wenn alles schön liegt in tiefer*
Ruh, Luba kommt rein und steckt ihrem Schützling noch eine
*   Kräftigung zu.*
Und dann das eine Mal dass die Kinder hatten keine Schuhe,
Die 'Organisiert' Schwester Luba im Nu.
Und so ruht unser ganzes Leben in ihrem Schoss und wir sind sie
*   ihr dankbar klein und gross.*
Viel zu sagen habe ich nicht mehr, jetzt noch einen Wunsch, schnell
*   komme die Freiheit für uns alle hier.*

Which, in a free translation to English says:

Sister Luba, the name fits like a glove,
You have all our respect and all of our love,

The Children of Belsen

From early morning till late at night
Not once do you let us out of your sight.

The day has barely begun
And already Sister Luba is on the run.
And where is she off to now?
To the kitchen to fetch our chow.
The children wait, asking when she'll be back,
And what's she'll bring today
To fill this and that little stomach.
How happy she is when the day's taking
Includes potato soup and bacon.
All take their seats, all are present,
Because eating makes our lives ever so pleasant.
No gate, no wall,
For Luba nothing is too strong or tall,
For she'll do anything
For the children under her wing.
If one gets sick, many weeks on end
Luba knows no rest until the child is on the mend.
Leni is ill, and now
Luba paces endlessly up and down,
And in the night, when all is still
She is still up to give the child a sweet 'pill'.
Once the children had no shoes —
Sister Luba organised* them, swell.
Our lives are in her hands, we know full well,

*camp slang for stealing

And all of us are grateful, big and small.
Much more there isn't to tell:
We wish you joy, health and happiness,
And may freedom come quickly for all of us.

Sister Luba was sitting enthralled in her chair. I went over to her and handed her the present, and I told her of the sacrifice all the children had made so we could buy the silk shawl for her. I then put my arms around her neck and as I kissed her I told her, 'We love you, Sister Luba.' By now Sister Luba and all the other sisters did not have a dry eye after such a show of devotion. Sister Luba got up and walked down the line of children and she thanked and hugged each and every one of them. We sat around the table to have our breakfast with Sister Luba. She did not go out that day. Instead she sent Sister Hermina who took Max with her to the kitchen.

Sister Luba was in our midst all day and some of the little girls were vying for a hug and a cuddle. It was a happy day, until late in the afternoon when two female guards visited. I was in the dormitory as usual when I was called to the dining room. When I entered I could see Sister Luba talking to the two guards who had their backs towards me. When Sister Luba saw me she came to me and took me by the hand and said, 'The guards wish you to recite the verse from this morning,' and she pushed me gently in their direction.

One of the guards was Irma Grese, who was feared for her brutality. Every fibre in my body warned me to be careful. These female guards were not the same as the ones who had visited us in the dormitory before. My instinct told me that these two women

201

were very evil. Somehow I gathered enough courage to recite the poem, but when I came to the last line which said 'And may freedom come quickly for all of us', I hesitated and said instead, 'I wish you a happy birthday from all of us.'

Where in the world I found the words I do not know. I could only speak a few German words and I firmly believe that some power from above formed the words in my brain so I could say them. Sister Luba looked very relieved and the guards told me that it was a very nice verse, but they did not look sincere. I was allowed to return to the dormitory. But that was not the end of it.

Two days later I was again requested to come to the dining room. There I saw Sister Luba with some of her helpers standing in front of a mean-faced SS officer who was seated on a stool. Irma Grese and the other female guard who had listened to my verse stood next to the SS officer. Sister Luba's face was flushed and her mouth was pulled in a straight line so I knew something was very wrong. Irma Grese turned to me when I entered and said, 'Übersturmführer Herr Fox wants to speak to you.'

She pushed me in the direction of the SS officer. He was a very skinny, short man, who wore glasses over his piercing dark eyes and had jet-black hair. He wore no cap, his uniform was black and he carried a short leather whip in his right hand. As he was seated his eyes were at the same level as mine. He stared at me intently and then in a gentle voice he asked, 'What is your name?'

'Hetty Werkendam, Herr Übersturmführer.'

'What is your name?' he said again very softly. He stared straight into my eyes. They reminded me of a snake and I started to feel alarmed.

With my heart pounding I said again, 'Hetty Werk …'

'Esther, you mean, Esther, and not Hetty!' Übersturmführer Fox screamed.

I reeled back in shock but managed to whisper, 'Yes, Esther.'

'I have heard that you have made enquiries about your father,' he said.

'Yes, Herr Übersturmführer.'

'And what is your father's name?' he asked me very gently.

Again he stared into my eyes as if he wanted to hypnotise me.

'My father's name is Maurice Werkendam.'

'So,' he said softly, 'Maurice Werkendam?'

I nodded my head in agreement, but then Fox exploded in fury, 'Moses you mean, Moses, not Maurice.'

I was shaking with fright, and without turning I could feel that Sister Luba and the other sisters were also afraid of what could happen to me. Then Fox calmed down again and asked me very softly: 'How old are you?'

I recalled Sister Luba's warning, but he knew my birth name and my father's birth name so he must have checked the records, so if I told him I was thirteen he would know that I was lying.

'Fourteen, Herr Übersturmführer,' I answered.

Fox looked at the two female guards when he heard my answer, but before he could say anything else Sister Luba came forward and stood beside me.

'Herr Übersturmführer, the little one has special permission from the Commandant to be in the children's house,' she said, with her dazzling smile.

This was news to Fox and after consulting in a low voice with the two guards he told me I could go. Sister Hella pulled me into the next room as I was shaking like a leaf. I burst into tears and pressed my face into her body for protection. Sister Hella held me tight and tried to comfort me. I could hear Fox screaming something at Sister Luba which I could not understand. Thank God, Fox and his ladies soon left, but not before he ordered Sister Luba and Sister Hermina to wear prisoners' garb in the future, threatening that he would personally punish them if they did not obey.

Sister Luba was furious after they left.

'Who has been informing the SS about the children's house?' she asked. 'It must be someone in our midst.'

But how could one of us do such a thing? Or could it have been those two female guards who visited the dormitory? They had seemed to pump the children for information. On the other hand there were plenty of people jealous of the position Sister Luba held, and jealousy and hatred of those who were in a more fortunate position in the camp were the order of the day.

Sister Luba was very upset that she was not allowed to wear civilian clothing any more, as she was now known as a prominent. Sister Hella and Maria were put to work at once. Sister Luba had soon acquired through her connections a few male jackets in grey and white striped material. Maria carefully tore them apart and together with Sister Hella made an excellent fitted sports jacket and straight skirt from them. Sister Luba looked quite good in it, and she wore her faithful blue blouse to complement the outfit.

Seeing the final result, Sister Luba resigned herself to her fate and on the first day she wore it I told her how dapper she looked. She smiled at me and gave me a big kiss. From that day on she wore the suit as if it were a Paris creation.

Nine

'Criminals! Pigs!'

For some mysterious reason the SS had decided that all the dead bodies had to be piled high upon a wooden structure. The inmates from the men's camp had been put to work. Trucks with wooden planks had arrived and the poor prisoners worked laboriously to pile up the corpses. From early morning to late at night they worked under supervision of a big kapo and some SS guards. Many prisoners died from exhaustion, and they were piled up with the other bodies.

The weather had become pleasant and the sun was shining over the now-familiar landscape. One sunny day I decided to have a closer look at the pile of bodies, so I left the barracks and crossed the narrow road which separated us from the field. During the night a lot of prisoners had died and fresh heaps of bodies were scattered around. I stepped over a few and was looking to see if there was anyone there I may have known, when out of the corner of my eye I saw two tall women walking past towards the sick bay.

Their posture was erect, they looked strong and healthy, and their high cheekbones suggested they came from Eastern Europe. They did not give me a glance but continued their walk. Then I noticed a small elderly woman shuffling along from the opposite direction. In her hands she held a small piece of bread. She was obviously in a very bad state, as she was mumbling or singing softly to herself. The two tall women passed her, but ten or so steps later they turned and ran back towards the luckless woman. They knocked her to the ground and, in a swift movement, grabbed the piece of bread and ran away with it. I was shocked and stood nailed to the ground. It had all happened so fast. The two women were already out of sight. When I could move again, I walked up to the old lady. She lay where she had been knocked over and did not appear to be breathing any more. She must have died from the brute force and the subsequent fall on the road.

Her body was blocking my way and after some hesitation I gingerly stepped over her. The feeling of shock was still lingering in my body and I decided to go to the toilets just outside our barracks. It was not far – I could see it from where I was standing.

When I entered the latrine it was pitch-dark inside as there were no windows. I let my eyes become accustomed to the dark and then walked to the end of the building. The latrine appeared to be reasonably new and had not been used very much. Tree stumps had been used so one could sit down, and behind it gaped a large deep hole in the ground. I could not fathom the depth as the only light in the latrine was from the doorway. Just as I was about to sit down I could hear Polish-speaking voices approaching the building. The entrance darkened as two people entered the latrine and, to my shock, I realised that they were the same two women who had beaten down the old lady for the small piece of bread. The hairs on my neck stood up as I realised the danger I was in. I had been the only witness and now I was in this empty building with these dangerous women. The women entered but they did not notice me in the gloom. I held my breath and did not move a muscle. The women were deep in conversation.

I expected them to take their places on the tree stump next to me but something very strange happened. Neither woman sat down – instead, they lifted their skirts and stood upright to urinate against the wall. When they were finished, they dropped their skirts again and left the latrine. I sighed with relief that they had not noticed me. Then I realised what was so different about these women. They were not women at all; they were men walking through the women's camp in disguise, and they used their superior strength to steal food. I walked as fast as I could back to the safety of the children's house.

I had gone to the kitchen many times with Sister Luba so I knew the way through the camp and the procedure to pass through the SS checkpoint. One day I decided to go to the food store on my own to see if I could get something extra for Max and Jacky, as our food supply was dwindling. A group of some twenty Polish and Hungarian children had arrived about a week ago, crowding our dormitory and cutting into our food rations, as the SS did not increase our quota. The air held the promise of spring as I set out on the long walk.

The women's camp was large and the barracks had not been built in straight lines but were scattered on different angles amid wooded areas with large trees. It could not be compared with the Sternlager where the barracks were built in a straight line in a much smaller area, which was very overcrowded. This must have originally been designed as a holiday place, I thought, as I walked over the road which snaked through the camp. And what a holiday place did it turn out to be, I muttered to myself.

When I passed the morgue I could see the mountain of dead bodies spread over a large area about the size of a football field. On my left were the two hospital barracks. Max and Jacky, who had gone on an unauthorised walkabout, had told me a few days ago that Aunty Bets was in there, so I gave the hospital special scrutiny as I passed and indeed I could see Aunty Bets sitting up in her bed at the window. I stopped and waved to her. At first she took no notice but then she recognised me and waved back. (From then on, I always made it a point to wave to her when I went past, until one day she was not there any more.) I continued on my way, taking my time, as this was the first time that I had walked on my own through the camp.

A short distance away two prisoners were cutting into a corpse. I walked away as fast as I could from this depressing sight. Despite the many barbaric things I had seen, this shocked me deeply. I knew without doubt that whatever happened I would not commit cannibalism. Never! Never!

When I neared the gate of the women's camp, I noticed barracks on the hillside. I could hear screaming and crying and, as I came nearer, I could see about twenty women lined up in a row. One by one the women had to bend down over a stool with their trousers down. A kapo was lashing each woman with a long whip on their buttocks with full force. I could hear the sweep of the lash as she meted out the punishment. The row of women were forced to watch the atrocities while nearby, smiling broadly, stood a female guard.

I ran towards the gate to escape this evil sight. I knew that once I had passed the gate the trees would dull the sound of the screaming women. After a while I slowed to regain my breath. Thank God, I could not hear the sound from the women's camp any more. It was peaceful in this part of the camp. There was no one in sight. I was alone and did not meet another soul. No one had been on the gate either. Through the trees I could glimpse the road on which we had arrived in Belsen. It seemed such a long time ago, but it was only a year and two months.

As I neared the SS checkpoint my heart started to pound. This would test whether I was able to wander through the camp or not. As I had done with Sister Luba, I went over to the small building where the SS was monitoring everyone who came or left.

Two SS officers were seated behind a desk at the open window facing the road. I walked up to them. They looked at me and one said, 'Where are you going?'

'I am from the children's house and I am going to see Herr Fritz at the food store.'

'Have you got a number?'

'Yes, number 10564.'

'You may go through,' he told me after making a note in a book.

Well, that was easy, I thought, as I walked through the gate. It was not far to go now.

The food store was just over the road on the left. I was lucky, Fritz was standing at the door when I arrived. I took the bull by the horns and asked him point-blank.

'Good morning, Herr Scharführer. Can you please let me have a salami for the children's house?'

He looked down at me and I gave him my best smile.

'Do you belong to the children's house?' he said.

'Jawohl, Herr Scharführer,' I answered.

He turned around and called to someone in the storehouse to bring him a salami. The person asked Herr Fritz, 'A small one or a large one?'

For a moment Fritz hesitated and then said, 'A large one.'

The person disappeared into the storehouse, and Fritz told me that he had work to do and he also left. I was standing at the door for what seemed a long time before the person returned with a large salami.

'What took you so long?' I asked him.

He told me that he had shown the salami to Fritz to make sure that this is what he wanted me to have. He handed me the salami. This time I was prepared to carry it home without it being seen. The salami slid into my father's sock, which had been sewn onto the end of my pocket, and was undetectable as it hung in the wide leggings of my slacks.

I set off 'home' again. Passing the SS checkpoint I waved from the road and the SS officer waved back, indicating that I could pass through. So far, so good. As I neared the gate of the women's camp I could see there was no one there, so undisturbed I continued towards the children's house. There was no one in sight at the barracks where I had witnessed the brutal treatment of the woman earlier. I did not dare let my thoughts linger on the sore bottoms those poor women would be nursing.

I started to hurry as it was getting late in the afternoon and the light was fading already. A grey fog started to drift down and, although I could still see the road clearly, the barracks slowly got lost in the mist. I knew I still had to pass the mountain of dead bodies, and other dangers lurked for me if anyone had the slightest notion that I was carrying a salami. People would kill for a small piece of bread. I started to walk faster but shortage of breath made me slow down again.

'Stay calm,' I told myself, 'if you run someone will see you and know you are scared.'

I knew that in Belsen you must never show that you are scared, otherwise the stronger ones would take control or kill you. So I forced myself not to run. The eerie quiet of the morgue on my left told me I was nearly home and there it was, I could see it, a small light shining over the entrance. Despite my good intentions, I started to run the last part of the way towards the safety of the children's house.

When I entered the dormitory all the children were already in the room. Our evening ration had been given earlier that night. Max showed me the slice of bread waiting for me on my pillow. My pillow was not clean as I had slept on it for many months now, but who cared, it was food. The younger children were crowding around me as they were always happy to see me. They were hanging on to my arms and my coat so I could only make slow progress towards my bed in the far corner of the room. Arriving at my bed I gave them all a big hug and told them to be good because I had something special for them. I climbed up onto my bed and removed the salami from my pocket. It had a deep mahogany colour from smoking and it smelled delicious. I hid the salami behind my back under the blanket and ate my slice of bread. Someone had got me a cup of water. When I had finished I called Jacky and Max over and showed them the salami.

'Where did you get it?' Max asked.

'From Fritz at the food store,' I said. 'Go and get a knife please.'

The children had grouped around my bed, all wanting to see the beautiful salami, and I could see in their eyes the desire to have a piece. Someone handed me a knife and I told everybody to line up. I cut the salami and handed a small slice to each child who wanted it, but I gave a bigger slice to Max and Jacky as they were my brothers. Everybody enjoyed the salami as it was salty and peppery and this was what our bodies desperately needed. We had been deprived of salt for such a long time that even this small piece of salami helped to strengthen us a little bit. Slowly the group of children dispersed. They were so grateful that I let them share the food. I only had a very small piece of salami left and I hid it in my locker to give to Max and Jacky the next day.

Sister Mala came into the dormitory to put the little ones to bed and as the lights would soon be dimmed we all followed. Sister Mala guarded us through the night, and sometimes when I woke up I could see her sitting with another woman having a whispered conversation.

In about the middle of March we were told that the Red Cross was going to hold an inspection. It was amazing how things changed. Our barracks was cleaned from top to bottom. Sister Luba acquired some more helpers. All our clothing was inspected by Sister Hermina with the help of Zosua and Helen (they looked after the dormitory and the sick children during the day). I helped with inspecting and sorting out the clothing that each child should wear during the Red Cross inspection. If things needed to be mended they were taken to Sister Hella and Maria, and dirty clothing was washed. A messenger had arrived from Frau Stania, the camp elder, with strict instructions. We had to be cleanly dressed and appear to be happy. If someone from the Red Cross asked us if we were being treated all right we were to say, 'Yes'. If they asked if we had enough to eat we had to say, 'Yes'. For the next few days we were constantly told what we had to do and not do. Sister Hermina told us that on the day we would eat our main meal at lunchtime.

When the day finally arrived the dining room held a feast for the eyes. The long tables were covered with white sheets and every child had a thick slice of white bread with butter put before them. The door opened and three men and one woman entered the dining room. Each had a white band with a Red Cross on the left arm. They were accompanied by Frau Stania, the lady doctor and some other medical staff.

To our great surprise, Mr Weiss also entered with the group. How happy I was to see him again. I sat on the end of the table and we found a chair so that Mr Weiss could sit with us. As it happened, the visit of the Red Cross fell on the Jewish Passover and Mr Weiss read from the prayer book he had brought with him before we started our meal. There were no matzos (unleavened bread), but that was not important now – we had life-sustaining white bread. Mr Weiss also carried a large box of chocolates, apparently provided for us by the Red Cross. A woman dressed as a nurse with a white apron came over to Mr Weiss and took the box from him. She told him that she would distribute the chocolates to the children. I knew this woman. She was the dental nurse who had assisted my dapper dentist. I did not like her then and I did not like her now.

Mr Weiss asked me lots of questions. Were the sisters good to us? How did we spend our days? I told him how we lived and, of course, I asked him if he knew if my father was back in Belsen. Mr Weiss told me that about twenty men from the diamond transport had returned from Mauthausen but he did not know who they were.

'It is difficult to find out,' he said. 'The Häftling camp is separated from the Sternlager by the Hungarian section and so it is not easy to find out.'

But he promised to give it a try.

213

The room was overcrowded. The children chatted excitedly. The Red Cross people were talking to Sister Luba and the other sisters, whose faces were smiling brightly. One of the Red Cross people could speak German. Frau Stania also stood near the Red Cross people so as not to miss a word that was spoken.

Then the Red Cross people came over to the table to speak to the children. One of them came to me and asked my name, which he wrote down in a notebook. He then wanted to know if the camp management was good to us, if we got enough to eat and if anyone beat us. I answered, 'Yes' to the first two questions and 'No' to the third. The man smiled at me and wrote notes in his book. Then he was called away as the party was leaving to inspect our dormitory and the rest of the barracks.

Some of the rooms opposite the corridor were used by some Romanian women who had arrived only a few weeks before. One of them had a beautiful baby who I had been to see a few times. I knew Sister Luba was giving food to the woman and her child, although she was not allowed to enter our side of the barracks.

Mr Weiss stayed behind with us while the others were inspecting the rest of the barracks. When the dental nurse came back from the inspection tour, he introduced me to her.

'I know her already from the dental clinic in the Sternlager,' I said.

The woman looked at me intently and seemed to recall.

'I am not working in the Sternlager any more. I am now in charge of the SS clinic,' she said. 'Show me your teeth,' she commanded.

I made a very bright grin to expose my front teeth.

'The teeth do not look too bad, but I do not like the colour of your gums,' she said. 'They look too red. Come and see me at the clinic one day and I will see what I can do.'

I firmly closed my mouth and made up my mind at once that I would never see that woman. She was so false, I knew that if we had met in different circumstances I would not go to her even if I lost all my teeth. The children who had witnessed this exchange all came over and the woman was obliged to look at all their teeth. Max got the same verdict as me. His gums were also too red. No wonder! We went short of everything, most of all proper food and vitamins.

The door of the dining room opened and Sister Luba returned with Sister Hermina from the inspection. Mr Weiss was told that the party had already left the barracks. Reluctantly he rose, then took hold of both my hands and looked down at me,

'You are a brave girl, Hetty,' he said. 'I will see what I can do to find out about your father and let you know.'

We hated to see Mr Weiss go. I closed my hands more firmly into his but he gently removed them. He had to go. The dental nurse had left already, so with a last pat on my head he bade us goodbye and quickly left the room to catch up with the others.

We felt so lonely after he left but we had one consolation: we all had a large piece of chocolate. For once Sister Luba let us keep it to eat it as we liked, but she warned us to go easy as it could make us sick if we ate the lot all at once. Soon we all returned to the dormitory where we discussed the happenings of the afternoon. The bigger children felt optimistic about the future. It had been the first time in many months that we had had contact with people from outside the camp.

What a show the SS had put on, with the help of all of us, to deceive the Red Cross. That night we had no dinner but it did not matter as by then we had eaten most of our chocolate. I still had half of mine and, as I could not eat any more, I hid it in my locker for the next day.

The visit from the Red Cross aroused a wild longing to be free. The confines of the barracks pressed into me, so I decided to try my luck once more at the food store. It was about the middle of March and the weather was very mild for the time of the year. When I sneaked out of our barracks, it was early in the morning and the camp was very still. As I passed the morgue I noticed that the pile of bodies had increased considerably, but I did not pay much attention to it. By now I was used to seeing corpses with their eyes wide open and their mouths stretched in hideous grins. Maybe it was their way of saying that they had been released from the barbaric torture and deprivations of the camp. I passed the hospital and stopped to seek out Aunty Bets, but she was not at the window any more. I did not dare go into the barracks to ask about her, so I turned to the row of bodies lying along the road to see if I could spot her among them, but I did not see her. I stood for a while scrutinising the dead women's bodies. I felt sad as I was sure she had passed away. I remembered Aunty Bets as a soft and friendly woman with a smile for everyone. Her husband, Uncle Harry, whom the children called Uncle Rabbit behind his back, always had a friendly smile for us too.

I turned and continued on my way. I had still a long way to go. I passed barracks with no one in sight. I passed smaller divisions within our camp enclosed with a wire fence like our barracks. I had been told that some Hungarians were in there. They had special treatment. There were also separate barracks for the Ascher and Soep families.

Again no one was at the gate when I left the women's camp. Through the trees I could see the bathhouse and next to it the store for clothing and other amenities. In the store worked Polish prisoners under the control of Frau Hilde. Where was everybody? I wondered as I walked down the main street. But then I saw, directly opposite the SS checkpoint, the pitiful hunched figure of a prisoner, no more than a skeleton in grey-striped garb, holding up a large pumpkin at eye level. At his feet was a sign which read, 'I stole from you'. I had witnessed many evil things in Belsen, but they did not lessen my pity for this poor creature. His hollow cheeks and dull and lifeless deep-sunken eyes shook me to the depths of my soul. As I came closer I could hear the SS shout at the luckless man, 'Hey, keep those arms up, thief!' and I could see him raise the pumpkin a few inches higher. I could feel his pain. That pumpkin in his hand must have felt like it weighed a ton. I had no idea how long he had been crouching out there, but a man in good condition could not sit in that position holding up a large pumpkin for long. This poor skeleton had so much will to survive that he endured this torture, but how long could he keep it up?

I walked up to the open window, averting my eyes from the prisoner. I gave my number to the SS officer.

'You had better be good if you do not want to be punished like him,' he said.

I nodded and gave him my best smile. I was allowed to pass and soon I arrived at the store, only to be told that Fritz was not there. The two Dutch ladies from the Albela camp were not there either and the Polish kapo on duty did not want to give me any food whatsoever.

'Come back when Fritz is here,' he told me.

How disappointed I was. I had started out on the long walk hoping that perhaps I could get another salami. Reluctantly, I turned to go back to the barracks. As I neared the SS checkpoint, I noticed that the poor prisoner was now on his knees, but still holding up the pumpkin.

As before I waved to the officer and he nodded that I could be on my way. I was very upset that I had nothing extra to eat for Max and Jacky, but I kept telling myself that I would try again soon. Food had been getting very scarce in the past few days. Sometimes Sister Luba came back with no food at all, and our rations were cut to one slice of bread a day, which we received at night.

Without realising it, I had already passed the gate of the women's camp and was getting close to a two-storey house standing in a clearing. I could see a wooden cart, usually used to carry dead bodies, parked in front of a wooden chute suspended from the top-floor window into the cart. As I came closer I could see two prisoners catching bread loaves as they came down the chute, and at the same time repeating the numbers of each loaf which was accounted for at the top by the other prisoners. I could hear them count aloud, 'eighty-seven, eighty-eight' in Polish. On seeing all that bread in the cart I walked over and stood beside the SS Scharführer directing the operation. The Scharführer scrutinised me for a second and then smiled. My mind was made up. I was going to steal one of those loaves. I did not want to consider the consequences if I failed. I edged closer to the cart and felt the wooden side touching my chest. I moved my legs one step back so there would be room to hide a loaf under my coat. I stood very still next to the Scharführer who took no further notice of me. Two male prisoners faced me from the opposite side of the cart, catching the loaves from the chute and placing them end up in neat rows in the cart. They were counting aloud. In fact, they were repeating the numbers announced from the building. Three men were handling the bread loaves upstairs and two were downstairs. Then my opportunity came: the men downstairs disagreed with the man at the top about the number of loaves they had sent down.

'Eighty-nine loaves,' one man said.

'No,' the man opposite me said, 'eighty-seven loaves.'

The man on the window started to argue loudly in Polish. I made out that I was very interested in the argument and lifted my head to look at the men upstairs. I could not understand a word that was being said and neither could the Scharführer. He demanded to know from the men upstairs what the problem was. They told the Scharführer that they had sent down eighty-nine loaves, not eighty-seven. This resulted in a strong denial from the men on the cart. I knew that this was the moment. I kept my head up as if I were looking at the men upstairs. The two men in front of me had turned their backs to me. Together with the Scharführer they looked up to the men at the window. I stood deathly still and slowly moved my left arm to get hold of a loaf inside the cart. My hand enclosed the bread and, ever so slowly, I gently lifted the loaf high enough to clear the side of the cart. Except for the movement of my arm I stood motionless next to the Scharführer. The loaf had cleared the side of the cart and in the same slow motion I brought it down until it was hidden under my wide coat. I released my breath. The men were disagreeing about the count while the Scharführer gave them a piece of his mind. I remained a few seconds longer at the cart, and then ever so slowly I took the first careful steps on my way.

The Scharführer was so intensely engaged with the arguing men that he did not even look at me when I left. For the first ten metres

I expected to hear that my theft had been discovered, but when that did not happen I quickened my pace, and when the arguing men were out of earshot I ran and did not stop until, out of breath, I arrived at the dormitory.

The children looked up in alarm when I burst through the door, but this soon turned into happy smiles as I held the loaf high above my head while I was practically dancing towards my bed. I was elated as not only had I 'organised' a whole loaf of bread but I had also outwitted the SS Scharführer by stealing the bread from under his very nose. Soon the children had grouped around me, wanting to hear every detail of my escapade and bombarding me with questions. One of them asked me if I had been scared, and it was then that the enormity of my deed sank in. If I had been caught in the act, the punishment would have been severe and God would have had to have mercy on me. I shivered and put the thought out of my mind. But what if the Scharführer remembered that I was from the children's house? Better to leave no evidence around, so I took the knife, cut the bread into chunks and handed them to all the children around me. Max and Jacky got the biggest. When every crumb was devoured I felt more at ease, and as the hours went by I knew that the missing loaf had not been connected with me.

Overnight the weather changed abruptly. Cold blustery winds and sleety rain swept through the camp, creating more misery for the prisoners. We heard of the long hours the adults endured on roll-call from early morning to late in the afternoon, when the bleak clouds made the night fall earlier. Without proper clothing and food, many prisoners succumbed during these cruel hours, and when the kapos mercilessly beat these poor people and they failed to get up, they were left to die in the mud and slush where they had fallen.

Two days after my escapade with the bread loaf, Judy and Mickey came to tell me that Jacky had slipped out of our compound about an hour before and gone to the building where they stored the bread in order to 'organise' a loaf. He had returned a few minutes ago and had apparently been caught in the act by the SS officer. I came down from my usual position on the bed to find out whether Jacky was all right, when he entered the dormitory surrounded by other children. I demanded an explanation as to why he had left the compound. Jacky shrugged his shoulders and his eyes looked defiant.

'You did it, so I wanted to do it too,' he said.

'But Jacky,' I said, 'don't you realise that what you did was very dangerous?'

Jacky nodded.

My anger subsided and I asked what had happened.

'I got hold of the bread and ran away with it, but the Scharführer ran after me and caught me. He took the bread from me and gave me a few very hard whacks on my head while he was screaming at me, and then he let me go,' Jacky said.

'How are you now?' I asked.

'I'm all right,' Jacky said while he lifted his face proudly. 'It didn't hurt at all,' he lied.

I put my arms around him and begged him not to do it again.

The weather was bad and the children could not play outside, so the dormitory became a bit crowded, but on the bright side, the room temperature was bearable from the heat our bodies radiated. The smell of unwashed bodies and bedding in the dormitory must have been horrendous, but we did not notice it any more. We huddled together with the ones we felt closest to.

Leni, who had been sick since the beginning of February, had not been able to leave her bed for weeks. We kept her company and in turn brought her her daily slice of bread, but the poor girl could hardly eat any more and was wasting away. She would patiently chew a few bites of bread, but the effort was too much for her at times. Bella, who had the most patience, usually tried to feed Leni each morning, but she was allowed, with our blessing, to keep the rest of the bread which Leni could not eat. Bella always kept it for her brother, Bram, who visited us every day, and although he could not stay the night, he was part of our group.

There was always someone near Leni's bed and we assisted her down so she could use the potty. It was pitiful to see how skinny she was, but she never complained. Leni was so weak that when she used the potty her lower bowel would extrude from her body. When this occurred, we would panic. We wanted to spare Leni any pain or discomfort. Sister Zosua or Helen would come to help, and ever so gently, by pushing together what was left of Leni's buttocks, they forced the bowel to retract into her body. While this was happening we felt helpless, but there were always willing hands to assist Leni back to her bed. We were so young but we were so wise. As the days wore on, we became used to helping other little children, who, through malnutrition, were not able to keep their lower bowel inside their bodies. A particular boy called Gerry became very adept at it and he was called upon if the younger children had this problem.

It was the third week in March when Judy and Louky came to tell me that Jacky was very sick. I immediately went to his bed to see for myself. Jacky was dozing but when I called his name he struggled into a sitting position and looked at me with fever-glazed eyes.

'How are you, Jacky?' I enquired. 'Are you very sick?'

'I'm not feeling so good,' Jacky said. 'I have this terrible headache. Can you get some water for me?'

'Of course,' I said. I turned to Louky and told him to get a cup of water for Jacky straight away. I told Jacky to lie down again while I fetched him some aspirin that I still had in my locker. When Jacky was settled down again I asked Judy to keep an eye on him for me as I had to go with Sister Luba to the kitchen, but by the time I reached the dining room she had already left with Iesy and Gerry. I did not mind at all as it was freezing outside. I went back to my bed as from there I could keep an eye on Jacky and watch what was happening outside.

The mountain of bodies was growing bigger every day. Food became scarcer. Our SS benefactor, Maximillian, had been able to get us a few large sacks of flour, which were delivered during the night. Sister Hella, Maria and the Witch had been cooking little dumplings during the night so they would not be discovered by the SS. This had become our only source of food during the past few days. The difficulty was keeping the stove in the dining room going so they could heat the water to boil the flour balls. All the beds in the dormitory were already minus one or two wooden slats, as this was our only source of fuel for the stove. The pan previously used as a toilet had been scrubbed clean and was now used to cook the dumplings. We did not care, nor did anyone think it wrong, that we used the pan as we needed it in order to eat.

I decided to have another look at Jacky, so I climbed down from my bed and walked towards him. Louky was standing near Jacky's bed and he moved to let me pass.

At that particular moment we heard a great tumult in the dining room. Everyone in the dormitory froze, fearing danger. The door to the dormitory was flung open and in stormed Rau, the Arbeitsführer. His face was contorted and he was foaming at the mouth. He was yelling, 'Criminals! Pigs!' and he started to hit out at us with a rubber truncheon. With his arm raised above his head he looked me straight in the eyes as he rained down the lashes. In his anger he missed me but poor Louky got it right on the top of his head. I could hear Louky's breath escaping as he reeled under the brutal onslaught. Terror reigned in our dormitory but then it was over just as suddenly as it had started. Rau had left. We could hear him screaming down the corridor as he was leaving the barracks. For a few seconds no one spoke as we were still terrified. I turned to Louky and asked if he was all right. He looked very pale but managed a weak smile to reassure me that he was okay. I called Iesy over to take care of Louky as I wanted to go to the dining room to find out what had happened there.

The dining room was in chaos. Tables and chairs had been overturned and the stove was burning with its door wide open with parts of the wooden bed planks poking out. In the corner of the room Sister Hella was lying on her bed with her mother, the Witch, attending her. Hella was a terrible sight. She had big blue swellings near her eyes and her upper arms were covered with weals and bruises, as she had raised her arms to protect her head from the brutal bashing she had received from Rau. Maria, who had received a few blows, was in a much better condition and she was able to tell me what had brought on the wrath of Rau.

Sister Hella had been at the stove pushing down the planks of wood into the fire when Rau had entered the dining room. There had been no warning of his coming, so he had surprised Sister Hella in the act. We had no tools with which to cut the bed planks into smaller pieces so we had to burn them in their full lengths, pushing them down as they burned up at the bottom.

The sight of burning 'German property' had outraged Rau, prompting his frenzied attack. But Rau never needed much excuse for such behaviour. He was feared right through the camp for his cruelty towards the prisoners. Thank God there had only been the three of them in the dining room: Sister Hella, her mother and Maria. I returned to the dormitory to find everyone recovering from the shock. Jacky appeared to have slept right through all the commotion. He felt very hot so I placed a wet flannel on his forehead to help ease the fever.

I had no idea at the time that Jacky was sick with typhus. As the days went by, more and more of our children, including myself, came down with this grim disease brought about by the lice and bedbugs which attacked us during the night. You could not see the bedbugs during the day but at night they bit us, so we woke the next morning with angry, red, itching weals all over our faces and bodies. I looked at the children and their unwashed hair and faces. I decided to do something about it and told them to go and wash their faces and hands and to meet me at the entrance of the corridor so I could inspect their hair for lice. I told someone to bring a chair, and I got my mother's dressmakers' scissors from my locker, a comb and the nit comb.

I started with the boys. Their hair was nearly shoulder-length by now. I snipped away and became more adept at what I was doing as the hours went by. After I had shortened their hair considerably, I pulled the nit comb through it. The boys were reasonably clean.

Not many had lice in their hair, but when I started on the girls later in the afternoon it was a different story. The little girls were not too bad. They slept in a different part of the dormitory from the older girls. I was getting very tired so when the little girls were done I called it a day.

The next morning I continued with the older girls. First I did Phoebe. I cut her hair and then inspected her head for lice. Phoebe shared my bed and I was pleased to find only a few in her hair. I removed these with the nit comb and then killed by squashing them between my finger and thumb nails. I delighted in the sound of the 'click' telling me they were dead. Little did I know that by doing this I was endangering my life!

That morning I shortened the hair of most of the girls, until I came to Bella. Bella had thick shoulder-length black hair and before I even touched it, I could see the nits stuck on the outside layer of it – the lice were nearly walking away with her. I asked Bella if her head felt itchy?

'Yes,' she said, 'but what can I do?'

'To start with, you can wash it under the tap outside,' I told her.

'Brrr,' Bella said. 'Too cold.'

I had to agree with her. I told her to sit still and I would see if I could help her. I pulled the nit comb through her hair and the result was terrible. The entire comb was covered in lice from small to large ones. I gave up any attempt to kill them but shook them off the comb onto the floor. Once the lice hit the floor they scattered in all directions, so I and some other girls nearby tried to stamp on them with our shoes. I was wrong to shake them off the comb, but although I had seen a lot of lice in the camp, the multitude in Bella's hair revolted me to the extent of throwing up.

I told Bella that I could not do it. Bella, who was a very casual, easy-going girl shrugged her shoulders, indicating she was not offended.

At that moment Bram, Bella's brother, entered the barracks, which was a convenient diversion. Bella got up from the chair and went to her bed to retrieve the slice of bread which Leni had not wanted to eat that morning. She had saved it for Bram. The brother and sister were very close, and each was always there for the other when needed.

I called a halt to being a hairdresser and went in search of Sister Hermina. I found her in the dining room talking to Sister Hella, who was slowly recovering from the beating she had received from Rau. Her eyes were not as swollen any more and she managed a wan smile for me. I told Sister Hermina about the condition of Bella's hair and the lice which infested most of us. I urged her to do something about it. Sister Hermina said she would tell Sister Luba to see what could be done. True to her word, two days later four large containers with a gooey yellow ointment arrived, and we were told to smother our hair with it of a night.

It was a revolting remedy but it had to be done. Everybody smeared their head with the gooey stuff that night except for those who were already very sick. Jacky had been one of the first to contract typhus, but over the past few days a few more children had taken to their beds. We also smeared some of the ointment over the joints in the bed frames in an attempt to kill the bedbugs, which gave us no peace at night. The boys grimaced as the gooey mass penetrated their hair. The girls looked disgusted, piling their hair on top of their heads to avoid contact with the messy stuff on their skin or neck. The older children helped the little ones until we all looked like yellow circus clowns. That night we were in bed later than usual but finally quiet returned and everybody drifted off to sleep.

Ten

'The English are coming!'

One late-March night, just as the lights were about to be turned out, Sister Mala climbed on a stool so that she stood out above the dormitory beds. She requested silence. When it became quiet she told us that the British army was getting nearer and was only about a hundred kilometres away from Belsen. We could not believe it. Someone asked her how she knew this. She told us that they had a clandestine radio in the men's camp and that this was how they had received the information. My God! Could it be true? Could we possibly be free soon? We all talked at once, but Sister Mala warned us to be quiet because the SS were getting very jumpy.

During the past few weeks we had had many air-raid warnings as English reconnaissance planes had flown over the camp. The SS had given strict instructions not to show any lights during the night, and we were warned that they would shoot anyone who did not comply. We blacked out our windows with a few blankets every night so that Sister Helen could burn a candle. She needed the light as quite a few children were seriously ill with typhus.

The SS started to patrol the camp at night. The air reconnaissance increased as the front line came nearer. At times we could hear the thunder of cannons; it was like music to our ears. Every night Sister Mala reported to us how close the freedom forces were.

'Children,' she would say, 'seventy kilometres,' and the next night, 'sixty kilometres.'

For us, it could not be soon enough. The condition of the camp deteriorated by the day. Food was so scarce that the prisoners looked for every green leaf on trees or grass blades on the ground. People died where they stood. No one cleared the bodies away.

It was 30 March 1945. Sister Luba was exhausted and Sister Hermina took over the task of going to the kitchen to beg for food. She asked me to go with her, and we set off on the long road towards the kitchen. Snow had fallen during the night and the entire camp was covered under a thick blanket of new snow. Our footsteps made no sound. The sky was lead-grey. The air was crisp and it was very still. After about an hour we arrived at the kitchen where Sister Hermina had a long conversation with a Polish man. I could not follow what they talked about, but when we left Sister Hermina told me that she could return later in the afternoon to pick up some containers of food for the children's house. This was good news and I chatted happily with Sister Hermina, whom I loved very much.

We were walking through a lovely wooded area as we neared the gate of the women's camp when I noticed some dark spots in the snow. On closer scrutiny I realised that they were beautiful large potatoes. I shook my hand loose from Sister Hermina, who had been holding it snugly in hers in her coat pocket, and darted towards the half-buried potatoes. With a cry of joy I started to pick up the potatoes from the ground. One, two, three I had in my hands already. While I was bending down to pick up some more, a dark shadow fell over the pristine snow and a shiny pair of black boots came into my line of vision.

When I slowly straightened up with the potatoes still in my hands, I was standing face to face with the notorious female guard Irma Grese. My blood turned to ice and my heart began pounding.

'Well?' she said, demanding an explanation.

Before I could answer her Sister Hermina said, 'Please, the little girl was not stealing. She thought it was a shame to leave good food lying in the snow and she picked it up for the children.'

For a moment Grese looked into my eyes as if to ascertain whether Sister Hermina was telling the truth, then to my complete surprise she said, 'All right, you can pick a few more.'

I could not believe what I heard and made no move to pick up more potatoes.

'You are allowed to pick up some more potatoes,' Sister Hermina said.

I did not trust Grese and, expecting to get a hiding, I bent down and picked up two more potatoes. Sister Hermina prompted me to thank her. I looked up to the woman who had my fate in her hands and said, 'Thank you very much, Frau Hauptaufseherin.'

She nodded, indicating that we were allowed to leave.

I had picked up six potatoes in total and had dropped them into my pockets. They were very heavy and I could only walk slowly. My legs started to ache from my ankles to my calves. I told Sister Hermina and she took four of the potatoes from me and put them in her coat pocket. With less weight to carry, I tried to walk faster but could not. My feet were dragging and I developed a terrible headache. I could not understand what was wrong with me. Sister Hermina was walking in front of me, urging me to hurry, but I could not.

At long last we arrived at the barracks. I went straight to my bed and somehow managed to climb up. Thank God I still had some aspirins left, and after a little girl brought me a cup of water I took one. With unsteady hands I took off my jumper and slacks and found a flannel pyjama top of my mother's in my locker which I put on. It was much too large for me, but who cared? By now I was shaking uncontrollably, and I realised I had a high fever. I crawled under the blanket and made myself lie deathly still in an attempt to ease the headache. After a while it seemed to be a little easier and I noticed that Max had also taken to his bed.

It appeared that the news of my illness had spread quickly, as a steady stream of children came to my bed to ask how I was feeling. This was a blessing as they were able to bring me cups of water when I craved them. Max was complaining about his headache and I struggled to the foot end of my bed so I could get to my locker. I got out an aspirin for Max and handed it across to him. Someone got him some water and after a while I could see Max dozing off in an uneasy sleep. Thank God, Jacky was much better and he was sitting up in bed.

The fever took hold of me again. My whole body ached and my legs felt like lead. The hours must have gone by without me knowing as Phoebe climbed onto our bed to get ready to sleep. The slightest movement she made disturbed my feverish slumber. I asked Phoebe to move away from my body as much as possible and to sleep on the edge of the bed.

Phoebe and I had been sharing the bed for nearly three months now. We slept head to tail, and up until now we had not had any problems as we were both small girls and had derived body heat from each other during the freezing nights. But now the slightest movement Phoebe made disturbed me. I had a very restless night with the fever raging through my body.

Just before the light went out that night Sister Luba had come to my bed and laid a cool hand on my burning forehead. She looked very worried and put a wet flannel on my forehead to cool it down.

Phoebe woke up early and brought me some water. The water was very cold so I managed only a few sips. The rest of the water was used to wet the face washer to cool my head. Someone brought me an extra pillow to raise my head. The headaches were awful and I dared not move a muscle. I had learned before I became sick that the first four days were the worst and, if you survived, the fever would break on the tenth day, after which red spots would cover your arms, legs and stomach. I lay on my back with my arms resting against my thighs. My legs were aching so much I could not move them. Now and then I opened my eyes a little. My vision was so blurred that I closed them again. The light was hurting my eyes as well.

The day passed slowly although I had no idea of the time. It must have been night as Phoebe had come back to bed. Her climbing onto the bed had awakened me, but then when she crawled under the blanket she moved so abruptly that my body could not cope. I asked her to lie still. Phoebe, who was not sick, tried not to move, but a healthy body turns regularly while sleeping. So when she turned again, sick as I was, I lost my temper, raised my voice and told her to lie still. Leni, whose bed was directly behind mine, called out and told Phoebe to come and sleep in her bed so I could rest properly. Phoebe groped in the dark and slowly crawled past my head into Leni's bed. What a relief it

233

was to lie undisturbed and very still. I dozed off and must have lost all track of time.

The headache was so bad at times that it seemed as if I was in a black well. It used to become so quiet in my head that I heard nothing at all. I knew only that I was still alive. When I came back from the darkness I could hear snatches of conversation. One conversation I clearly understood was when Sister Helen said, 'They have closed down the water again, the hellish bastards.'

During the long hours when the fever took hold of my body and mind, someone had given me sips of water and renewed the flannel with cold fresh water, but after a few minutes the flannel became hot so I pulled it off. The weight of the small cloth on my forehead was too much for me. I had no idea how many days I had been sick when the voice of Sister Luba told me to wake up. Slowly, my head cleared a bit and with an effort I opened my eyes. I did not feel well. But Sister Luba insisted.

'Hetty, wake up. The doctor has come to see you,' she said.

I opened my eyes for a second or two and vaguely saw Sister Luba and Doctor Bimko standing near my bed. I closed my eyes again, drifting away.

'Open your mouth, Hetty. I am going to give you some grape sugar that the doctor has brought for us,' Sister Luba said.

I opened my mouth and felt a spoonful of a very fine, cold substance.

'Swallow it,' Sister Luba coaxed.

I made an effort to get the substance down my parched throat.

'Here, have a sip of water,' she said, supporting my head as she held the cup to my mouth.

The cold water helped me to swallow, but I was relieved when she lowered my head onto the pillow again. With my eyes closed I could hear her and the doctor go to Max, and to all the other children in the dormitory who were sick. The next night and the following night all the sick children received another spoonful of grape sugar in an attempt to give us some energy to fight this dreadful disease.

I had no idea how many days had gone by but one morning I woke up and realised that the fever had left my body. I slowly raised my right arm and noticed the telltale red spots of typhus on it. I inspected my left arm and found the red spots there as well. I looked across at Max and asked how he was doing.

'I've still got a slight headache,' he said, 'but it's much better than before.'

I looked at the bed below Max's and saw Robby looking up at me with feverish eyes.

'Give Robby some water and then please climb onto my bed and go into my locker to find some aspirins for Max and Robby,' I said to a child who had come in with a beaker of water.

The aspirins were found and when I was satisfied that Robby and Max had been looked after, I turned onto my side facing the window and fell into a deep, healing sleep.

I must have slept the whole day despite the horrific noise and screaming I heard outside my window in my sleep. Even in my sleep I realised that the water had been turned back on and that the women out there were parched from thirst, but nothing could rouse me. I woke up to hear a little voice calling my name. I slowly opened my eyes and saw Judy and her sister Mickey looking up at me.

'Do you feel a little better now?' Judy asked.

'Yes, Judy, a little bit.'

They both smiled happily at my answer.

'Judy,' I continued, can you get me a beaker of hot water? I have to have a cup of tea.'

Judy and Mickey left for the dining room where I knew the Witch would have a pot of water on the stove. I dozed off again for what seemed a long time before Judy and Mickey returned. I struggled up onto my elbows. It was quite an effort and the first time I had raised my head since I became ill. Judy handed me the beaker of hot water, letting it rest on my mattress. I asked her to take out my small tea tin from my locker and to open it, as I did not have the strength to do it. Judy opened the tin, I put my fingers in, withdrew a small amount of tea and dropped it in the beaker of hot water. I brought the beaker of hot tea slowly towards my lips and carefully took a small sip. When the warm tea ran down my throat it felt so good. It was the first warm drink I had had in many days.

Max watched me from his bed opposite and said in a weak voice, 'What are you drinking, Hetty?'

'I'm having some tea. Would you like some?' I answered.

'Yes,' Max said.

I took a few more sips and then handed the beaker to Judy so she could give it to Max.

Little Robby, whose bed was below Max's, looked up at me with longing in his eyes.

'Would you also like some tea, Robby?' I asked.

He nodded, so I told Max to leave some for him. Max complained that he wanted more tea.

'Okay,' I said, 'give a bit to Robby and we can make some more.'

So when Robby had drunk the last of the tea, Judy and Mickey left to get some more hot water. I sank back down on my bed totally exhausted. The tea party had taken every little bit of energy I had. For the first time I became fully aware of what took place around me. I looked out of the window and saw a group of prisoners pushing a cart piled with dead bodies in the direction of the crematorium. It looked like it was icy-cold outside. The SS guard had a white band around his left arm. He was rugged up for the cold and he had lifted the collar of his coat to protect his ears. But the poor prisoners! How frightful they looked. Skin over bone, they wore only cotton prison pyjamas and they had to do this gruesome job. The pace was slow but, to my surprise, the Scharführer was uninterested and did not push the men to hurry. The men were too frail to push the cart any faster anyway, and they had to keep stopping every few metres to catch their breath. It was a truly macabre sight.

Sister Hella stood next to my bed. Her whole face was smiling, she was so happy that I was on the way to recovery. Beside her stood Judy and Mickey.

'How are you, my Hettylein?' Sister Hella asked. 'I am so glad you are out of danger, and Max too,' she said, turning towards him.

She walked over to Max and kissed him, and then shook up his pillows so he would be comfortable.

Judy, who had been holding the second beaker of hot water, moved closer and handed it to me. She climbed onto my bed and retrieved the little blue tin with the small amount of tea inside. She opened it and held it out towards me so I could take out a fingertip of tea and drop it into the hot water. I took a few sips before I allowed Judy to hand the beaker of tea to Max. For the first time I felt some strength returning. Max was clearly enjoying the drink, again leaving some for Robby, which Sister Hella gave to him.

After the last drop of tea was consumed, Sister Hella told me that all the SS guards had the white bands around their arms as the English army was very close and the SS guards would surrender. Everybody was waiting apprehensively for what would happen in the next few days. Sister Hella told me that a few days ago male prisoners had dug a huge hole in front of the sick bay barracks further up the road and that is where the cartload of bodies was being taken – to a mass grave.

I looked outside. A slushy snow was falling and daylight was fading fast.

'What time is it?' I asked.

'About six o'clock,' someone told me.

Six o'clock and the prisoners were still pushing the cart with bodies! When would they be able to go back to their barracks?

Someone brought me a small, flat piece of hard-baked flour. It looked like a biscuit but besides being rock-hard, the taste was indescribable as the flour was only half-cooked. It had been cooked and dried on top of the stove in the dining room. There was nothing else to eat. I was told that this had been the only food available for four days and that water was hard to get as well. It had been off again for two days. Still, the ghastly conditions could not dampen the pervasive feeling of expectation.

We could hear hurried footsteps in the corridor. Silence fell in our dormitory. The footsteps went past our door towards the dining room. We started to speak again as no danger seemed imminent, but then our door opened and Sister Hermina entered with a messenger from Frau Stania. It became quiet again and

Sister Hermina told us that our camp would be inspected by the English army the next day. The order from the Commandant was that no one was allowed outside the barracks tomorrow. We were to observe absolute silence during the inspection. Anyone disobeying this order would be shot.

The messenger left after delivering this order, but Sister Hermina remained and repeated the order so that we all understood the seriousness of it. It was time to go to sleep. Most of our children were still extremely sick, though some of us were on the way to recovery. We did not talk much that night as we were all busy with our own thoughts. I asked myself if it really was true that freedom was so close. I was very tired by now and wanted to go to sleep. As I turned my face towards the window I saw that the prisoners were still moving a cart with dead bodies by the light of a kerosene lamp.

The next morning those who were well enough were up early. You could feel the tension, but we still had some hours to wait before the kapo posted outside our barracks screamed the order to be mouse-still. Everybody in the dormitory froze. Not a sound was heard. For a few minutes the silence continued, but then we could hear heavy footsteps approaching. I held my breath, looked out of the window and there they were.

Two SS guards with drawn bayonets marched quickly on either side of a young English soldier carrying a small white flag, who proudly held his head up high. The SS guards were looking very grim. The English soldier looked straight ahead but now and then his eyes darted over the mountain of dead bodies. The small group passed our barracks very quickly and as I saw them disappear into the distance I wanted to call the English soldier back to give me reassurance that freedom was just around the corner.

As soon as the inspection was over, everybody in the dormitory started to talk at once. Iesy, who had recovered earlier, made an effort to walk over to my bed. He was still very weak and had found a stick to support himself. He lifted his head towards me. His deeply sunken eyes with dark lines around emitted a burning light of happiness and hope.

'Hetty, get well soon, as it will not be long now and we will be free again.' He laughed as only Iesy could laugh when he was sure of something.

I could only nod my head.

Max had not been able to see the inspection party from his bed as he was not near the window.

'What did he look like?' he asked, meaning the English soldier.

'He looked good to me,' Iesy said.

'I liked his nose which he so proudly stuck in the air,' I added.

Everybody who was listening laughed.

Sister Luba entered the dormitory and requested our attention. When we quietened down, she told us that no one was allowed to leave the compound. When Sister Luba's mouth was set in a straight line, she was demanding unquestioning obedience. The happy mood disappeared as we realised that we were still vulnerable.

Before she left, Sister Luba came to my bed to see how I was recovering. She also looked at Max and Robby and the children in the far corner who were still very ill.

Quiet returned to the dormitory when the children who were not sick left to play outside. You could hear their excited voices, just like normal children at play. Max and Robby had dozed off again, and Iesy had climbed up to his bed to have some rest. I was wide awake but lay very still. The happenings of the morning seemed to have drained the little strength I had. I looked out of the window only to see the mountain of dead bodies, but today there were no prisoners clearing them.

It was as if time stood still. Nothing moved outside. There were only the grey skies and dead bodies. I closed my eyes and in my mind I could see the English soldier with the fierce-looking SS guards. The brief glimpse of them as they marched past my window would be etched into my memory for the rest of my life.

During the day someone brought me the dry flour cookies, but I refused them as I did not have the strength to chew them. So I ate nothing. I was past the stage of feeling hunger. I just wanted to lie in bed and rest. I did not realise how thin I had become and how weak I really was. As usual, some of the children came to my bed now and then to see how I was and to get anything I wanted, such as a cup of water or the potty. They helped me and held me up if I needed the potty, and not even an experienced nurse could have given me better help than the willing hands of the nine- and ten-year-old girls.

Night set in, bringing sleep, and with sleep came forgetfulness and healing for the sick.

Saturday 14 April 1945 dawned and the camp telegraph informed us that the SS guards had already been replaced with Hungarian soldiers in the watchtowers. The camp itself was very quiet. It was as if everything was in a haze, unreal, waiting for things to happen. I was sleeping a few hours at times, nature's way of making me better. As night approached Sister Luba came to my bed and asked if I was well enough to get out of bed and walk. I did not know, as I had not been able to get up before.

'Why?' I asked. 'What's wrong?'

Sister Luba whispered that Maximillian had sent a message that the gate near the crematorium was unlocked and that he would send two trucks to get the children out at midnight, as the SS had laid explosives around the camp to blow it up after the prisoners had been given poisoned bread. Perhaps it was the lethargy which sets in after a terrible illness, I don't know, but I told Sister Luba I did not want to go because I did not have the strength. Sister Luba surveyed the room with so many sick children and decided to abandon the escape plan. She kissed my cheek and told me to sleep.

When Sister Luba left, Max wanted to know what we had been whispering about. I told him, 'Nothing, really.' He did not believe me but refrained from asking further questions.

'I think I'll get up tomorrow,' he said.

'Are you sure you're up to it?' I asked.

'I'll try,' Max said. 'I'll use a stick just like Iesy.'

Sister Mala told us to be quiet and go to sleep. She turned out the light but I could not sleep. The night was not peaceful. I could hear machine guns firing in the distance and wild screams. Sister Mala doused the candle she usually kept burning to allow her to see a sick child when needed. She did not wish to attract attention to us during the shooting. I tried to look through the window but it was pitch-black outside. I was so scared that I pulled the blanket over my head as if to ward off evil.

I must have slept, as I woke to the noise of some of the other children. What a relief – daylight. Max had realised his plans to get out of bed. He was up and about, talking to Leni. When he saw that I was awake, he stumbled over to me, holding on to the bunks to prevent himself from toppling over. I told him to sit on Robby's bed so he could get the weight off his feet for a while. Max sat at Robby's feet and looked up at me.

'How are you today?' he asked.

'I'm not strong enough to get up yet,' I answered.

'Maybe you will be tomorrow,' Max said optimistically.

Iesy also came over and asked how I was.

'Did you hear?' Iesy asked.

'What?'

'That gun firing during the night,' Iesy continued. 'They were those Hungarian guards. They shot dead four hundred people last night. They wanted to go over the fence.'

'How horrible. Is that what all the screaming was about?' I asked Iesy.

'Yes,' he said.

We were stunned at the news.

'Why did the prisoners do it when the English are so close?' I queried.

'Yes, why?' Iesy said. 'They must have lost their minds at the last moment,' he concluded.

Max got up and asked Iesy to walk with him to the dining room to see what was happening there. Robby told me he wanted to get up as well, so I called Judy and Phoebe who were nearby and told them to dress Robby warmly. How thin he looked when he emerged from under the blanket. His clothing was too big for him but I was happy to see him on his feet again. Judy took Robby for a walk.

When they left, little Yiddele came shyly towards me. This little three-year-old boy had arrived in our barracks with a Polish and

Romanian group of children a few weeks before. They were well fed and healthy. I could not converse with Yiddele as I could not speak his language, but before I became ill he had attached himself to me.

'Hello Yiddele,' I said. 'It's good to see you. How are you, darling?'

Yiddele looked up at me with big eyes. I had no idea whether he understood me. He was either happy to be close to me again or he was lonely. He never moved from my bed. After a while I told Phoebe to bring a Polish girl to speak to him. The Polish girl came and with sign language I asked her to speak to Yiddele. She bent down and spoke Polish to him, but he looked at her the same way he looked at me and did not speak. After a while the Polish girl gave up. She looked at me and shrugged her shoulders as if to say, 'I cannot help,' and left.

The camp telegraph informed us that the previous night at midnight most of the SS had left the camp. Frau Stania, the camp elder, and many prominents and kapos had gone with them.

It was my mother's birthday, 15 April 1945, and my thoughts lingered on her. Where was she now? I prayed that she would be all right.

The dormitory was very crowded. A lot of children had recovered or were on the way to recovering from typhus, but most of them were not strong enough to venture outside. They chatted among themselves and a feeling of happy expectation prevailed.

It was way past lunchtime but there was nothing to eat. We had had nothing for breakfast either but no one thought about food. An electric feeling was in the air.

It was half past three. I was lying back on my pillow. The excitement had tired me out completely.

'Hetty, Hetty,' I heard.

I lifted my head and I could see Inge trying to get past a group of children. Inge was the Dutchwoman of German origin who, with her friend Gretel, had written Sister Luba's birthday poem for me.

'Oh, Inge. How good it is to see you again. Where have you been all this time?' I said.

'I have been very sick but I wanted to see you so much I had to come.'

I looked at Inge. She still looked sick and she was very thin.

'Come, Inge,' I said, 'sit on my bed. Here, use the stool.'

Inge climbed onto the stool with difficulty and between us we managed to get her onto my bed. After we both got our breath back, Inge asked, 'Are you all right, Hetty? You still look very sick.'

'I'm fine,' I said. 'Just a bit weak still.'

Before Inge could say anything else, there was a loud disturbance in the corridor. A woman was screaming hysterically in Polish. Silence fell in the dormitory. Then the door flew open and someone shouted, 'The English are here, the English are here!'

For a moment, no one moved, but then everybody who could walk left the barracks and ran as fast as they could towards the fence to see our liberators.

I was sitting on my bed unable to move. My heart was pounding. I would have given anything to be with them, running towards the fence. I looked out of the window and saw that our group had disappeared out of sight already. Only Iesy was still visible, struggling on, leaning on his stick and behind him, as quickly as his little legs could carry him, came Yiddele.

The sight of Iesy struggling through a field of dead bodies and little Yiddele following him brought tears to my eyes, and as I turned towards Inge the realisation that we were free hit me. 'We are free, Inge. We are free,' I cried out.

We were both crying as we embraced each other, rocking to and fro. Freedom! Freedom! At long, long last we were free again.

After a few hours most of the children who had run towards the fence returned to our dormitory and told us of the events which had taken place when our liberators had entered the camp. They told us that tanks had come up the main road and an announcement was made over a loudspeaker telling us that we were free. They also told us that English soldiers had immediately taken control over the kitchens, as there was a rumour going around that the SS was cooking poisoned food for us and, therefore, the kettles had to be cleaned out first and tomorrow there would be food. How they found out all this information no one asked, as we really did not care. We were free and the future looked good again.

After promising to return soon, Inge left at about five o'clock to see what was happening in the camp and to find Gretel.

It was getting dark when Max entered the dormitory. He proudly showed me two pairs of woollen socks and a jumper.

'How did you get them?' I asked.

'The prisoners raided the storeroom,' he said 'and I went in and helped myself.'

I looked at him and realised that he had gone to the far end of the camp. Where in the world did he get this strength from? He had only got up that morning and walked with the aid of a stick, and yet he had run to the fence and, by the sound of it, he had walked a great distance. He was much stronger than I was. I could not even attempt getting out of bed, let alone walking. Typhus must have affected me more than some of the other children.

That night there were no restrictions on bedtime and the sisters left us to our own devices. Nobody thought of food. Adrenalin kept us going. But in the end, exhaustion took hold. The little ones were put to bed by the older children as I gave out orders from the top of my bed. At long last sleep set in and peace reigned in our dormitory.

Early the next morning there was an exodus from our barracks. All the boys left to find food and to make contact with our liberators again. The little ones stayed behind and played in the compound. During the morning Sister Luba and Sister Hermina came in to see how we were recovering. They did not stay for long as they wanted to go to the kitchen to find something for us to eat. We had had nothing to eat for two days. Tea had arrived early in the morning and the beaker of hot, sweet liquid had tasted, as my Uncle Max used to say, 'as if an angel landed on your tongue'. You could feel the healing effect as the warmth descended into your empty stomach.

My recovery was slower than some of the others and I was content to lie in my bed in the now quiet dormitory. It must have been about midday when I had my first visit from our liberators. Surrounded by some of our children he came to my bed and introduced himself as Reverend Ted Aplin, a priest from Canada. Communication was difficult as I did not speak English. He asked me if I was okay.

I could understand 'okay' and nodded. The priest then asked me something about Leni. I could not answer him and the reason that I knew he was talking about Leni was because he was pointing at her.

'That's Leni,' I told him.

He studied Leni and I could see the pity in his eyes. Our Leni looked so frail. She was only skin and bones. A photographer came in and the priest told him to take a picture of Leni. Jacky, who was sitting on the lower bunk, craned his neck so he would be in the picture as well. After taking some more pictures the priest and the photographer left. The children who had come in with the priest to see what was happening also left the dormitory to play outside. The weather was mild and the sky its usual grey.

About an hour later, a very excited Max came in, and with him was a tall English soldier wearing a purple beret (the sign of the Parachute Division, I was told later). They came straight to my bed and Max said, 'Hetty, this is Max Monash and he is a cousin of our Dad.'

'Really?' I asked the smiling soldier, who had a black moustache and warm brown eyes.

'Yes,' he said, 'I believe so. Your father is Maurice, is he not?'

I nodded. My eyes scanned his face, failing to find a family resemblance. Max Monash asked me many questions about my father and if I knew of the whereabouts of different family members. I could only tell him that I did not know what had happened to them. After about a half an hour Max Monash left with Iesy and Max. He promised to come back the next day. Before he left he gave me a large block of chocolate, which I shared with some of the children.

When the dormitory became quiet again, I realised that what had impressed me most was the healthy outdoor look Max Monash had. He looked so clean, and through the open neck of his shirt I had glimpsed his name tag, as well as a golden Chai.*

I wish I was strong enough to get up, I thought. There seemed to be all sort of things happening outside the barracks.

---

*a Chai is a letter from the Hebrew alphabet, and means 'life'. A Chai made from gold is given to newborn babies as it is supposed to protect them from harm. Many men still wear it as adults.

As promised, Max Monash returned the next day. With him came a few people from the Red Cross. Among them were a young Dutchman called Jaap Ebeling Koning and a pretty Dutch nurse. All the others were English. Jaap's charismatic appeal resulted in a group of children gathering around him. They touched him to make sure he was real and asked him a thousand questions at once. Jaap was wonderful with the children and gave them all a block of chocolate with the warning not to eat it all at once.

After a while Jaap told the healthy children to go and play outside as the sick children in the dormitory needed quiet and rest. Jaap then came over to my bed to ask how I was getting on.

What a kind and wonderful person Jaap was. He was about twenty-one years old and had joined the Red Cross when the south of Holland was liberated. He had a lovely smile that instantly told you that he could be trusted. Jaap stayed on longer than the others. The living conditions in our barracks had not improved and the smell of sickness and unwashed bodies must have been nauseating, but he did not care and his happy smile lifted our spirits.

Tuesday 17 April 1945 started with more tumult. It was a beautiful day. The windows of the dormitory were wide open so the warm, fresh air could enter. In the early hours of the morning trucks laden with dead bodies drove past our barracks. Some SS men could be seen sitting on top of the bodies. The truck was heading towards the mass grave near the crematorium. While this was happening a huge bulldozer arrived and started to dig a second mass grave just in front of my window. A group of about forty Hungarian soldiers marched up to the front of our barracks and were told to line up in two rows. An English officer conducted what appeared to be a roll-call, as one by one Hungarian soldiers would step forward and call out. I had no idea what it meant, but this went on for about an hour until they were marched away towards the morgue.

When the hole for the mass grave was large enough, a truck arrived with decomposed bodies. Six SS men were sitting among the corpses. They were told to unload the truck and put the bodies into the mass grave. The English guards were tense and furious after seeing the atrocities that had been committed by the Germans. If an SS man did not move fast enough or dropped an arm onto the ground while carrying a corpse, they would lash out at them with the butt of their rifles and tell them, 'Take care, boy, take care.' The SS showed signs of being under pressure. Their previously spotless uniforms were dirty and in disarray.

One SS man still had his cap on, which made an English soldier posted just in front of my window so furious that, with a swipe of his rifle narrowly missing the man's head, he removed the cap. It spiralled into the air, landing on my windowsill. On seeing the result of his action, the English soldier ran towards my window and, after saluting me, removed the cap with the end of his rifle.

Throughout the day, the SS brought the slimy and decomposed bodies to the mass grave. These SS officers, who had always stayed at a safe distance from the macabre mess so they would not contaminate themselves, were now standing knee-deep among the foul-smelling, decaying corpses.

I only witnessed the burial, but was later told that at the morgue where the bodies were loaded onto the trucks, the English soldiers occasionally gave the SS a good hiding for not handling the corpses with more respect.

A woman prisoner spotted Dr Fritz Klein among the SS group. She called out to him, 'Dr Klein, how does it feel to be at the other end of the stick?'

'Wait. One day you will come back to me in Auschwitz,' he answered.

That fanatical beast would not accept defeat.

Dr Klein had been in charge of the Experimental Barracks in Auschwitz where he used prisoners as human guinea pigs. He had also been responsible for deciding which prisoners were still fit enough for the work teams, as well as who would go to the gas chambers. He was later condemned to hang by the British Military Trial at Luneberg.

The next morning the burying of the dead continued, but the English did not hit the SS any more, by order of their superiors and the Geneva Convention. What a shame. The prisoners had enjoyed it.

It was mid-morning when Sister Luba came to see me. She had a small scrap of paper in her hand on which a message was written in German. Sister Luba told me that Maximillian (our SS bene-factor) was hiding in the toilet block close to our barracks. She needed civilian clothing for him so he would be able to get away.

'He has helped us and now we have to help him,' Sister Luba said.

I told Sister Luba that all I had was one of my father's shirts, and I went into my locker to find it. I soon located the shirt and gave it to Sister Luba. She went away and about ten minutes later I saw Maximillian walking through the corridor past the open door of the dormitory. For one second our eyes met as he furtively glanced inside. He looked dishevelled and dirty but most of all he looked terrified. How he had changed since the last time he was here.

Then he was a powerful and arrogant man who could decide over life and death. Now he was reduced to a miserable coward.

Sister Luba came back to speak to me again. She told me that Maximillian was hiding in the little room at the beginning of the corridor.

'Hetty, I want you to write a letter to the English telling them that without Maximillian's help we would have starved to death in the last month, and asking the liberators to be merciful to him.'

She handed me a piece of paper and a pencil. I did not want to do it, but she insisted. I was still very weak and not strong enough to resist. Furthermore, I usually did without questioning what Sister Luba wanted, so I sat up in bed and wrote in Dutch:

This man, by the name of Maximillian, has helped the children of the children's house with food during the past month, so please do not be too hard on him.

I signed it with my name and age. I explained to Sister Luba what I had written and handed her the paper, which she carefully folded, and then left.

As I was still confined to my bed, I had no idea what was happening in the corridor, but I thought about the fact that we were hiding the enemy right under the noses of our liberators, who were still directing the burial of thousands of bodies just outside the windows of our barracks. I was not happy about it but what could I do?

I felt very tired after all this upheaval and decided to have some rest. I turned my back to the window as seeing body after body being dumped one on top of the other in the huge grave was upsetting me. Since our liberators were being restrained from harassing them, the SS were not as careful any more. At times they would drag the body over the ground towards the grave instead of carrying it. Limbs came away from the corpses in advanced stages of decomposition and, at times, the body thrown into the grave was minus a head.

It all became too much for me. I was still very weak from the devastating illness, and I seemed to be taking much longer to recuperate and regain my strength than the other children. I could not remember if I had had anything to eat that day or, for that matter, the past few days. Everything was shrouded in a haze. So many things had happened. Come what may, I decided, tomorrow I would get up.

The dormitory was deserted during the day as the children played outside in the sun or went walkabout through the camp. Only Bella, Mala, Leni, Maurice and I were still in bed. Bella and Maurice were still pretty sick, although they had passed the crisis point. Mala and I were much better already. Surprisingly, despite being so weak and thin, Leni had not contracted typhus.

Inge came to see me again in the afternoon. I scolded her for having stayed away for so long. She had recovered so much that she climbed onto my bed unaided.

'Where in the world have you been, Inge?' I asked.

'Well,' Inge said, 'after I left you on Sunday I looked for Gretel in the SS pharmacy. Then I found out that Gretel had taken control of the roundhouse, which used to be the SS sleeping quarters. She has set up an improvised hospital and I have been helping her.'

'You are sleeping in the SS quarters?' I asked. I shuddered, contemplating it.

Seeing the terror in my eyes, Inge reassured me that all the SS were gone from the building.

'The SS have been locked up. They have all been arrested,' Inge told me.

I was not convinced and had this frightful feeling that they might come back any time.

'Don't be scared, Hetty,' Inge said, putting her arms around me. 'The SS are gone now. We are free.'

After a while I calmed down and accepted Inge's reassurances. She stayed with me for about two hours. We talked and talked, but then she had to leave to see Gretel and help her if needed. Reluctantly, I let her go. I hugged her and told her that the next day I would try to get up.

'Good,' Inge said, 'I'll see you again soon.'

She gave me a farewell kiss, slid down from my bunk and was on her way.

The following day I waited until the dormitory was nearly empty and then prepared to leave my bed. From the locker I took out my grey chequered skirt and my jumper, and dressed myself on top of my bed, the same way as I had done for the past seventeen months. When I was ready I carefully lowered myself from my bed onto the chair next to it. From there I could easily reach the floor while still holding on to my bunk for support. As I shakily stood on the floor, my skirt dropped around my ankles, and it was then that I realised that I had lost a lot of weight and that my skirt was miles too big for me. My coat was hanging on the end of my bed and I remembered that under the collar was a safety pin used to pin up my collar when the bitter wind was blowing during roll-call. I transferred the safety pin from my coat for its new use: to hold up my skirt. So far, so good.

I attempted to walk but my legs felt so rubbery I could hardly stand up. I moved my feet slowly, holding on to the bunks on either side of the walkway.

'Good, Hetty, I'm glad to see you up again,' Leni said, who had been watching my progress from her bed.

I smiled up at her as I slowly shuffled past. By now I had reached the door, and when I entered the corridor there was no one in sight. I turned towards the dining room, holding on to the wall for support. When I reached the end of the corridor, I peeped into the dining room, but it was deserted. Everybody was out. I decided to go into the toilet, which was partitioned off at the end of the corridor by a crude wooden door. There was no such thing as a water-closet, only a bucket with a wooden plank over it. Nevertheless, it meant privacy. I did not want to use the bucket, but instead sat down on the plank, and it was from this place that I prayed and thanked God for our freedom and asked him to look after my father and my mother, to keep them safe and bring them home again.

My emotions overtook me and hot tears fell down my cheeks. After a while I calmed down and dried my tears with the sleeve of my jumper. I sat for a few more minutes and when I left the toilet I closed the door firmly behind me.

Slowly I walked back along the dark corridor towards the open door and daylight. I wanted to get into the fresh air. As I neared the doorway an English soldier entered. For a moment he stood still, letting his eyes become accustomed to the darkness. He saw me and came towards me and asked in German, 'Are you Hetty?'

'Yes,' I answered.

'Good,' the soldier said. 'I want you to come with me. The

children have sent me. We asked them to sing for us but they won't do it without you.'

For a moment I hesitated. I still felt suspicious and fearful.

'Where are the children?' I asked.

Sensing my unease, the soldier smiled at me and said, 'You do not have to be scared, I'll take you to them. They are just a bit further up the road.'

He stuck out his hand to help me down the few steps into the compound, and I walked very slowly towards the gate. Seeing that I could not walk very well the soldier did not waste any more words. He lifted me in his arms and carried me down the road to where the children had gathered around an army jeep. He carefully sat me down on the end of the jeep.

The children soon crowded around me, and Max told me that the soldiers wanted us to sing for the radio but they had not been able to decide what to sing. After some deliberation, 'Ferdinand Was a Bull' was chosen. This was a song from the Dutch singing duo Johnny & Jones, who were sent to Auschwitz. And, of course, we would also sing 'Barracks Seventeen'.

After a few false starts and under the direction of two soldiers, the song was recorded. When the soldiers were satisfied with the recording, one of them asked me some questions in German and then suggested we record it. I told him that my German was very limited, but he said that was okay.

Most of the children had returned to the barracks by now and it had become quiet enough for my interview. The soldier who had carried me over was still there and he smiled encouragingly at me. The recorder was ready and the soldier asked the first question:

'What is your name?'

'Hetty Werkendam,' I answered.

'How old are you?' he asked.

'I am fifteen years old.'

The interview* continued; we did it twice to make sure it had come out all right. The soldiers thanked me and the one who had carried me earlier took me back to the barracks.

I was very happy about it all but little did I realise that this interview would be broadcast all over the world. I was later told that family and friends from as far away as Buenos Aires, Belgium, Holland and Sweden heard me speak on the radio, and this way the few family members who had been spared found out that I was still alive.

*see prologue for full interview.

Eleven

'Bang, bang, bang – finished!'

It was Saturday 21 April 1945, my father's birthday. The sun was shining brightly when early in the morning ambulances and trucks arrived to take us away to another place. Soldiers with Red Cross bands on their arms came into the dormitory and told us to leave everything behind. We could only come in the clothes we were wearing. They told us that this was to prevent the typhus from spreading. We panicked about where were we going.

The trauma from earlier evacuations were still fresh in our minds. Those who could walk and were okay went onto the trucks first, including Max and Jacky. I called out from the window for them to take me as well, but the truck moved on without me. I came down from my bed as quickly as I could, but I was still too weak to walk very far. When I stopped to catch my breath, a soldier lifted me in his arms and took me to the waiting ambulance. I looked around and saw that Leni and Maurice were already inside. Both were lying on a stretcher, and about ten other children were sitting on the floor.

All of a sudden I realised that I had left Robby inside. I made an attempt to leave the ambulance but was prevented from doing so by a Red Cross soldier. I begged him to find Robby for me. I was quite hysterical by now and kept calling for Robby at the top of my voice. Seeing my distress, the soldier told someone to go inside to find Robby for me. He also told the driver, who was most anxious to drive off with his load of sick children, to wait. After about five minutes the soldier who had gone in search of Robby returned with him and Yiddele as well. How happy I was to see the two little ones. They were lifted into the ambulance and they both snuggled up to me. How in the world could I forget about them? I scolded myself.

The ambulance started and we left this place of horrors. The ambulance had no back doors so we could see where we were going. Soon we left concentration camp Bergen-Belsen behind and were driving on a bitumen road. After a very short drive we entered what we were later told was a recuperation camp for German officers.

On first impression, it looked like well-kept red-brick two-storey buildings with gardens and lawn areas. Our ambulance stopped in front of a building that appeared to be a garage. Soldiers and nurses helped us out of the ambulance and took us into the garage which had sunlight streaming through its high windows. I was lifted onto a table where a doctor examined me. My weight was recorded as thirty-four kilograms. I was then told to stand still and a soldier came forward with what appeared to be a vacuum cleaner. The nurse held the hose under my skirt while the soldier puffed a cloud of grey powder. The process was repeated in the front and back of my jumper, and my hair got a dosing of this strange-smelling powder (DDT) as well. I stood there in the grey haze until the nurse guided me outside where I was glad to breathe clean air again.

Outside were long tables with lots and lots of clothing in every size and colour, and everybody could pick out clean things to wear. Near the tables I saw the woman with that lovely baby who had lived opposite the corridor in our barracks. She was wearing the beautiful Hungarian skirt which Sister Luba had given me before I got sick with typhus.

It was then that I realised that I had forgotten to take my mementoes from my locker: Herman's Swann pen, his watch with his photograph on the dial face. I had left them all behind in the panic to get into the ambulance to follow Max and Jacky. I was so upset that I started to cry. Tears were never far away lately. Sister Luba, who had come on an earlier truck, asked what was the matter. Through my tears I told her.

'Come,' Sister Luba said, 'our new house is about a hundred metres from here.'

She took me by the hand and slowly we walked across a large grass field towards a two-storey building. Sister Luba promised that she would send someone down to the camp to find the pen and the watch. I knew well enough that once we left the children's house the ex-prisoners would swoop like vultures to see if there was anything which could be of use to them.

We entered our new home and I was so happy to see Sister Hermina, all clean and dressed in a white nurse's apron. Her thick wavy hair was pulled back from her face and she looked really pretty. She smiled when she saw me come in with Sister Luba. I told her straight away of my distress at losing the precious mementoes of my friend Herman. She put her arm around me, and Sister Luba told her that she would send someone back to see if they could be found.

Sister Hermina took me to the kitchen, the first room next to the entrance. Inside the kitchen was a long table with chairs around it. She told me to sit down, and after a few seconds put a bowl of porridge in front of me and a beaker of hot tea. I could only eat about two spoonfuls.

When I was finished Sister Hermina took me up a flight of stairs. I had to pull myself up holding on to the bannister. I entered a lovely room, which had only two beds with snow-white sheets. I could not believe my eyes.

'Can I sleep here?' I asked Sister Hermina.

'Yes,' she said. 'One of the Hungarian girls will share the room with you.'

I went over to the bed and stroked the white sheets. They smelt so nice. Sister Hermina said that we must go down again to see if the other children had arrived.

My God, I thought, where are Max and Jacky?

I had also forgotten about Robby and Yiddele again. I followed Sister Hermina downstairs, holding on to the bannister with both hands. The hall was crowded as most of the children had arrived now. Sister Luba was standing in the middle. There were also some English nurses who helped to find everybody a place to sleep in one of the many rooms of the building. I saw Iesy and asked him if he had seen my brothers.

'Yes,' he said. 'They went to explore the camp, but they are okay. They'll come back,' he assured me. 'Don't worry.'

It was strange to sleep in a separate room instead of a dormitory. I also felt far removed from Max and Jacky. But the cool sheets and clean pyjamas felt so good that I soon fell asleep and did not wake up until late next morning

The Hungarian girl had gone already. I dressed and went downstairs. Sister Luba was standing in the hall with a very angry expression on her face. I asked her what was the matter.

'That French woman, Maria, was given food and shelter in our barracks and now she is taking over from me,' she said.

I looked over to where Sister Luba was pointing and I could see Maria talking animatedly to two French Red Cross nurses. I started to walk towards Maria when Jaap Ebeling walked in with a very nice Dutch nurse. I explained the situation to Jaap and urged him to do something about it. Together with Jaap I walked up to Maria and the French nurses. To my surprise, Jaap could speak fluent French and, after a short conversation, Sister Luba's position was restored. Jaap introduced Sister Luba and myself and made it clear that Sister Luba was in charge of the children's house.

The weather was drizzly and the sky was grey. Most of the children were playing and running around on the soaking grass in front of the house. I walked across towards the children, but by the time I got there I was so tired that I went back to the house.

It took a great effort to go up the stairs again. A nurse came to my assistance and helped me to my bed after she had removed my overcoat and shoes. She covered me with a blanket and tucked me in before she left. Slowly I could feel the chill which had crept into my body while I was outside receding and a warm glow taking its place. I dozed off and must have gone into a deep sleep because when I woke, it was already late afternoon.

The Hungarian girl came back when darkness fell. She was a big girl and advanced for her age, or at least my age. She was already very sophisticated and she had arrived in Belsen about four weeks before the liberation. She had not lived throught the long months of deprivation, hunger and despair. She had not contracted typhus either. She was robust and energetic. We could converse in German with a very limited vocabulary. When she entered the room she unloaded packet after packet of cigarettes from her pocket and the inside of her blouse onto her bed. I watched in astonishment.

'What are you doing with all those cigarettes?' I asked. 'Do you smoke?'

'No,' she answered, 'but when I get home these cigarettes will be worth a lot of money and I can buy food with them. I am asking every soldier for cigarettes.'

I had never thought of this. Children from Eastern Europe were much more streetwise than those of us who came from the West. It seemed to me that we had different mentalities. This had become very clear to me in Belsen. I still remembered the Polish woman who had knocked on the dining-room door in the barracks. I had opened the door to find this woman holding something wrapped in a snow-white cloth.

'Meat,' she whispered, and lifted the corner of the cloth to reveal a beautiful heart. In my innocence it did not occur to me that something was wrong, so I called Sister Luba to speak to this woman. Sister Luba came to the door and asked the woman what she wanted, but when she showed her the heart, Sister Luba exploded with fury and demanded that she leave immediately. The woman ran off. Sister Luba then told me to be very careful as this heart was a human heart. It was then that the realisation set in. Where else could this woman have got it? The kitchens certainly were not carrying this kind of food for prisoners.

My thoughts returned to the present, and when the Hungarian girl (whose name I did not know) stashed the cigarettes in the nearly full pillowcase, I decided that I would also ask for cigarettes to take home with me.

I was sitting on a chair in the hall. My right arm was hurting as I had been writing non-stop for three days. Jaap Ebeling Koning had come in one day and asked me if I could write down my experiences in Bergen-Belsen. He explained it was a request from English military headquarters to ensure that the horrors of the camp were properly recorded for the future. How could I refuse a request from our liberators? I had agreed and Jaap brought me pen and paper, and installed me in a small room next to the stairs. It had been very quiet and I was not disturbed. Now and then a nurse would bring me tea or a sandwich. They asked how I was progressing and told me to take it easy. Now I had completed my story and I was ready to give it to Jaap.

I was still tiring quickly and was not able to eat well. The Red Cross nurses would in turn attempt to persuade me to try some porridge or anything else I wanted. One morning I had asked them for a fried egg. For many months in the camp I had a great desire to eat an egg. The nurse who sat next to me smiled happily when she gave my request to the cook, but when the egg was put in front of me a few minutes later, I could not eat it. The smell of food made me sick and no persuasion could make me taste the egg.

From where I was sitting in the hall, I could look through the open front door and see the children playing on the field. Max and Jacky and some other boys had left in the morning to go 'exploring', as they called it. Now and then they would return and bring me the latest news of what they had seen and experienced. Iesy told me of a tall English soldier who had bright red hair. Uncle Tinus was his name. He urged me to get well very soon so I could meet him.

The drizzly weather continued but I decided to go outside for some fresh air. I noticed that some English soldiers were erecting swings for the children. How wonderful our liberators were. I watched them for a while but then I could feel the chill in the air penetrating my clothes again so I returned indoors.

I was about halfway down the hall when I heard someone call my name. I turned and saw Maurice. It dawned on me that I had not seen Maurice around lately.

'Hi, Maurice,' I said. 'Where have you been?'

'I've been in the hospital,' he answered. 'Leni is dead, Hetty, Leni is dead.'

He looked so skinny and his coat was miles too big for him. His shoulders were drooping and the tears were running down his hollow cheeks. My weakness forgotten, I ran to him and put my arms around him, while he unburdened his immense grief with his head on my shoulders. I could feel his pain and cried with him. After a while I recovered and gently urged Maurice to do the same. When Maurice lifted his tear-stained face, I asked him, 'When did she die?'

'About two days ago.'.

'Do you know where they buried her?' I asked.

Maurice shook his head, unable to speak.

'Don't worry,' I told him. 'We'll find out.'

Maurice nodded again, still not able to speak. I told a nurse who was walking by that Maurice had just come from the hospital and needed a bed. She took Maurice down the corridor, but not before I told him that I would wait for him here in the hall.

I honestly do not know what happened to me during this emotional release with Maurice, but afterwards I felt much stronger and capable of doing things for the children again. Maurice needed me, and I had to be strong to be able to find Leni's grave for him. When Maurice returned, we both went to the kitchen where, for the first time, I was able to eat a bowl of porridge without feeling sick.

When we left the kitchen Maurice decided that he wanted to have a rest. I went to Sister Luba's room to tell her the sad news about Leni. Her room was next to the kitchen and when I entered there were lots of people inside. As well as Sisters Luba, Hermina and Hella, there were three English officers and one Canadian officer present. They were trying to make conversation with some hilarious results. The men would burst into laughter when one of them could not find the words to express themselves properly to the women, who could not speak English.

Above the conversation you could hear the radio. It was German radio and the broadcaster was announcing that the Russians were approaching Berlin from the east and northern gate. The room fell silent and everybody listened to the news. The announcer was calling all boys of twelve to be mobilised to defend Berlin against the Russians. You could hear the urgency in his voice as he commanded the boys to come forward. He kept on announcing the advances of the Russians as they entered the city of Berlin, and it sounded as if a street-to-street fight took place because he was telling the boys what street to go to next to stop the attacking Russians.

Suddenly the broadcast was interrupted: an English voice announced that Hitler was dead, immediately followed by the English national anthem. The Canadian officer, who had until now lounged lazily in his chair with one of his legs thrown over the armrest, jumped up and stood to attention, bringing his hand up in a salute. The other soldiers followed his example. After that someone said they had better get back to their stations as there may be some movement now that the Russians had entered Berlin and the Führer was dead. After the soldiers left, we talked about the latest development, but it really did not matter to us what was happening in Berlin, as in our case the war had ended on 15 April 1945.

It was a warm spring and our usual group was standing in the hall when Iesy declared that he wanted chicken soup. 'So why don't we go and steal a chicken from a farmhouse?' he said.

Everybody agreed but I said, 'First we have to find where Leni is buried.'

Our group that day consisted of Iesy, Max, Jacky, Maurice, Louky and me. We crossed the field and walked through a wooded area towards the outskirts of the camp. Small tents, which housed the English soldiers, had been erected under the trees. Although it was daytime some of them were sleeping and others were seated in front of their tents. A soldier called us over to make some conversation. This proved to be difficult as our English was limited to a few words, however, we were able to establish where we could find the cemetery. One of the soldiers gave me a toothbrush and a small round tin of toothpaste. Max asked to be given a toothbrush and toothpaste as well, as we had not been able to brush our teeth for many months. Soon we had all been given a toothbrush from the other soldiers who had come over to us. Thanking them for their kindness we started out on our walk to the cemetery. We walked slowly through the trees. How good it felt to be walking about in freedom.

Before long we noticed on our right a small clearing with a white picket fence and we could see it was a graveyard. We entered the cemetery and a man crossed the clearing and came towards us. He asked us in Polish what we wanted, or that is what we thought he asked. Believing that he may be the guardian of the cemetery, I handed him a piece of paper with Leni's name on it. He walked away to a small shed under the trees and when he returned he pointed to a place in the second row of freshly dug graves.

The first long row of the mass grave was already full, and Leni's body had been placed in the second row which had started not long ago. We all stood in silence at the spot the Polish man had indicated and reflected on the sad fact that Leni was not able to be with us in freedom.

Maurice stood with bowed head but did not cry. He had no tears left. I could see that he was relieved to know the place where Leni was resting. I turned around and noticed the trees nearby and registered in my mind the distance Leni's grave was from the entrance. I wanted to remember where we had to leave our Leni behind.

After we left the cemetery, we stood outside deliberating about what to do next, when Iesy reminded us that we still had to find a chicken. We followed the road and slowly our moods lifted as we left the cemetery behind us. Fifteen minutes later we came upon a farmhouse. It must have been lunchtime as the farmer and his family were having their lunch on the grass in the warm sun. As we approached the woman got up and said something to the other people before she went into the house. Slowly the rest of them retreated to the house except for a young girl of about twelve years old. She remained seated and looked at us curiously. She, like the others of her family, looked chubby and rosy with health. No, they had not starved during the war. They were well fed. How could one believe that they had not heard or known what had happened in Belsen only a few miles away?

The father came back from the house to tell the girl to come inside. Iesy approached the father and asked if we could have a chicken. The father shook his head and urged his daughter to hurry. They quickly moved into the house and closed the door firmly behind them. For a while we stood there, undecided about what to do next. Here and there we saw a chicken scurrying beside the house but we still had the terror of 'the regime' inside us, and despite our earlier bravado, we were too scared to take one.

We continued our walk. The country road was deserted with the sun shining over the fields stretching out before us. Except for the singing of the birds, no other sound was heard. Jacky and Max walked up front, Iesy and Louky followed, with Maurice and I making up the rear. After a while Max and Jacky stopped walking and turned, waiting for us to come near.

'As far as our eyes can see there is no other house in sight, and Jacky and I are very tired. I think we had better get back to the house,' Max said.

Iesy was unhappy, as in his opinion we were giving up too soon. Maurice and Louky also wanted to go back, as without noticing it we had wandered a long way from the recuperation camp. We could no longer even see it in the distance. I was standing at the rear of our small group when I saw a movement in the high grass. Suddenly, two English soldiers approached us with drawn rifles, looking very menacing as they came near. I felt the hair rise on the nape of my neck and realised the danger we were in.

'Stop! Do not move!' one soldier called.

The six of us stood frozen on the spot. While the first soldier kept us covered, the second soldier asked for our papers and where we were going.

'No papers, children of children's house, Bergen-Belsen,' I told him.

That seemed to mean something to him, as he turned around and called something to what appeared to be an empty field. Six other soldiers became visible and approached us with their guns at the ready. They formed a circle around us and one soldier who looked as if he was in charge asked roughly, 'Where are you going and who are you?'

I was terrified and started to tremble. Iesy said, 'We are the children from the children's house of Bergen-Belsen.'

The soldiers discussed this answer and then one said, 'Go, go, go!' and pointed in the direction of our camp.

We did not need to be told twice – we ran as fast as our legs would carry us. Unwittingly, we had walked straight into the path of a patrol party. We had forgotten that there was still a war going on, and we must have crossed the demarcation line of the forty square kilometres the Germans had surrendered unconditionally to the English before Belsen was freed.

We were out of breath when we passed the cemetery, and when we could see the English sentry in the distance we knew we were close to our camp again. We told each other how lucky we had been. We could see the soldiers' tents when we heard a motor-cycle approaching fast. We looked over our shoulders and when the soldier on the bike came into view, we heard him shouting, 'Hey, hey.'

We did not wait a second longer but started to run away. The soldier kept calling:

'Hey, children.'

Iesy must have recognised the voice as he turned around and then called out to me, 'Hetty, it's Uncle Tinus, the one I told you about.'

We all stopped running and turned towards Uncle Tinus, but from a safe distance.

The soldier stopped his bike but did not get off it.

'Children,' he called out, 'the war is over.'

We looked at each other but could not understand what he was trying to tell us. Uncle Tinus then raised his arm pretending it was a rifle and called out, 'Bang, bang, bang – finished!' waving his arms in the air.

Max understood it first.

'Hetty,' he screamed, 'the war is finished!'

Iesy ran halfway back to Uncle Tinus and called out to him, 'Bang bang over?'

'Yes, yes,' Uncle Tinus said, and he restarted his bike and drove off to spread the good news.

We jumped up and down from happiness and screamed our throats hoarse, and then we ran towards our building, yelling out the good news as we passed the soldiers' tents.

'The war is over, the war is over,' we told Sister Luba as we burst into her room, but we had to translate it into German, as she could not understand what we were trying to tell her. What happiness! We laughed, we kissed, we danced and we sang. All the bottled-up emotions came rushing out and we thanked God for saving our lives.

The next day on the field across from our house twenty cannons were lined up in two rows of ten facing each other. We heard that there would be an official ceremony to herald the end of the war. The morning after, trucks arrived and soldiers unloaded stacks and stacks of ammunition next to each cannon. Without needing to be told, the children kept a safe distance from those destructive-looking cannons, but we watched every move made by the soldiers.

At six o'clock that night we all lined up to see the show. Jeeps arrived with high-ranking officers to witness the salute to the end of the war. There was no dais or microphone. We could faintly hear a man speaking, after which all the British military present gave three loud cheers, then a trumpet sounded 'The Last Post' and a deathly silence fell around us for two minutes. At seven o'clock exactly a command was given and a soldier waved a white flag. The soldiers, who had stood to attention next to those dangerous-looking cannons, sprang into action and, with a fluid movement acquired through experience, they loaded the cannons. A further order was shouted and the noses of the first ten cannons were pointed skywards and simultaneously fired the first round. This was immediately followed by the second row of cannons. Each cannon shot their ammunition into the air twenty-one times. The noise was unbearable. We covered our ears but to no avail. The earth was trembling, the air was black and smelled putrid, but then it was over and quiet descended. The soldiers lowered the cannons and covered them with hoods, and the truck returned to pick them up.

Within the hour the field was empty except for twenty heaps of empty gleaming brass shells which the cannons had ejected after each shot. We walked up towards them to inspect them more closely. Soon some people picked up a shell as a souvenir. Max,

Jacky and I did the same, each carrying a shell which had heralded the end of the war. For me it was quite a weight so Iesy came to the rescue and carried it to my room for me. There I sat, gently stroking the shiny shield and tried to contemplate the amount of destruction these shells created. But this shield had signalled our freedom and I picked up the now-harmless shell and planted a big kiss on it.

A week after the end of the war it was made known that the Russians wanted their people to return at once. Polish and Ukrainian ex-prisoners could request to return as well. They were given forty-eight hours' notice and advised that the train would leave Celle station at seven o'clock that night. We were informed about it through the camp telegraph at first, but later the Red Cross sent their messengers with more details. There was no one in our children's house who wanted to return, and Sister Luba would not even consider it. The next day the camp was quieter and not so crowded, so a lot of people must have returned to Russia and Poland

Now that the war was over, most of the soldiers were relieved of duty and had more free time. Many of them visited the children's house and they brought us presents and sweets. They put up a table tennis table on the field and Jacky became quite an expert.

One day a film crew arrived and I was the only one around, as usual sitting on my chair in the hall. They asked me to come outside on the swing, where a nice soldier gently pushed me. After a short while I had to ask him to stop as I was getting dizzy. I was still not completely recovered, although I was eating much better. The children who had been invisible a moment earlier now seemed to appear as if by magic. They all wanted to have a turn on the swings so they could become film stars.* I went inside to call Sister Luba; she was the heart of the children's house and had to be in the film with us. The film crew turned their camera on the table tennis, where Jacky performed like a pro. Max, who was looking on, told his partner Gerry how to play. I was watching, and I must admit that Jacky was the champ.

The weather was not kind and I could feel the chill creeping up on me again so I decided to go indoors, just as the film crew handed Sister Luba a huge bell to ring, 'So the children will come home.' I was nearly pushed over when all the children answering the call came rushing through the doors. The film crew requested the bell-ringing sequence time and again. At last they were satisfied and packed up and left.

The days and weeks went by and slowly we became stronger. Our cheeks filled out and our bodies became fuller. The warm, sunny days helped to restore our health and our minds to a certain extent. At times, one could still hear a child screaming in terror during the night but slowly we emerged from the trauma and devastation we had experienced until a month ago. By now I had convinced myself that the SS would not come back and that we were really free from danger.

I had asked Jaap a few times when he thought we could go home, but he had smiled and told me to be patient. I adored Jaap and so did all the children. We crowded around him whenever he came and we felt a sense of loss when he had to go again.

Earlier Jaap had told us to write letters to anyone we wished to inform that we were still alive. I had written a letter to the Pomstra

---

* This film is in the British Imperial War Museum and forty years later I saw it for the first time.

family in Amsterdam advising them of our whereabouts, and also telling them our worries about the welfare of our parents and our doubts that they would be still alive. Jaap collected all the letters written by the children and assured us that they would be delivered.

The month of May entered its fourth week. The recuperation camp was no longer crowded as a lot of ex-prisoners had been repatriated.

In about the middle of the week Jaap came to see us with Captain Samuel Gazan. The captain was Dutch and he had joined the Allied forces during the war. He was surprised and very happy that we had survived the horrors of Belsen, and when he left he promised us that he would arrange for our quick return to Holland. Jaap escorted him to his car and returned to us after the captain had driven off.

We besieged Jaap with questions, which he patiently tried to answer.

'When do you think we will leave, Jaap?' I asked.

'Soon, I think,' he answered with a smile. 'I'll let you know when I find out.'

He ruffled my hair and I leaned against him. My thoughts were in turmoil now that the day was coming that we would return to Holland, leaving everything we had become accustomed to. I looked up at Jaap and asked, 'Do you think we could take Sister Luba with us?'

'I believe we could take her if she wants to come,' Jaap said.

We looked at each other, then, without saying a word, we both turned and walked to Sister Luba's room. Sister Luba looked up in surprise when we entered followed by Max, Iesy and Louky. Her smile turned to concern when she sensed that something important had happened. Iesy told her that Captain Gazan was arranging for our speedy departure to Holland and that we did not want to leave her behind.

'Sister Luba, you must come with us to Holland,' he said.

We all nodded our heads in agreement. Sister Luba was deeply touched by our devotion and without hesitation said, 'Yes, I will come with you to Amsterdam.'

One by one she hugged us, and happiness was shining from our eyes. We were going home and the woman who had become our second mother and saved us from starvation in Belsen was coming with us.

The days were disappearing fast now. Inge and Gretel decided to come with us, and Jaap told us at the end of May he might be released so that he could accompany us to Holland. I was so happy when he told me this news as I had dreaded the moment when we would have to say goodbye. Jaap had been so good to us since we first met and all the children adored him.

On the last day of May Jaap came to tell us that we had to be ready on the morning of 3 June by ten o'clock. This was it. The moment was near when we could leave all the nightmares and trauma behind us and return to our country. All the children were informed and excitement ran high. Iesy and I decided to go for a last stroll in the woods to say goodbye to all those friendly soldiers who were still camping there.

We went from one tent to another and the soldiers wished us a safe journey and a happy homecoming. Some of them gave us their addresses in London and asked us to write. After waving a final goodbye, Iesy and I walked back towards the children's house. Iesy was a bit upset that we had missed Uncle Tinus as he had been away on a mission.

'Never mind,' I said, 'the others will tell him that we came to say goodbye.'

We were now clearing the woods and crossing the field opposite our house. I noticed that an ambulance had stopped in front of the door and that the driver hurried inside. The back door of the ambulance was open. The little children needed no invitation and had scrambled into the ambulance, with some of them sitting precariously close to the open end. I could sense a disaster in the making, as the soldiers had a habit of tearing away at the start of the motor. I started to run across the field towards the ambulance and Iesy, sharing my concern, started to run with me. I was calling out to the children, 'Get inside, get inside!'

From the corner of my eye I could see the soldier hurrying from the building and entering his cabin without noticing the children sitting in the rear. Out of breath I reached the ambulance, jumped onto the step and screamed at the children, 'Move inside, move!'

Iesy also jumped onto the step next to me and told the children to move away from the open door. The urgency in our voices made the children move into the body of the ambulance, and not a moment too soon.

The engine roared and with a violent start the ambulance moved off. The start was so swift that Iesy and I went over backwards and with a severe thud we both landed on the road. My bottom hit the ground first and my head snapped down after. For a moment I lay stunned, not able to move, but then with an effort I got back on my feet, nursing my extremely sore bottom. Iesy had met with the same fate but was a bit slower to get up, and I recalled the thud I had heard when Iesy's head hit the pavement.

Sister Luba and Sister Hermina came running out when they heard the hubbub as the children had all screamed in panic when they saw us fall.

The driver had stopped at once and came round to the back of his vehicle where he noticed all the children in the rear for the first time. Sister Hermina helped Iesy to his feet, asking him if he was okay. Iesy still looked dazed from the very accident we had tried to prevent happening to the children. The driver asked me if I was all right. I nodded – I had still not found my voice. The pain when my bottom had hit the road had been excruciating, and the shock had vibrated through my spine. The base of my spine was so painful that I could hardly move, but when I gently massaged it, it became a bit more bearable. The driver looked so crestfallen that I gave him a smile and said, 'I'll be okay.'

'You want to come for a drive?' he said.

I declined. 'Fancy falling out of an ambulance,' I scolded myself.

Despite the mishap the children still wanted to go for a drive around the camp. This time Sister Hermina and Sister Hella went with them for the ride, just to make sure there were no further accidents. Iesy and I went inside to have a rest. Iesy had an enormous swelling on the back of his head and Sister Luba applied a towel with cold water to it. My bottom was hurting.

The next day went by fast. We had no packing to do as the only things we possessed were the clothes we were wearing. We were full of anticipation, and the hours could not go quickly enough for us to leave this place for ever. Sister Luba ordered everybody to bed early that night.

I could not sleep. My thoughts kept me awake. We are going home in the morning, I kept telling myself. But where are my father and my mother? Are they still alive? I had made an unsuccessful attempt to find them through the Red Cross. I kept turning from side to side and sleep eluded me. My heart was pounding and I could not relax. The night seemed endless, but at long last I could see the dawn breaking and I slid carefully from my bed so as not to wake the Hungarian girl. I suddenly thought of Sister Hermina, who had always been so good to me, and Sister Hella and her mother, Zosua, and Helen – they had all become dear to me and today I had to say farewell to them. Tears came to my eyes even thinking about it.

I went downstairs. The house was quiet, but when I neared the kitchen I could see a light. The cook, Cookie, was there before me. She gave me a warm smile when I entered the kitchen. Cookie was from the English military. She was about forty years old and a sturdy, strong woman. She had been allocated to us from the very first day we arrived, and she made sure that we were eating good, wholesome food. It was wonderful that Sister Luba did not have to worry about our food any more and this had given her more time to attend other matters. It was incredible that we all were so healthy after the typhus epidemic.

Cookie put a steaming cup of tea in front of me and asked, 'Fried eggs or boiled?'

I shook my head. 'It is too early for eggs, just toast and jam will do, please.'

'You're going home today,' Cookie said. 'Are you happy?'

'Yes, I am so happy that I couldn't sleep last night, but I am also very sad.'

'Why?' Cookie asked, looking surprised.

'Because I have to say goodbye to a lot of people I love and who care for me. I know that I'll never see them again,' I said.

Cookie came and sat opposite me at the table.

'Hetty,' she said, 'you're going home and I hope you will find your father and your mother again, so forget the past and look to the future. We fought to have a better world. Now you make it so, you hear me?'

I nodded my head.

'Now drink your tea,' Cookie ordered. 'I have to attend to the breakfast because in a moment the whole bunch will be in.'

I drank my tea and, after thanking Cookie, I went back to my room. The Hungarian girl was awake when I entered.

'Hello,' she said. 'Are you packed?'

'There is nothing to pack, only my vest and my coat,' I said.

'Here,' she handed me two new panties and a carton of cigarettes. She pulled the pillowslip off my pillow and put the cigarettes and the panties inside it. 'Give me your vest and anything else you are taking.'

I handed her my vest, the toothbrush and the small tin of toothpaste. They were all my worldly possessions. The pillowslip looked empty.

'Wait,' I said. 'I must take the brass shell.'

I dived under the bed to retrieve it and and put it in the pillowslip as well. I was ready to leave. We both went downstairs to find out what was happening. I carried the pillowslip, which felt a bit heavy now. Downstairs it was very busy. Most of the children were dressed and waiting in the hall. They milled around me, asking thousands of questions. Although we all knew that we were going home to Holland, we were apprehensive, as most of us remembered the traumatic time we went through before we were picked up by the SS. We were also leaving the home we had become accustomed to. I assured them that it was wonderful to go home.

'And remember,' I said, 'Sister Luba is coming with us.'

I was able to quieten their fears and soon the excitement was at a peak. We had been told that we would leave at ten o'clock. Inge and Gretel arrived at about half past eight, they had nothing to carry except either the clothes they wore.

Jaap arrived at about eight o'clock and told me he was coming with us.

What a surprise! I hugged him and asked, 'Is it okay with the army?'

'Yes,' he said. 'I can come home with you, they have released me.'

Jaap had become very dear to me since the liberation, as well as being a trusted and kind friend of all the children. When the good news spread that Jaap was coming with us, the children were elated and crowded around him.

The hall had become very full now. All the sisters, Hermina, Hella and her mother, Maria, Helen, Zosua and a few English nurses and Cookie had come into the hall to spend the last minutes with us.

Sister Luba and Sister Hermina were standing close together. Tears were in Hermina's eyes as she softly talked to Sister Luba. At her feet was a large army bag, which she had filled with flour, sugar and a few bread loaves. Cookie had made lots of sandwiches for us to eat on the road. Suddenly the trucks were there. One by one the children walked past the sisters and thanked them for their care. When my turn came, I thanked and kissed Sister Hella and her mother, after which I passed all the sisters until I came to Sister Hermina. I buried my face in her stomach while I was hugging her around her waist, and I did not want to let her go. I was crying bitterly – the pain of saying goodbye to this wonderful woman was too much for me. I lifted my tear-stained face and Sister Hermina bent down to me and said, 'My darling Hettylein, stay well. I love you.' She kissed me and I hugged her more tightly, then with a great effort I let go and went outside to the trucks.

Sister Luba and I were the last to climb into the second truck. Gretel and Inge were already on board guarding the children. Captain Gazan and Jaap were in charge of the first truck. The engines started and the trucks began to move. All the sisters and nurses had come outside to wave us a final farewell. 'Goodbye, goodbye, auf wiedersehen,' we called until the small group was no longer visible. At long last we were on our way.

At two o'clock on 3 June 1945 we arrived at Nüneberg airfield. Some soldiers helped us down off the truck. We stood huddled together and observed the planes coming and going. The airfield had a single runway and its only building was a galvanised iron shed. Captain Gazan entered the shed to find out when a plane would be available to take us to Holland. He returned about fifteen minutes later and told us that we would be leaving when the next plane arrived.

At about half past two a few soldiers guided us through the field towards the waiting plane. It had two engines whose blades were lazily going around, and its tail rested on the ground. On its side was painted a large circle in red, white and blue. A door at the rear of the plane was open and small steps were leading up to it. We climbed the steps and entered the plane. It was the first time any of us had been on a plane. There were long benches on each side of the plane along the metal body, with wooden ribs showing and small windows.

Soon the door was securely closed and we set off down the runway. We were seated on the long benches with no seat belts. This military plane had no luxuries. No one was scared as the engines roared and the plane took to the air. The plane was not soundproof or pressurised. The sound of the engines was deafening and we had to scream to each other to be heard. Soon the plane reached its required height and the shaking we had felt earlier stopped.

We could see the enormous damage the Allied bombers had done to the German cities as we flew over them. We were very happy to see this and Robby, who stood next to me on the bench looking down, said, 'Schön, schön.' I looked at him, studying his little face as he pressed his nose to the window of the plane. What a lovely boy he was and I loved him so dearly. As if he felt my gaze, Robby turned towards me and pointed his little finger at the window and repeated, 'Schön, schön.' I nodded and pulled him down to me. He snuggled up to me, his little hand holding mine tightly.

Although the engine noise was loud, some of the children had managed to fall asleep. We had been flying for more than an hour by now and, although it was a novel experience, most of us wished that we were at our destination. After about another half an hour, we could hear the engines slowing as we started our descent – that's when the trouble began. Most of the children started to cry out in pain as they developed intense earache. We were told by one of the crew to open our mouths wide and swallow air. But nothing helped. We pressed our hands against our ears, hoping it would get better.

The captain of the plane told us it would not be long now and we had to sit down as we were landing. The captain had been speaking to the children who had walked over to him during the flight. There was no partition between the cockpit and the body of the plane, and the boys had shown the most interest in all those dials.

A few minutes later the plane landed in Eindhoven. Willing hands helped us down the steps as we set foot on Netherlands' ground again.

Twelve

'Is that you, Hetty?'

We were ushered into a building and towards a long table where a few men and women kept records of our arrival. When it was my turn I sat down on the chair with Max and Jacky standing close beside me. The lady asked me my name, my date of birth, and my last address in Holland before our deportation. She asked for the name of my parents and in which camp we had been. She wrote everything down and then she wrote out a white card, gave it to me and told me to see the doctor, pointing towards a man dressed in a white coat. I waited for Max and Jacky to be interviewed and when they received their repatriation cards, we walked over to the doctor together. A nurse told us to take off our tops and one by one we were put in front of an X-ray machine to screen our lungs for tuberculosis or other illnesses.

The process was quick. The doctor called out his findings, which the nurse noted on our repatriation cards. A second doctor checked our throats, ears and hands. The nurse recorded everything. Thank God, Max, Jacky and I were free of TB. A few of our children were not so lucky and they were immediately separated from the healthy children.

When it was Sister Luba's turn to be interviewed, we struck trouble. We had not given a thought to Sister Luba's nationality. She was Polish and had no right to enter Holland. This had not even occurred to us in our desire to take her home with us. I went to Sister Luba's assistance, as she could not speak Dutch, of course, and told the person who interviewed her that Sister Luba had to stay with us. She was our second mother and we did not care if she was Polish, Russian or Chinese. She had saved our lives and we wanted to keep her with us.

The entire administration staff became very embarrassed by it all as the children thronged around Sister Luba, insisting that she should be allowed to stay. In the end, a tall gentleman dressed in a gaberdine raincoat came into the room and the staff asked him for advice. He took one look at the agitated faces of the children and told the staff to allow Sister Luba to come with us. What a relief! Soon we all left the room and boarded a waiting truck. We were driven through Eindhoven to a building that appeared to be a school.

We entered a large room with straw mattresses on the floor covered with grey army blankets. Toilet facilities were outside and in front of the 'dormitory'. There was a small room that looked like a kitchen but there were no cooking facilities, tables or chairs to sit on. The whole place looked desolate and grey. When Sister Luba saw how we were received she became very upset and asked me, 'Why did this man (meaning Captain Gazan) take us away from our comfortable house in the recuperation camp? This is a terrible place. Even in Belsen I made sure you had beds to sleep in and now you all have to sleep on the floor.' Sister Luba's mouth was set in a straight line, telling us she was very angry.

The news that children had arrived from Bergen-Belsen spread like wildfire through Eindhoven and scores of people came to the school to meet the children. There were people everywhere and the children mingled with them.

The people of Eindhoven opened their hearts and doors, and took most of the children home with them. The repatriation staff was kept busy recording the whereabouts of the children. Only a few children were left behind in Sister Luba's care. Our usual group of Max, Jacky, Iesy Louky, Gerry, Maurice and I did not even contemplate leaving Sister Luba.

As night fell we turned to the dismal-looking dormitory and made ourselves comfortable on the straw mattresses. Henneke and Sid had attached themselves to Inge, scared of the strange surroundings. Henneke was crying constantly, with her brother Sid attempting to comfort her. After a while Henneke fell asleep. Nobody had bothered to bring us any food and it was only thanks to Cookie that we did not go hungry that night.

We were up and about at dawn the next morning, only to discover that the Dutch authorities had locked us in for the night. Inge climbed out of the window to investigate exactly where we were and to get us some assistance. We hung around until someone came to open the door and brought us some milk and sandwiches. It was a meagre meal. We could not even make a cup of tea from the tea Cookie had put in the bag, as there was no way to boil water.

At ten o'clock that morning the man in the gaberdine raincoat came to see us again. He brought with him a very important-looking military person who asked me a lot of questions about Sister Luba. He then went to speak with Sister Luba in fluent

German. This seemed to satisfy him and he left soon after. 'The gaberdine man', as I called him, stayed with us a while longer. He told us that he was the head of staff, Dr J van Waldre de Bordes. He asked us a lot of questions about Belsen and told us how happy he was that we were safely back in Holland.

When I asked him when we could go to Amsterdam, he told me that Amsterdam was not open for repatriation. There was a lot of sickness and not enough food available, so we had to be a bit patient. During the morning more and more people came to the school and took children home. Jacky went with one couple to Den Bosch, a small city not far away. Amid all the confusion Inge came to me and said, 'Hetty, I can get a lift to Amsterdam and I'm leaving right now with Gretel and Captain Gazan.'

I was shocked.

'Why Inge, I don't want you to go,' I cried out. I realised how much I had become attached to her. 'Please, Inge, don't go,' I begged her.

'I'm going now, Hetty. I want to find out if my little girl is still safe with my doctor in Amsterdam,' she said, already walking towards the truck.

When the truck drove off, the tears were streaming down my face and my heart was breaking, while Inge waved goodbye through the open window.

Jaap came by later in the morning. He told me that he was also leaving us today to go back home to his family in Arnhem. How sad I was to say goodbye to this friend who had won our hearts and our trust as no other liberator had. I knew that I would never see him again, but I also knew that his memory would always remain in my heart.

Sister Luba was not happy. She was restless and had not taken kindly to the authorities, who left us to cater for ourselves. No proper food had arrived. There were no proper ablution facilities. The sleeping quarters were disgusting and were riddled with fleas and lice. We soon became infested again. The situation did not shock us as we had experienced worse, but Sister Luba was furious and could not excuse the unhygienic conditions. She was also upset because the reason that she had come with us to Holland was to be near us. This need was taken away when the children were fostered out.

I could hear Sister Luba talking to Iesy and Max in the little front room-cum-kitchen. I could hear Iesy loudly protesting about something with Max joining in. My curiosity was aroused, so I went to join them. As I entered the room I could see the upset faces of Max and Iesy, and the determined look on Sister Luba's face. I looked questioningly from one to the other and Iesy burst out, 'She wants to go back to Belsen. You talk to her please, Hetty, tell her we don't want her to leave!'

My heart contracted.

'No, Sister Luba,' I said, 'you must not go. You must stay with us.'

But I could see from Sister Luba's face that I could not change her mind. We were desperate. The loss of Sister Luba would mean the loss of our security. All the people who had played such a vital part in our lives during the past eight months had gone away. All the sisters in Belsen, Inge, Jaap and now Luba. Our whole world collapsed, and all our pleading and tears did not help us. Sister Luba wanted to leave as she did not feel needed any more.

When Dr van Waldre de Bordes came to see us later in the afternoon, we told him the sad news that Sister Luba wanted to return and we implored him to persuade her to change her mind. He walked over to Sister Luba and handed her a copy of a letter he had despatched to the Commander in Chief of the Security Forces of the Netherlands. In the letter, he requested permission for Sister Luba to remain in Holland, as she had saved more than forty children from starvation in Belsen.

Sister Luba took the letter but insisted that she wanted to go back to Belsen. For an hour the doctor tried to persuade her and to find out the reason she wanted to leave. Sister Luba told him of her disappointment at how we had been received, and how we had been dumped in this school and left to our own devices. She told him that she was not needed any more as all the children had gone except for the few who did not want to leave her. The doctor promised to get her a beautiful big house the next week and to bring all the children back to her, but nothing could persuade Sister Luba to change her mind. By the time the doctor left, he had promised Luba that he would arrange for her return to Belsen.

Two days later Sister Luba left. We went with her in the truck to the airport where an official was already waiting, urging her to hurry. The plane was ready to take off. The farewells were quick and painful. A kiss and a hug for all of us and she was hurried away towards the plane. We stood in stunned silence watching the plane take off with the woman who had become our mother in Belsen. We felt bereft and no one spoke on the way back to the school, each busy with our own thoughts. It was the end of an era and the start of an uncertain future. None of us knew if our parents were safe.

The next day Max and I decided to go to Nuhnen. Through the Red Cross we had found out that my father's sister, Aunty Jet, had been in hiding in this small village during the German occupation.

She had been in hiding together with her good friends, Sal and Kay. Max had asked the doctor for some money to pay for the bus fare. Iesy decided to come with us, as the prospect of hanging around the school all day did not appeal to him, especially now that Sister Luba had gone.

We had to change buses a few times, but at last we arrived at the little village. Where do you start to find someone if you have no address? A man on a bicycle was coming our way and Max stopped him. We asked if he knew in which house our Aunty Jet, Sal and Kay B. had been given safe haven during the war. He knew straight away who we were talking about and he pointed to a house halfway down the road. We hurried towards the house and entered a large farmyard. A woman who saw us came towards us and asked if she could be of help.

'We are looking for our Aunt Jetty Werkendam. We believe she found shelter here' Max said.

'Yes,' the woman answered. 'Jetty, Kay and Sal stayed with us for one year, but they left and went to Jetty's brother Abraham in Brussels.'

What a disappointment this was. Although we were pleased to hear that Uncle Appy was still alive, I had looked forward to the reunion with my favourite aunt. It had not occurred to us that Aunty Jet would leave the village soon after the liberation in 1944.

There was no point in staying around so we walked back over the country road to the bus stop.

We got the travel bug once we had had a taste of being able to move around the country unrestricted. Max and I decided to go to Den Bosch to see Jacky. We had not seen him for about a week and we were worried about him. So, with the name and address of the

291

people who had taken Jacky, Max and I set out to pay him a surprise visit.

Den Bosch was a pleasant city with a tram running through the main street. Willing helpers directed us to the street we were looking for.

When we arrived at the address, we pressed the gleaming brass bell of the first floor. The front door was opened by someone pulling a long rope and at the top of the stairs stood a woman asking, 'Who's there?'

'Is this the home where my brother Jacky is living?' I asked, peering up into the dim light of the stairway.

'Yes, Jacky is with us. Are you his sister, Hetty, and his brother, Max?' the woman said, coming halfway down the stairs.

We nodded.

'Please come in,' the woman said.

So Max and I climbed the stairs to enter a spotlessly clean apartment. You could see your reflection in the shiny wood of the furniture and there seemed to be nothing out of place. The woman ushered us into the kitchen where a middle-aged man was reading the paper on the kitchen table.

'Look who we have got here, Father,' the woman said. 'This is Hetty and Max, Jacky's family.'

The man got up from his chair and stuck his hand out to greet us.

'So you have come to see Jacky,' he said, 'but he is not home at the moment. The neighbour took him to the shop a while ago, but he won't be long now. Please sit down and Mother will make you a cup of tea.'

He indicated two seats, and I was grateful to sink into one of the chairs. I was still getting tired very quickly. The woman put a kettle of water on the stove. Soon the table was laid with a lovely table-cloth, dainty cups and a plate of sandwiches. The latter were very welcome, as Max and I were hungry after our journey from Eindhoven. What wonderful people they are, I thought. We were made so welcome. The friendliness showed in their eyes. If my Grandmother Hetty and Grandpa Zadok had found these people instead of those bastards who had betrayed them, they might still have been alive.

Jacky's arrival interrupted my reverie. He looked well; he had put on weight and his clothes were clean. He was happy to see us. We told him of the departure of Sister Luba. Jacky was never a person to show much emotion. He shrugged his shoulders and said, 'Well, if that's what she wanted, then let her be happy.' He changed the subject and asked, 'When are we going to Amsterdam?'

'Soon I hope,' I said.

'Not to worry,' the father said, 'we'll make sure Jacky is there.'

By now it was time for Max and I to leave. We wanted to be back at the school before darkness set in. We bade farewell and 'Mother' and Jacky walked with us to the bus stop just to make sure that we went in the right direction.

The following days went by very slowly. The few of us who had remained at the school saw each other only in the morning or night. Every day the boys explored Eindhoven, except for Iesy, Max and myself – we stuck together. The doctor came to see us every day to enquire how we were doing. Whenever he came we asked him when we could go to Amsterdam.

Finally, one morning he told us the long-awaited news: we would leave for Amsterdam in two days' time. All the children had to come back from the foster homes and somebody must have worked very hard, because on the morning of our departure all the children except for those in hospital or destinations other than Amsterdam were present for our trip.

When the bus started on its way there were lots of goodbyes from the people who had taken children into their homes and their hearts.

The journey to Amsterdam took hours. All the bridges in Holland had been blown up either by the bombs of the Allied forces or the retreating German army, and all traffic had to be ferried across the rivers. It meant many hours of delay but at last we drove into Amsterdam. It was about four o'clock when the bus turned into the Dr Henry Polaklaan and came to a stop at the Jewish hospital, from which we had rescued my grandparents just before a German raid. The doors of the hospital were closed and only about eight to ten people were there to welcome us home. Six people were there to collect some children who were related to them, and the other four people were from the Dutch Resistance, which had done much heroic work during the occupation. The bus driver handed a list with our names on it to one of the women who seemed to be in charge.

Some of our children recognised their relatives and went over to them where tearful reunions took place. Robby clung to me and I picked him up, understanding his panic among these strange surroundings and people. An elderly couple came up to me and asked if this was Robby Englander.

'Yes,' I said, 'this is Robby.'

'We are his grandparents,' the woman told me.

My heart stopped as I realised that I had to surrender Robby. Sensing that he had to leave me, Robby clamped his little arms around my neck, nearly choking me in the process. He buried his head in my shoulder and cried bitterly. His grandmother looked bewildered and stretched her arms out to Robby, who screamed even louder. I told Robby's grandparents to be patient for a few minutes so I could calm him down. With Robby in my arms I walked to the edge of the group and started to talk softly to him. I told him that those people were his grandparents and they loved him as much as I did.

'You do not have to be scared, darling,' I told Robby. 'Now dry your tears and go with them and I'll soon come to see you again.'

Robby calmed down. He trusted me and believed what I told him. Slowly I walked towards his grandparents. I gently disengaged Robby's arms from around my neck, and before I handed him over to his grandmother I kissed him and whispered, 'I love you, darling, be good.' For a second it looked like he would resist, but then he gave in and went into the arms of his happy grandmother.

Most of the children had already left, either escorted by a member of the Resistance or with a relative. Maurice came to tell me that he and Phoebe were going home with their aunt Anna.

'Goodbye, Hetty,' Maurice said. 'I'll soon be going to England to my uncle.'

I nodded. Maurice had told me that many times before. We both knew that from this moment on our lives would go separate ways. I put my hand in his and reached up to kiss him on his cheek.

'Goodbye, Maurice,' I said. 'Write one day, will you?'

Maurice nodded. Our eyes met, he turned and walked away with Phoebe and his aunt. After about an hour only Iesy, Max, Jacky and I were left. All the other children had found a destination for the time being. The woman in charge was called Miep and she asked Iesy if he had somewhere to go.

'Yes, I've got the address of my uncle in Amsterdam South.'

'Good,' Miep said, 'my friend will take you there on the back of her bike. Hetty, have you got somewhere to go?'

'Yes,' I said, 'I have to go to the Pomstra family's place. They live on the President Steyn Plantsoen.'

Max and Jacky interrupted me to say that Miep wanted to take them home but they would not go without me.

'It's okay,' Miep reassured them, 'I'll take Hetty home as well. Now does that sound better?'

Max and Jacky beamed and looked relieved. Miep picked up all the papers and put them in her bag. Iesy had left with Miep's friend. Our farewell was swift. As usual, Iesy had been very demonstrative. He came to me and kissed me on both cheeks. 'Look after yourself, okay?' I nodded, realising that our close-knit group had disintegrated on our arrival in Amsterdam. Iesy climbed onto the back of the bike and waved goodbye as he disappeared down the street.

Miep was ready to go. We loaded the army bag that Sister Luba had left behind onto the bike and my pillowslip with my only possessions, and we walked towards Miep's home. It was nearly seven o'clock by the time we arrived. Miep lived on the Amstel River, next to Theatre Carree. Wearily we climbed the stairs to the first floor and entered a gloomy-looking apartment.

Miep's friend arrived soon after us. She had delivered Iesy safely to his uncle. We sat in the front room overlooking the Amstel. Miep and her friend had gone to the rear of the apartment, and when they returned we were given a slice of bread and a cup of water. Miep apologised that she had no tea to give us, as there was still a great shortage of tea and food in Amsterdam.

'But we have tea for you,' I told Miep, 'in the army bag.'

We filled Miep's small pan with sugar and a cup with tea. Her friend returned from the kitchen fifteen minutes later with steaming cups of tea laced with lots of sugar.

We were very tired, as it had been a long day. I kept telling Miep that I had to go to the Pomstras. Now that I was so close to them I could not wait to go and see them.

Miep told us that there was a curfew on at the moment, like there had been during the German occupation. Nobody was allowed on the street after eight o'clock until the next morning at six o'clock. However, Miep, who had been a very active member of the Resistance, had permission to be on the street after the curfew. She told her friend that she would take me on the back of her bike to the Pomstras.

So shortly after the curfew started, Miep and I rode through the deserted streets of Amsterdam. Miep had fastened a small pillow to the back of her bike to soften the bumps in the road. The bike had wooden tyres and the ride was rather hazardous. When we rode through the Sarphatistraat towards the Weesperplein it was not so bad as the road was bitumen, but when we turned into the Wieboutstraat, the ride became very bumpy and painful. We had been stopped by the BS (Dutch Security Guards) who carried guns, just as we turned into the Wieboutstraat. But after he saw Miep's identification pinned to the front of her dress and enquired why we were on the streets, he allowed us to continue on our way.

I cannot describe in a few words the emotions I felt when we rode over the Wieboutstraat. I had walked home that way from school with my friends many times – friends whose lives had ended so violently. Although it was about half past eight, it was still daylight and I could clearly see the diggings people had made on the land next to the road in search of coal during the winter. The area we drove past had been used for decades as a place for the trains to park and reverse before the new railway line and subways were built just before the war started. The road was not in good repair and the shaking and bumps were, despite the pillow, very painful to my already-sore bottom. When we rode past Luyks, the mustard factory, I knew we did not have far to go. Then we were in the subway where I had once played when it was being built. At the end of the subway we would ride into the President Steynplantsoen.

'We are here, Miep,' I said. 'The house is on the left, number 4.' Miep slowed down and my eyes scanned the row of houses, all with their neat white curtains. My eyes found the apartment where the Pomstras lived and, as if by magic, Mrs Pomstra appeared at the window. She saw me and after a second recognition dawned. After I climbed stiffly from Miep's bike, she securely locked the wheel before we pressed the bell of the Pomstras' apartment. The door sprang open and we ascended the stairs.

My heart was pumping loudly. How would I be received? Would they be happy to see me? We had reached the last stairs and I could see Mrs Pomstra standing at the top. When I was about halfway up the stairs, Mrs Pomstra asked, 'Is that you, Hetty?'

'Yes,' I answered.

'And your brothers?' Mrs Pomstra asked.

'They are okay,' I told her, 'they are at Miep's house at the moment.'

I had reached the top of the stairs when Mrs Pomstra said, 'How wonderful, my girl, that you are all alive because your father and your mother are alive as well.'

I reeled backwards under the impact of the shock, and Miep prevented me from falling down the stairs. I looked up at Mrs Pomstra. 'I don't believe it! You are not telling me the truth.'

'No,' Mrs Pomstra said, 'come inside and I'll show you the letters your parents wrote to us.' She put her arms around my shoulders and kissed me on both cheeks before guiding me inside.

Miep introduced herself to Mrs Pomstra and after I was seated on a chair, trying to control my shaking, Mrs Pomstra put three letters on the table in front of me. I recognised the letter I had sent from Belsen through the Red Cross. In the other two letters I recognised the handwriting of my mother and my father. I picked up my mother's letter first and with a shaking hand, I opened it. She had written to the Pomstras:

Dear family Pomstra,
I am in Sweden in Malmö and I do not know where my husband or my children are. I think they are dead and I am alone in the world.

She continued the letter in the same trend, in the belief that she was the only survivor. I then opened my father's letter. His letter was not addressed to the Pomstras. He wrote:

My dear wife and children,
I am alive, I am alive and I am sure you are too.

I burst into tears and the years of trauma, of deprivation, of horror and suppression all flooded to the surface as I read those words written by my wonderful, optimistic father. In his unshaken belief that we all were alive, the war had finally come to an end.

Postscript

There was life after Belsen.

The Pomstras took us in. The two-bedroom apartment was crowded with the addition of three children, but the neighbours made an attic room available, which had a very comfortable and clean bed. Max, Jacky and I slept there without a problem.

We had to get used to the Pomstras' family lifestyle. This meant sitting up straight at the table for meals after we had washed our hands. Mr Pomstra made us join in thanking the Lord for the meals that were put on the table, and after each meal he would read a passage from the Bible before we were allowed to leave.

Food was still scarce in Amsterdam so the army bag with the flour and sugar came in very handy. Mrs Pomstra was very good at obtaining potatoes with the extra ration tickets the government gave us. Every morning I had to peel about four kilograms of potatoes, and Mrs Pomstra taught me how to peel a potato so as not to lose too much potato with the skin.

Max went to Central Station in Amsterdam every day and stayed there from early in the morning until late in the afternoon. There he would read the list of names of those who had returned from the camps in Germany. Each night he would come home dejected, but the next day he would be off again in the hope our father or mother would return to us.

Then in the first week of July I arrived home from a visit to a friend when Mrs Pomstra told me that my father had arrived at Central Station that morning, and the doctors who examined him had transferred him to a hospital. Soon Mrs Pomstra and I were on the tram on the way to see my father. She told me that Max and Jacky had seen my father at the station and later in hospital.

A nurse directed us to the room where my father was lying in bed, supported by pillows. I rushed up to him and put my arms around his thin frame. He looked so skinny. Tears of happiness filled his eyes and all he could say was, 'You have grown so much, Hetty.' We both cried. The feeling of relief that our ordeal was over left us without words.

When we had recovered, my father told me that when he had to leave us on 4 December 1944 he had been transported with four hundred men to Sachsenhausen, but after a few days he and another man had been separated from the diamond group. He had told Uncle Max to volunteer to join him but he wanted to stay with the diamond group. This decision determined Uncle Max's fate – he died in Belsen.

My father was sent to a camp near Berlin where he was put to work in a Siemans Cable factory.

When the war came to a close the Germans took the entire camp on a death march. My father had to walk from Berlin to Mecklenburg-Schwerin, which was about two hundred and twenty kilometres to the north-west.

At the start of the march he had met up with Gary, a young man who had been employed by us in Amsterdam, prior to our deportation. The march took a big toll on the hungry. When the prisoners could not continue to walk or dropped down on the road, the SS shot them without mercy.

At the end of the second day, my father said to Gary, 'I cannot go any further, I am finished. I will step out of the column. Gary, please tell my wife and children I love them.'

'No, Mr Werkendam,' Gary said, 'don't do it. Think of your wife and children. Here, lean on me. We are both going to make it, you will see.'

Gary persuaded my father to go on. Leaning on Gary, he had only taken about then more steps, when right in front of him he found a strong stick from a tree. He picked it up and by leaning of the stick when making each difficult step, he had managed to stay on the march for seven long days before they were liberated by the United States army.

On 3 June he had flown with Gary from Nüneberg to Brussels at about noon – we had missed each other at the airfield by only a couple of hours.

About a week before coming to Amsterdam he had met up with his niece, Doortje, in Brussels. Doortje had been in Auschwitz and, after she returned to Amsterdam, had travelled to Brussels in the hope of finding some family members. She had told my father that his three children were back in Amsterdam.

'What about my wife?' he had asked her.

'I don't know,' she said.

'Is my wife dead?' he asked.

'I don't know,' she repeated.

From that moment on my father had no rest, and he travelled to Amsterdam to be reunited with us on the first available transport.

My father was a very sick man. His legs were swollen with oedema but after a few days in hospital, wild horses could not keep him away and he came home to the Pomstras.

Not being a person to sit home for long, he persuaded Mr Pomstra to find him a bicycle so he could go with Max each day to Central Station to see if my mother had arrived on one of the many boats coming from Sweden with refugees. The first few days we had to help him on and off the bike and in order for him to stop and get off he used to wrap his arms around the lamp post in front of our door to bring the bike to a halt. But after a week his health had improved and he was able to get on and off the bike by himself.

Months went by, and every day Max and my father would return from Central Station without news of my mother. We knew she was in Sweden but communication was still difficult in post-war Europe.

It was three long months before my mother finally came back. What joy, what happiness! She had put on an enormous amount of weight, as the Swedes had fattened up all the ex-prisoners. We hugged her and touched her every few seconds, and my father was on cloud nine now that he had his family around him again.

My mother's transport from Belsen on 5 December 1944 had been sent to Beendorf concentration camp. There she had been put to work deep in the salt mines to build automatic pilot instruments for German planes. She was liberated and sent to Sweden, with most of the women from the diamond transport, when a high-ranking Nazi (believed to be Himmler) gave them to the Swedish diplomat Count Volker Bernards Dotte in exchange for a box of vodka.

The Pomstras were beautiful people. They had a full house and we must have inconvenienced them at times, but never was there a cross word. Their hospitality was unsurpassed and their kindness helped to heal some of the pain we felt at having lost close family members.

My mother had been to see the mayor of Amsterdam to ask him for assistance to allocated us a home of our own. Our previous home around the corner from where the Pomstras lived was occupied by another family. After a long wait we were allocated an apartment, fully furnished, which the government had confiscated from a Dutch Nazi. (Later we purchased furniture from the Dutch government.) Can one express the happiness we felt that we had a home of our own again and we could go to sleep at night without fear of being raided?

Amsterdam was dead. There was no commerce and all the shops in the city were boarded up. Slowly, ever so slowly, things changed. Here and there shops opened up again in the Amsterdam central business district (CBD).

My father decided not to return to the markets but to start a large fashion shop in the CBD. The son of Polak & Son, his main supplier previously, had returned and found piles and piles of fabrics in his stores, apparently amassed by the German liquidator of the business. What a windfall that was. The business prospered as my father and mother manufactured badly needed garments for the Dutch population, who had gone without for many years.

I had returned to school but it became clear to me, as well as my brothers, that studying was out of the question. We were still too mentally affected to concentrate on the curriculum. All five of us spoke very slowly and it was only after many years that we could say our brainpower had recuperated to the state that we could speak normally again.

Aunty Jet offered to teach me how to cut diamonds. She was one of the best in the business and my father advised me to take up her offer. I had two enjoyable years learning all about it, and I do believe that I became very good at it. But factory work did not appeal to me as it kept me inside all day. I wanted to be outside. So I persuaded my father to let me join the fashion world and to help out in the shop. At night I studied dress designing. I loved working with the beautiful garments we sold.

The years passed quickly and when Max was called up for military service in 1951, he decided to emigrate to Australia instead. He had fallen in love with a girl who had emigrated in February, and by April that same year Max was on the boat to Sydney. He did not even wait for my marriage, which took place on 17 May 1951.

Six months later Jacky was on the boat to join Max.

My daughter, Julia Louise Maja (Maja was from the first two letters of Max and Jacky) was born on 10 February 1952. Then disaster struck as my wonderful young husband became ill and never recovered.

Four months after Julia was born my parents decided to emigrate to Australia, as the political situation in Berlin worried them and they believed another war was imminent. I had to stay behind because my husband was sick.

It took two long years before the Australian government reluctantly allowed me to enter the country and, as I was by then a single parent, I had to sign an undertaking that I would never request any assistance or pension from the government.

In 1972 I was given an award as the most successful migrant. When I asked, 'Why me?' I was told that I had come to Australia with a little girl but never asked for assistance and I had been an achiever.

Fifty years after our liberation, 'The Children', as we call ourselves, came from every part of the world to be once more with the woman who had so valiantly saved our lives in Bergen-Belsen.

Luba Frederick, seventy-six years old, was to receive the highest decora tion from Queen Beatrix of the Netherlands for humanitarian services in difficult circumstances.

Thirty-one 'Children' attended the reunion and the tears were flowing freely as we embraced each other after so many years.

Although we were all fifty years older and had our own individual life experiences, we still, after all those years, quickly recognised and hugged each other and became, before thirty minutes had passed, the same close-knit group we had been in Belsen.

On 15 April 1995, on the exact anniversary of the liberation of Bergen-Belsen, in the Town Hall of Amsterdam, Sister Luba was decorated by the Deputy Mayor in the name of Queen Beatrix. When he pinned the silver medal on her, all her Children and the many guests gave her a standing ovation.

The Deputy Mayor said, 'This recognition is long overdue,' and he thanked Sister Luba in the name of all the people of Holland for her gallant work.

We had a few exciting days together in Amsterdam until the moment came when we all had to say goodbye once again.

The memories of this reunion will stay in my heart until the end of my days.

A fiftieth anniversary commemoration was also held at Belsen. Ex-prisoners went to Belsen from all over the world to show their respect for those who had suffered and succumbed to the brutal treatment of the Nazis.

I had no intention of going there ever again, but when (my little) Robby asked me to accompany him as he was in a wheelchair, having lost one leg from the after-effects of Belsen, how could I refuse? Also, Maurice wanted to find Leni's grave, and I believed that I could help him with that.

So I found myself in the bus on the way to the place which, at times, still gives me nightmares. In the bus were women and men who had travelled from the USA and Canada. I was the only one from Australia.

The bus stopped and someone said, 'This is Bergen-Belsen'. No one moved, you could hear a pin drop in the bus as each of us had to meet our moment of truth and walk once moce through the gates. But then the driver was told to continue on to another destination, and after about five minutes I realised that we had entered the recuperation camp. After fifty years the buildings looked the same, except that now there was no one about. It was clean and empty.

After a few minutes we left the camp and we came to the small cemetery in which I remembered Leni was buried – together with 17,000 people who died after the liberation from the effects of malnutrition and from typhus, along with seventy doctors and nurses who contracted typhus whilst trying to help the poor victims.

As I alighted from the bus I noticed a much-decorated English military officer and a small man in a black suit standing next to the gate, and I walked up to them.

I asked the officer if he had been one of the liberators of Belsen. 'No,' he said, 'but this gentleman next to me was one of them. In fact,' he continued, 'he was the young soldier who was sitting on the bulldozer pushing all those dead bodies in to the mass graves. You must have seen it many times on television.'

I was introduced to Frank Chapman, and before he knew it I put my arms around him and hugged him, and thanked him, after all those years, for liberating me. I had been unable to do so at the time, as I had not been able to get out of my bed to meet the liberators.

Then Frank pointed out the one person in the crowd I had never forgotten. The image of his profile was engraved in my mind, and when I saw him after all those years I ran up and embraced him in the same way I had with Frank. I thanked and kissed, after fifty years, Dick Williams, the proud young soldier who was the first to enter Belsen with the white flag on 13 April 1945.

Later that day a luncheon was given to the ex-prisoners by the British Armed Forces, who are still in possession of the forty square kilometres of land surrendered in April 1945 by the German generals. At that luncheon I again met Helen and Zosua, who had helped Sister Luba look after us.

The solemn commemoration on 26 April 1995 took place in the grounds which were once Bergen-Belsen. The concentration camp is no more and only the silent mass graves tell the terrible story of what took place there during the barbaric regime of the Nazis.

I had great reservations about entering Belsen once again, but, surprisingly, it did not rekindle the horrors as I had imagined. Instead it was as if all those mass graves were telling me, 'We are at peace now.'